The
INTERNATIONAL GROUNDS
OF RUGBY LEAGUE

The
INTERNATIONAL GROUNDS
OF RUGBY LEAGUE
by Trevor Delaney

First published in Great Britain in 1995 by
Trevor R. Delaney, 6 Elmwood Terrace, Ingrow,
Keighley, West Yorkshire BD22 7DP

British Library Cataloguing in Publication Data

A catalogue record of this book is available from the
British Library

ISBN 0 9509982 4 9

Typeset in Garamond ITC
Printed by Thornton & Pearson Ltd, Bradford.

CONTENTS

Page

The Contributors   6

Acknowledgements   7

Introduction   8

Chapter One
Soccer and other venues by Trevor Delaney   10

Fulham 10; Chelsea 10; Cheltenham 11;
Park Royal 12; Newcastle 12; Gateshead 13;
Birmingham 14; Coventry 15; Nottingham 16;
Glasgow 16; Edinburgh 16; Liverpool 17;
Plymouth 17; Highbury 18; Herne Hill 19;
Hull City 19; Old Trafford 20; Elland Road 22;
Wembley Stadium 25.

Chapter Two
England by Trevor Delaney   30

Bradford 30; Castleford 37; Cumbria 39;
Halifax 43; Huddersfield 47; Keighley 53;
Kingston-upon-Hull 54; Leeds 59; Leigh 65;
Manchester and Salford 68; Oldham 75;
Rochdale 78; St. Helens 80; Wakefield 85;
Warrington 87; Widnes 90; Wigan 93.

Chapter Three
Australia by Tom Brock   108

Sydney 108; Brisbane 120; Wagga Wagga 129;
Parkes 131; Townsville 132; Melbourne 135.

Chapter Four
France by Robert Fassolette   139

Paris 139; Bordeaux 144; Marseille 146;
Nantes 147; Lyons 148; Toulouse 149;
Grenoble 151; Roanne 152; Perpignan 153;
Carcassonne 154; Pau 155; Albi 156;
Narbonne 156; Avignon 157; Beziers 158.

Page

Chapter Five
New Zealand by John Coffey   160

Auckland 160; Christchurch 167;
Dunedin 172; Greymouth 174;
Palmerston North 175; Rotorua 176;
Wellington 176.

Chapter Six
Papua New Guinea by Dave Hadfield   178

Goroka 179; Mount Hagen 180;
Port Moresby 181.

Chapter Seven
The South Pacific Islands by Trevor Hunt   182

The Cook Islands 182; Fiji 183;
Kingdom of Tonga 184; Western Samoa 185.

Chapter Eight
Wales by Trevor Delaney   187

Merthyr Tydfil 188; Aberdare 188;
Tonypandy 188; Ebbw Vale 189;
Pontypridd 190; Cardiff 192; Llanelli 193;
Swansea 194; Abertillery 196; Bridgend 197.

Subscribers   201

Index of Grounds   202

THE CONTRIBUTORS

TOM BROCK Now retired after 40 years service with the administration of The Commonwealth Scientific and Industrial Research Organisation, Tom Brock was appointed South Sydney Rugby League Club's official Historian and Archivist in 1990, the first such appointment by any New South Wales club. After serving on Souths' schools committee from 1973, he was elected a Life Member of the club in 1993, and in 1994 he received the *Spirit of South Sydney Award* for outstanding service as an honorary official. He is or has been a contributor to *Code 13, The Rabbitoh, The Weekly Southern Courier* and *The Oxford Companion to Australian Sport,* and was Consulting Editor for Ian Head's book *South Sydney - The Pride of the League* and a researcher for the videos, *History of South Sydney* and *That's Rugby League.*

JOHN COFFEY From the rugby league stronghold of the South Island's West Coast, John Coffey has covered the game for *The Press* newspaper in Christchurch since 1963, making his first tour, aged 21, in 1967. He was the sole New Zealand journalist with the only Kiwi team to win a test series in both Britain and France, in 1971. The author of *Modern Rugby League Greats* (1991) and other books, John has contributed to the Australian *Rugby League Week* for more than 20 years and to other national and overseas publications. The New Zealand Rugby League has recognised him as its official historian. His newspaper assignments have included Commonwealth Games and international cricket, yachting, athletics, and boxing.

TREVOR DELANEY Since 1984 Trevor Delaney has published and edited several rugby league publications which have dealt with either the history of grounds, the background to the split in rugby football, or rugby league's general heritage. This is his fourth book, the first being *The Roots of Rugby League,* followed by *The Grounds of Rugby League* (1991), and *Rugby Disunion - Broken-Time* (1993). In 1990, he was the first person to identify the original rugby league World Cup, which had been found in a ditch twenty years after being stolen from a Bradford hotel. This subsequently led to the trophy's recovery, thus enabling the International Board to repair in time for the Centenary World Cup.

ROBERT FASSOLETTE Now a fully-qualified P.E. teacher, rugby league coach, and referee, in 1968, as a fifteen year old, Robert Fassolette toured Cumbria with Roanne XIII. It was this experience which made him determined to improve his English in order to learn more about the game. After an injury put pay to his playing career, at the age of twenty he turned to refereeing and was immediately appointed technical adviser to the French senior referees, whilst also being the regional development officer for the Roanne-Alpes area. In 1985 he moved to Fontainebleau to coach the national military rugby league team at the prestigious Battalion de Joinville. Currently Robert is at the Sports Institute in Paris where he is taking a History of Sports Degree on the conflictual situation between both codes of rugby in France.

DAVE HADFIELD Dave Hadfield has been writing about rugby league for twenty years and has been the British correspondent for *Rugby League Week* since 1981. He is also editorial consultant to *Open Rugby* and since 1990 the rugby league correspondent of *The Independent.* His first book, *Playing Away,* a history of Australians in British rugby league, was published in 1992 and he is the editor and part-author of *XIII Winters,* a best-selling collection of essays on the game, and of the forthcoming *XIII Worlds,* a book of travel writing based around rugby league. He has toured Papua New Guinea twice.

TREVOR HUNT A freelance rugby league journalist and radio broadcaster, Trevor Hunt has been the most prolific and well-respected writer and commentator on the amateur game over the past twenty years, being a regular contributor to *Open Rugby, Rugby Leaguer, League Express,* and a host of rugby league year books. His expertise and public relations work has been recognised by him being appointed BARLA's media manager on three of their recent overseas tours, to the South Pacific Islands in 1990 and 1994 and South Africa in March of this year.

ACKNOWLEDGEMENTS

So many people have assisted me in the compilation of this book that I should like to apologise here and now if I have inadvertently failed to acknowledge anyone's help. As well as owing a debt of gratitude to my fellow contributors, I am also indebted to Robert Gate, the game's leading historian, who read the manuscript and willingly provided his unrivalled expertise and support.

As well as those people credited for the use of their photographs, I should also like to thank the following individuals and organisations. **Australia:** Matthew Arnold (South Queensland Crushers), David Barnhill (NSW Country Rugby League, Sydney), Ruth Bieri (Royal Agricultural Society, Sydney), Betty Bullard (Melba Studios), Ian Collis, Les Cruckshank (Townsville), Stephen Gough (Carlton Football Club Limited), Michael Greenwood (Parkes Shire Council), Ian Heads (Ironbark Press), Peter McAlister (Prime Television), Peter Mann (Wentworth Park Trust), Ern Toovey (Queensland Cricket Association), Ben Wall (Australian Rugby Football League, Townsville), South Sydney District Rugby League Football Club. **England and Wales:** Kirsty Beddard, Malcolm Billingham, Andrew Bubeer, Jim Burns, Brian Cartwright, Mary Charnock, Sam Coulter, Stuart Duffy, Harry Edgar and Trevor Gibbons of *Open Rugby,* Bob Evans, Eric Farr, Mike Flynn, Trevor Foster, Len Garbett, Russell Gaunt, Mike Haddon, Andrew Hardcastle, Gareth Harris, Clive Harrison, Les Hoole, Andy Hudson, Mike Haddon, Simon Inglis, Michael Inman, Ian Jackson, Tony Jesson, David Kay, Michael Latham, Stan Lewandowski, Diane Lister, Dave Mackin, Bill Madine, Tom Mitchell, Geoffrey Moorhouse, Graham Morris, Bill Nelson, Darrell Platt, Margaret Ratcliffe, Diane Rogerson, Irvin Saxton, Malcolm Scarth, David Schofield, Alex Service, Henry Skrzypecki, Kirsty Shockett, Mike Smith, Dave Twydell, Jack Wainwright, Graham Williams (Leeds), Graham Williams (Llanelli), and the following companies and organisations: British Amateur Rugby League Association, Howard and Seddon Partnership, Richard Lindsay Associates, David Lyons and Associates, Manchester United, National Museum of Film and Television, Oldham Economic Development Unit, Pontypridd Historical and Cultural Centre, Rugby Football League, Rugby Leaguer Newspaper, Wembley Stadium Ltd, Wigan Heritage Services, and Malcolm Wood (Woods Visual Communications). **New Zealand:** John Borren (*Daily Post,* Rotorua), Bill Browne (V. C. Browne & Son), J. B. Buchanan (*The New Zealand Herald*), Carey Clements, Richard Cosgrove (*The Press,* Christchurch), Rae Dozell (Rotorua District Council), Colin Dyer (Palmerston North Show Grounds), Peter Kerridge, and Bernie Wood (*New Zealand Rugby League Annual*). **The South Pacific Islands:** Akeripa Toalepaialii (General Manager, Apia Park), John H. Smith (Fiji Sports Council), Mataina T. Te'o (Nelson Memorial Public Library, Apia).

To conclude, I also wish to thank the many reference librarians in most of the town's and cities mentioned in the English, French and Welsh sections, the staff of A J Typesetting, Morley, and Thornton and Pearson Printers, and the subscribers who helped make this venture possible.

Trevor Delaney, Keighley, July, 1995.

INTRODUCTION

It cannot be claimed that this book includes every venue in the world where international rugby league has been played over the last 100 years. Much as the inclusion of past and present developments in such countries as Italy, Morocco, Russia, South Africa, Canada, and America would have painted a truer picture of the game's world-wide appeal, it has been found necessary to restrict our attention principally to the international and test grounds of the International Board's full-member countries, namely, Australia, England, France, New Zealand, and Papua New Guinea. However, with the inclusion also of the South Pacific Islands, where Fiji, Tonga and Western Samoa now come under the umbrella of the World Super League; a look at rugby league's reliance on soccer stadia in this country; and a brief history of rugby league in Wales, this makes for nearly 100 venues world-wide.

Neither can the writer claim to have travelled tens of thousands of miles in order to single-handedly research the various grounds which have qualified for inclusion. Having re-acquainted myself with the major English grounds and having visited a number in South Wales, I was pleased to leave the overseas travel and this painstaking research in the capable hands of Tom Brock (Australia), John Coffey (New Zealand), Robert Fassolette (France), Dave Hadfield (Papua New Guinea) and Trevor Hunt (South Pacific Islands), without whose willing help there would have been no international follow-up to *The Grounds of Rugby League*. This edition has therefore been a joint venture, which also differs from its predecessor insomuch as it pays attention not only to ground landmarks but international match action.

In respect of the latter, one of the greatest tasks, lightened by being able to refer to Robert Gate's *The Struggle for the Ashes* and Alan Whiticker and Ian Collis' *Rugby League Test Matches in Australia*, has been to read through literally hundreds of newspaper match reports. Simon Inglis' classic books on football stadia, *The Football Grounds of Great Britain* and *The Football Grounds of Europe*, have also proved invaluable sources of reference whilst compiling the first chapter and researching several grounds in the French section.

A criticism of the Northern Union in 1895 was the loss, from both the public's and players' point of view, of the interest and honour associated with the traditional international games. To attempt to remedy this deficiency, the game's founding fathers staged the first official international, played 12-a-side, between England and Other Nationalities, at Wigan on 5 April, 1904. It was not until A. H. Baskerville's side, which included the incomparable Australian, H. H. *"Dally"* Messenger, toured England in 1907/8 under the label of the All Golds, however, that international competition for the new sport was firmly established.

With one or two exceptions, the only grounds included in this book are those which have staged officially recognised internationals, World Cup games, or test matches. By no stretch of the imagination could they all claim to be world-class venues, the choice of many simply proving that in this country, at least, most international events have held far less status and interest with the public than major club games. For example, many internationals have been played in mid-week, and only in recent years have home Anglo-Australian tests attracted the kind of support historically associated with the Championship (Premiership) and Challenge Cup finals.

Prior to 1948/9 the term Northern Union or England was used for the Great Britain side, despite Welshmen and Scotsmen being included in the teams. In order to differentiate between England's games, the term Great Britain is therefore used throughout for genuine test matches. Except for the use of Celtic Park, Glasgow, in 1909, and Tynecastle Park, Edinburgh, in 1911, all Great Britain's home games have been played on English soil, although there have been numerous Welsh matches which have been played in the north of England.

In the heartland of the game last year, two related events were highly symbolic. Namely, that during the same week in August that Huddersfield played their opening match at the £16 million all-seater Alfred McAlpine Stadium, the bulldozers started to level Fartown's 103-year old main stand. Fartown, which is to be preserved for community sporting use, had struggled to meet the stringent safety requirements imposed since the Hillsborough and Valley Parade tragedies, the latter which might so easily have been enacted at Headingley in 1932 and several other rugby league grounds where ancient wooden stands have been burnt to the ground. Thus, with the raising to the ground of the spectator facilities at the Rugby League's oldest surviving venue, the game effectively lost yet another of its spiritual homes. Homes which, with the sale of the Athletic Grounds, Station Road, and Crown Flatt, and the anticipated loss of McLaren Field, Watersheddings, and, quite possibly, Central Park, and Lang Park in New Zealand, are fast becoming endangered. At the same time, the Fartowners, and the game in general were fortunate to be inheriting what, technically, might be described as the finest rugby league stadium to be built in this country. After a decade or two of staging major events it will be known whether the Alfred McAlpine has lived up to expectations and is recognised as a truly great rugby league venue.

Elsewhere, in revisiting most of the grounds which appeared in the 1991 edition, it is obvious that very little has changed over the past four years. Rather than providing new spectator facilities the emphasis has continued to be placed on meeting essential safety requirements. It is estimated that since 1985 at least £13 million has been spent on such remedial measures. Excluding the McAlpine Stadium, a great deal less, I would estimate, has been invested in new stands and new stadia during the same period, and most clubs fail to meet the modest requirements - a minimum capacity of 10,000, including a minimum 2,500 seats and cover for 6,000 - of the *Framing the Future* report. Within the next few years, however, there are sure to be radical changes as grants are now available for safety work through the Football Trust, and the Sports Council estimate that by the end of the century £2 billion of national lottery money will be distributed to sport.

Some of this will obviously find its way into rugby league, whilst, if it not entirely frittered away on meeting existing club debts and inflated player contracts, a percentage of Rupert Murdoch's millions could well be allocated for ground improvements. Furthermore, following the 1996 European soccer championships rugby league will have use of the enlarged soccer venues in the north, and by the end of 1998 the new national stadium should be up and running. By that time, we will also know whether the Odsal Superdome is a reality, or whether it was merely pie in the sky.

At the moment, however, with the advent of summer rugby and the repercussions of the Super League, it is the uncertain future of international rugby league that is of greater concern. Hopefully, by the time that this is read, a solution will have been reached between the warring factions which will safeguard the credibility of the game at international level, for it is fairly certain that only fully representative sides from both Australia and Great Britain, with the former chosen by the Australian Rugby League, are likely to have the whole-hearted support of the public and be able to fill our proposed national stadium or the Olympic Stadium in Sydney.

History has almost come full circle with the Rugby Football League's use of soccer and other stadia for its international events in England. The hiring in 1994 of Elland Road, Old Trafford, and Wembley for the tests against Australia hardly compares, however, with the Northern Union's ill-conceived venture of taking all the official tests, and the supplementary internationals, against the first Kangaroos in 1908/9 to soccer grounds in London, Birmingham, Newcastle, and Glasgow. This missionary work had followed hard on the heels of the first tour to these Isles by Albert H. Baskerville's All Blacks (hereafter referred to as the All Golds), with whom the legendary Australian Dally H. Messenger had guested.

A. H. Baskerville (centre row, far left) and his All Golds. Dally Messenger is seated third from left.

On that tour tests were played at Chelsea's Stamford Bridge and The Athletic Grounds, Cheltenham; and the Northern Union repeated the flag-waving exercise for the visit of the 1911 Australians. Then, as well as tests again being played at Newcastle and Birmingham, additional internationals were staged at Notts County's Meadow Lane (see below) and Fulham's **Craven Cottage,** where on Wednesday afternoon, 18 October, the robust Australians won 11-6 before a crowd of 6,000. The experiment which was said to have been *"as much to make money as to attempt to introduce their game to foreign parts"*, failed on both counts - it being 1980 before rugby league returned to Craven Cottage following the entry of Fulham (London Broncos) into the Rugby League.

Craven Cottage	
1911 England 6 Australia 11	6,000

Subsequently, with the exception of Plymouth in 1913, Arsenal's Highbury in 1921, Gateshead in 1934, and Wembley in the 1930s, full internationals in England have mostly been played on northern club grounds until quite recent times. This section is therefore intended to cover what might be termed non-rugby league venues on which internationals and tests have been played, concluding with Elland Road, Old Trafford, and Wembley.

LONDON The first Northern Union game to be played in London was the second test against New Zealand on 8 February, 1908 at Chelsea's **Stamford Bridge,** where there was a crowd of 14,000 despite the counter attraction of the England versus Ireland game at Richmond, which was the last home international to be played there prior to the opening of Twickenham. Nonetheless, many rugby union supporters made their way to Stamford Bridge due to the novelty of the occasion, but, unfortunately, the game failed as a spectacle,

Stamford Bridge circa 1922 - The Hulton Deutsch Collection.

10

The scoreboard on the balcony of Craven Cottage, from which the ground takes its name, during Fulham's inaugural match against Wigan on Sunday, 14 September, 1980. - Mike Haddon.

apparently due to the home players having been instructed to throw the ball about in order to please the crowd. However, the backs were badly off form and Dally Messenger played well enough not only to lead his side to an 18-6 victory but to attract the attention of Manchester United and Tottenham Hotspur, who both offered him huge sums to join them.

According to Simon Inglis, whose book *The Football Grounds of Great Britain* was a valuable source of reference for this chapter, Stamford Bridge was the second largest ground in England after the ageing Crystal Palace. One stand designed by Archibald Leitch held 5,000, with the rest of the bankings around the oval running track being able to accommodate in the region of 90,000 (the record of 82,905 being set in 1935). A British Empire X111 beat the New Zealanders 26-2 there on the evening of 23 January, 1952, when the innovation of a white ball was used. The 6,800 spectators were impressed by Huddersfield's powerful Australian winger Lionel Cooper, who scored a hat-trick of tries, but the union-orientated southern press were generally dismissive. It would be another thirty years before rugby league returned to the ground, when, because of a fixture glut, Fulham played their last game of the 1982/3 season against Cardiff (attendance: 3,321) under the Stamford Bridge lights.

Stamford Bridge
1908 Great Britain 6 New Zealand 18   14,000

CHELTENHAM Having had to learn the Northern Union rules, the All Golds lost 14 games on that first tour, but they still managed to win the series with victory in the ill-tempered final test on 15 February, 1908. This was played at the Cheltenham **Athletic Ground**, described as an *"exceptionally fine enclosure"*, which was used for athletics and cycling as well as being tenanted by the town's rugby union club. The owners, who took 10% of the gate, had especially erected a large covered stand but heavy rain throughout the day kept the crowd down to less than 4,000.

Unlike the New Zealanders, who went to Cheltenham on Friday, the Northern Union decided to travel south on the morning of the match. One player had to leave home at 3 a.m. for the five hour journey, and when the team arrived it was found that Wigan three-quarter Jim Leytham had not been able to get out of work. Arriving only 90 minutes before the kick-off the players then had to take lunch! Not surprisingly the home forwards were *"fagged out"* in the latter stages, when the game was marred by brawls, and the dismissal by Bill McCutcheon of the New Zealand forward Cross. This was claimed to be the first sending-off *"in the entire history of international football"*. Some locals were evidently puzzled by the new code, particularly the ball back

rule, and this first exercise of attempting to promote the game in the west was deemed to have been something of a failure.

The rugby union club, of course, could not have prevented the use of the Athletic Ground in 1908. But in the 1980s their ancestors managed to stop an amateur rugby league representative fixture taking place at the council-owned Prince of Wales Stadium, having negotiated a clause in their lease which effectively banned the playing of rugby league on the new complex. The Athletic Ground, which was situated between Albion Street and Fairview Road, was bought in 1929 by the local council, who subsequently sold it to Barratt Homes in 1982.

Athletic Ground	
1908 Great Britain 5 New Zealand 8	4,000

PARK ROYAL In terms of finance, the Northern Union's expansionist policy also received another set-back with their choice of Queens Park Rangers' ground at **Park Royal**, Willesden, for the first Anglo-Australian test on 12 December, 1908. This 22-all draw had everything and the spectators were said to have left the ground *"perfectly satisfied that they had received very good value for money"*.

Unfortunately, the test clashed with both the 'Varsity rugby match and the Chelsea-Newcastle United encounter. Furthermore, Park Royal, which was situated between Coronation Road and the Great Western Railway (G.W.R.) line, had no local population to call upon for such an event. Queens Park Rangers had built up a clientele in winning the Southern League that year but Park Royal - with its estimated capacity of 40,000, including 9,000 (nearly half of whom were seated) in the one grandstand - was very much dependent on patrons of the G.W.R., which had opened the ground the previous November. Therefore, it was apparently no surprise to find that when the teams came out for that historic test *"the enclosure had a strangely deserted appearance"*, there being only 2,014 spectators present who had paid the paltry sum of £70. The ground is now covered in industrial units.

Park Royal	
1908 Great Britain 22 Australia 22	2,014

NEWCASTLE Satisfaction was gained, however, from the use of Newcastle United's **St. James' Park** for the second test on

This undated photograph gives some idea of how St. James' Park would have looked at the time of the tests in 1909 and 1911. - The Hulton Deutsch Collection.

23 January, 1909, which one correspondent said *"demonstrated clearly and unmistakably the superiority of the Northern Union code"*. To help stimulate local support the test was advertised as *"England versus Australia"*, and this certainly seemed to work, as a crowd of 22,000 turned up to see the Australians more outclassed than the 15-5 scoreline would suggest. St. James' Park in those days had a capacity approaching 60,000 with a recently built 4,500-seater west stand (demolished in 1987) and open bankings on the other three sides.

It had been noticeable that the in-goal areas were *"dangerously narrow"* but the success of this first venture to the north-east guaranteed that St. James' Park was again hired for the first test in 1911. Although the crowd on this occasion dropped to only 6,500, they were fortunate to see history made by the Australians' first-ever victory over the home country, and (among other notables) the inauspicious debut of the *"Prince of Centres"*, Harold Wagstaff. Since then, St. James' Park has hosted only one other *"international"* rugby league match, namely the Australians 32-22 defeat of a Northern Rugby League side on the 1929/30 tour before a crowd of 9,690.

St. James' Park	
1909 Great Britain 15 Australia 5	22,000
1911 Great Britain 10 Australia 19	6,500

Redheugh Park in the late 1950s - Gateshead Local History Library.

GATESHEAD The north-east continued to be the target for rugby league expansion, with the promoters of the proposed Newcastle rugby league club hastily arranging an England-Australia international (non-test) at the Gateshead soccer club's **Redheugh Park**, Low Team, ground on 13 January, 1934. A remarkable match-winning try in the 77th minute by Leigh centre Harris climaxed a memorable afternoon. At the end of what was the Australian's final game in England, the players linked arms and sang *"Auld Lang Syne"*, with the crowd, numbering a healthy 15,576, joining in. A scheduled exhibition game between York and Hunslet in May, 1934 was cancelled due to the F.A.'s failure to give permission.

Redheugh Park was formerly a clay pit, which was developed by the local Council and officially opened on 30 August, 1930. The grandstand had been transported by rail from Harraby Park, Carlisle, the former ground of the defunct Carlisle City rugby league club. Once dogs were introduced in 1936 the large totaliser at the west end restricted Redheugh Park's capacity, the record attendance of 20,752 being set the following year. Gateshead failed to be re-elected to the Football League in 1960, and, with the added loss of revenue from the abandonment of greyhound racing, the ground fell into disrepair. A fire in 1971/2 speeded the club's departure to the Gateshead International Stadium. Redheugh Park was demolished shortly afterwards, and in 1990, when the site was used as a car park for the Garden Festival, any remaining mounds were levelled.

Redheugh Park	
1934 England 19 Australia 14	15,576

Newcastle played the first of their two seasons - 1936/7 and 1937/8 - in the Rugby League at Brough Park greyhound and speedway stadium before moving to the 24,000 capacity White City Stadium. The latter was built on a 12 acre site near Scotswood Bridge, Gateshead. On 17 April, 1937 a Northern Rugby League side met Wales in atrocious conditions at the White City Stadium, prior to Newcastle playing their first game on the ground the following month. Owing £1,200 to the game's authorities, Newcastle failed to be re-elected in 1939. Today the White City site is industrialised warehousing and light engineering.

The Rugby League still consider the north-east to be a potential growth area for the game with the **Gateshead International Stadium**, which hosted the pre-season Charity Shield games in 1991 and 1992 and Australia's 54-10 win over Great Britain Under-21s in 1994, being allocated its first full international in February, 1995. The scheduling of a Wigan-St. Helens Challenge Cup replay on the same evening devalued this European Championship game against France,

The Gateshead International Stadium on the occasion of the Charity Shield game between Wigan and Hull in 1991 - Gateshead Metropolitan Borough Council.

which the home side won 19-16. But the support given to this event, on an atrocious night, was deemed highly satisfactory and the stadium was confirmed as the venue for Australia's preliminary Centenary World Cup game against South Africa, when the record books seem likely to be re-written.

Built by the local council on reclaimed industrial land, the Gateshead Youth Stadium, as it was originally called, was opened on 27 August, 1955 by marathon runner Jim Peters. The first grandstand, constructed over the changing rooms, seated a mere 170. From such modest beginnings the stadium now seats 11,500, a figure which can be increased to 15,000 with temporary seating, as was the case in July, 1993 for the famous sprint between Linford Christie and Carl Lewis. After a new tartan track was laid in 1974 the stadium was made famous by the exploits of local 3,000 metre world-record holder Brendan Foster.

In June, 1981 soccer manager Laurie McMenemy officially opened the present £1.3 million 3,300-seater Tyne and Wear County Stand, which provides the only cover in the stadium, whilst the north and south grass banks were made into all-seater terraces in time for the 1989 Europa Cup athletics final, the eastern terrace having been converted in 1975. The electronic scoreboard, first used in 1987, cost £382,000. The complex also incorporates an indoor training hall at the rear of the grandstand; and the landscaped parkland area, the Riverside Bowl, which is the venue for Gateshead's annual cross country races and such events as cyclo-cross.

The International Stadium will be the base for a Gateshead Academy side next season, but developments in the north-east will take on a much higher profile should Newcastle United, with their 37,000 capacity St. James' Park, pursue their present interest in applying for entry to the Rugby League.

Gateshead International Stadium	
1995 England 19 France 16	6,103

BIRMINGHAM The deciding test in 1909 had taken place on 14 February at Aston Villa's **Villa Park**. Despite it being played on a Monday afternoon, and an obvious lack of pre-match publicity for this first game of Northern Union to be staged in this soccer stronghold, the crowd still numbered a healthy 9,000. However, for the majority of those present the fact that Great Britain clinched this first series 6-5, meant very little, these soccer followers being simply there for the amusement. And Villa Park provided the ideal setting, having been built on the site of the former Ashton Lower Grounds Victorian amusement park.

There had once been an ornamental lake where the pitch then stood, and the stand on the Witton Lane side covered what had formerly been a sub-tropical garden. Including the use of the banked cycle track, Villa Park had a capacity of approximately 40,000. This, however, was hardly tested when Villa Park, by this time owned by the club, was again allotted the final test of the 1911/12 tour. On New Year's Day, 1912, despite favourable conditions, there was a crowd of only 4,000 to watch the Australians chalk up nine tries in a then record 33-8 victory, to take the rubber for the first time. A first-minute injury to Wigan forward Ramsdale made the game one-sided. Many of the spectators, although appreciative of the individual performances of the Australians, were clearly no wiser about the game than they were three years previous, it being reported that, *"After the match one could hear expressions of admiration for the play of the 'outside left' and 'outside right'"*.

Villa Park	
1909 Great Britain 6 Australia 5	9,000
1912 Great Britain 8 Australia 33	4,000

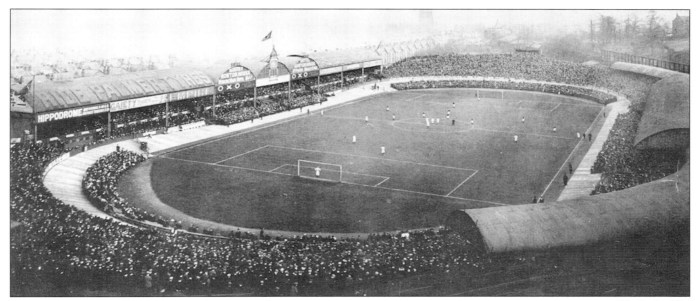

Villa Park, 1907.

COVENTRY There was hope in 1910 that the newly-formed Coventry club would have provided the Midlands' public with the necessary education on the finer points of the game. Earlier that year they had taken over tenancy of **The Butts** stadium, which was owned by the Coventry Cricket Grounds Company and had been home to the suspended Coventry rugby union club for the previous 30 years. In order to promote the new club, which finished 27th of 28 in their first season, an international was staged there on 10 December, 1910 when England, who included J. Tomes of Coventry in the pack, ran up nine tries in easily beating Wales 39-13. The poor weather kept the attendance down to only 4,500.

The struggling club were also granted the opening match of the Australians 1911 tour when a combination under the title Midlands and the South lost 20-11. After finishing bottom of the Rugby League in 1911/12 Coventry ceased membership and The Butts was re-let to the rugby union club. The stadium, which in those days had two stands with the pitch surrounded by an athletics track and a banked cycle track, still stands today behind the Technical College.

Action from Australia's game in 1911 against the Midlands and the South at The Butts.

The Butts	
1910 England 39 Wales 13	4,500

NOTTINGHAM Apart from the tests at Birmingham and Edinburgh (see below) two other internationals were staged on soccer grounds on that 1911 tour. As earlier referred to, the first was at Fulham's Craven Cottage, whilst the second was at Nottingham, which had its first taste of professional rugby on 6 December, 1911 when the tour-weary Australians were beaten 5-3 on Notts County's **Meadow Lane**. The council-owned ground included a 1,400-seater wooden stand which had been floated across the river from Trent Bridge cricket ground. Following the kicks to touch it is more than likely that the ball finished up in the open stream called Tinkers Brook, where someone was employed to fish it out with a long pole and wicker basket. Although there were a number of prominent rugby men present in the disappointing crowd of 3,000, the large majority had been drawn to the game through sheer curiosity - the keen tackling *"provoking constant ripples of merriment",* whilst many had no idea which side had won.

It seems that little had changed from 1888, when, in organising the first rugby tour to Australasia, England and Nottinghamshire cricketer Arthur Shrewsbury had advised his agent that Nottingham was not a rugby city. Instead, Shrewsbury suggested that any exhibition games should be played in Scotland, a part of the British Isles which has proved to be an even greater problem for rugby league development.

Meadow Lane	
1911 England 5 Australia 3	3,000

GLASGOW Ironically, the first occasion on which Northern Union football was played on Scottish soil (after the proposal in January, 1908 to stage a test against New Zealand was abandoned) coincided with a crisis involving the Scottish Rugby Union and their counterparts in London - the former having cancelled the Calcutta Cup game in January, 1909 due to England having approved of a three shilling daily allowance to the first *'All Blacks'.*

Not that this concerned the honest *"professionals"* involved in this additional international, which was played on Wednesday afternoon, 3 February, 1909, at **Celtic Park**, the present home of Celtic F.C. in the Parkhead district of Glasgow. This finished as a 17-all draw after a remarkable fight back by the Australians, who scored three tries in the last ten minutes, with Dally Messenger, the great personality of the game, having levelled the scores with his final conversion. Unfortunately, in this Mecca of soccer, and in one of the largest grounds in Great Britain, constant rain reduced the crowd to no more than 3,000, which apparently included many association and rugby personalities. The game, however, drew favourable comparisons with the other codes. *"It appears to us"*, said the Scottish correspondent, *"rather as attenuated Rugby football with the more cumbersome features eliminated...(it) is replete with nerves and exciting movements, many of which were yesterday executed to a fine science...."* But, despite such favourable comments the same critic had to conclude, correctly as history has so far proved, that, *"The prospects of Scotland being converted to the Northern Union game are about as remote as the conversion of the Jews to Christianity."*

Celtic Park	
1909 England 17 Australia 17	3,000

EDINBURGH Still, the Northern Union could but try and by playing the second test on 16 December, 1911 at **Tynecastle Park**, Edinburgh, they were said to have taken a bold step *"to place their special game in challenge with that favoured by the Scottish schools and aristocracy of the capital."* However, although the event had received favourable publicity and there were no major counter-attractions, there were still less than 6,000 present at what has been the home of Heart of Midlothian since 1886. A modest pavilion and stand had been built in 1903, but there was clearly no scoreboard, as it was reported that, *"The mode of scoring...seemed to puzzle many, and at the close there was some doubt, as one could hear, whether the match was lost*

The Tynecastle Park stand, built in 1903.

or drawn." Nonetheless, the game, which ended in an 11-all draw, was well received by *"Ruggerites",* the passing of the home backs being particularly appreciated.

It was suggested by *The Yorkshire Post* that,*"There is no antipathy to the Northern Union as such in Scotland,"* but, unfortunately, this was the last occasion, at a professional competitive level, when this opinion was to be fully tested - an application from the *"Glasgow Black Eagles",* who were to play at that city's White City Stadium, being rejected by the Rugby League in April, 1953. There are hopes, however, that a Scottish side, made up of students and established professionals, will prove to be successful in the emerging nations competition during the Cententary World Cup.

Tynecastle Park	
1911 Great Britain 11 Australia 11	6,000

LIVERPOOL The game has also had problems in establishing itself in Liverpool despite Everton's **Goodison Park** having staged representatives games during each of the Australians' early tours. Described by Simon Inglis as the *"first major football stadium in England"*, Goodison, with the familiar landmark of the St. Luke the Evangelist church set in one corner, was opened in August, 1892. At that time, Everton were the best supported club in the land.

On the evening of 15 March, 1893, in what was possibly the first rugby match on the ground, Northern Union founder-member Runcorn lost 9-0 to Swinton in front of a crowd of 10,000, when the ground's capacity was in the region of 40,000. On Wednesday, 18 November, 1908 the Australians beat the Northern Rugby League there, 10-9, in front of a 6,000 crowd. This was thanks to a last-minute drop goal from the incomparable Dally Messenger, who was a notable absentee when an additional international was staged at Goodison on 3 March, 1909. The main purpose of this game, which ended in a 14-7 win for England, was to help the tourists financially at the end of an arduous tour. Unfortunately, the snowy conditions reduced the crowd to only 4,500 and, with no attempt having been made to clear the pitch, the game was ruined as a spectacle.

During the summer of that year a new main double-decker stand was built which enabled a crowd of 69,000 to attend the 1910 F. A. Cup final. There have been two other tour fixtures on the home of the Toffeemen; on 25 October, 1911 when the Australians beat the Northern Rugby League 16-3 (attendance:

6,000); and on the 1921/2 tour when the Australians beat the Lancashire League 29-6 before a crowd of 17,000.

Goodison Park	
1909 England 14 Australia 7	4,500

Only one other international has ever been played in Liverpool, namely, at the **Stanley Greyhound Stadium,** Prescott Road (then home of Liverpool Stanley) on Wednesday afternoon, 10 April, 1935, when England beat Wales 24-11. One highlight of the game was the freak goal kicked against the gale force wind by England's full-back Billy Belshaw, who was playing on his home ground. The touch-judges just had time to signal a goal before the wind took the ball high into the air and back to the 25-yard line where it again came to ground! Built on the site of an old brickworks over the railway line from the present Police Athletic Ground, Stanley Greyhound Stadium is now covered by the Wholesale Fruit and Vegetable Market off Church Road.

Stanley Greyhound Stadium	
1935 England 24 Wales 11	7,100

PLYMOUTH: Despite the failure of the Cheltenham test in 1908, the west country continued to be a useful recruiting ground for Northern Union clubs, particularly Rochdale Hornets and Oldham. The latter had signed the former Plymouth forward Bert Avery, who was selected for the 1910 tour to Australasia, where he scored a hat-trick of tries in the only test in New Zealand. On Saturday 17 October, 1910, the day after they docked at Plymouth, the weary tourists, together with five players drafted in from the north to cover for injuries, staged a Wales and the West versus England exhibition match on Plymouth Argyle's present ground, Home Park. The crowd, numbering about 5,000, saw a last-minute penalty goal from Avery secure a 27-25 *"home"* victory. However, the 1911 Australians easily defeated a similar combination 23-3 at Bristol City's Ashton Gate on Saturday, 20 December, 1911, when the crowd was numbered in hundreds.

Such exhibitions therefore served very little purpose and it was not until the Rugby Union investigated the affairs of clubs in the Cornwall and Devon county unions that the Northern Union made any real progress in the area. In 1912 officials of Torquay Athletic, Newton Abbott, and Plymouth were suspended for making illegal payments to players and openly advocating broken-time, whilst the county treasurer was suspended for making false statements on hotel and travel expenses paid to the county team, all of whom were also suspended.

In the circumstances, the syndicate which controlled Plymouth R. U. club's ground at **South Devon Place** seized the opportunity of introducing professional rugby. After Huddersfield and Oldham had played a highly successful exhibition in May, 1912, terms were agreed with promoters of the proposed Plymouth Northern Union club, and the homeless rugby union side disbanded. Subsequently, Plymouth played two friendly games against Coventry over the 1912 Christmas holidays, and clubs were formed at Torquay, Teignmouth, and Paignton. St. Helens also travelled down and played two exhibitions on 8 and 10 February, 1913.

It also made sense to play a full international in the area, and this was staged at South Devon Place on Saturday 15 February, 1913, when England easily defeated Wales 40-16. On a perfect day for rugby a crowd of 7,500 were thrilled by England's display, which was dominated by the performances of the Huddersfield right-wing partnership of Wagstaff and Moorhouse, the latter who scored four of England's ten tries.

Unfortunately, a lack of progress in forming the proposed league led to the ground syndicate withdrawing their support from the Plymouth club, who disbanded in March, 1913. And when the Rugby Union lifted their suspensions the remaining clubs cancelled their plans. The Northern Union subsequently lifted their embargo on the signing of players from the region, and a number of western players were allowed to join northern clubs, including Willie A. Davies (Leeds) and D. Holland (Devon Albion to Oldham), both of whom toured Down Under in 1914. (For a full account see Graham Williams *How the West was Nearly Won* in *Open Rugby* 50 and 51.) In 1914 South Devon Place was renamed the Astor Playing Fields following the benevolence of Mr W. W. Astor (later Lord Astor), who ensured that they were not taken for housing. This recreation ground still exists today off Embankment Road.

South Devon Place	
1913 England 40 Wales 16	7,500

LONDON Flush with money after the first post-war tour to Australasia in 1920, the Northern Union made just two more attempts to interest Londoners in the game prior to the opening of Wembley. Northern Union officials, who donated the proceeds of the match to the Lord Mayor's appeal fund for famine relief in Russia, were full of praise at the

arrangements for the international against Australia on Monday, 10 October, 1921, at Highbury. Arsenal raised no objections to having their goal posts removed but found this was impossible as they were embedded in several feet of concrete. The rugby posts, which had been loaned by London Scottish, were therefore erected in front of the soccer goals, which were bound in canvas for the players' safety. Leigh's brilliant young full-back, Tom Clarkson, was England's hero, kicking a penalty from half-way to give them a 5-4 victory. The match, watched by a crowd of 12,000, generally created a good impression, so much so that there was talk of immediately arranging an Anglo-Welsh game in the capital.

The Australians perform their war cry at Highbury in 1921.

Highbury Stadium	
1921 England 5 Australia 4	12,000

However, this did not take place until Monday, 11 December, 1922 when England beat Wales 12-7 in an exhibition game at **Herne Hill Stadium.** Sir F. H. Sykes, M.P. kicked off and presented the winners with gold medals, the gift of Lord Colwyn. Unfortunately, the inclement weather kept the crowd down to about 3,000, with the proceeds, in aid of St. Dunstans' Hospital, amounting to only £250. Originally called the London County Athletic Grounds they were opened circa 1892 by a limited company of the same name. Although, of course, an athletic track was incorporated, the

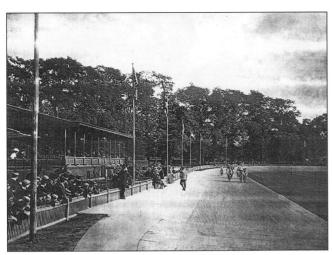

Cycling at Herne Hill c 1908 - Croydon Public Library.

stadium is best known for the cycling events which regularly attracted up to 20,000 in the early days. A world record was set there in 1926 and the slightly-banked track also hosted the 1948 Olympics. With some refurbishment the original small ornate grandstand has survived to this day.

Herne Hill Stadium
1922 England 12 Wales 7   3,000

Apart from Wembley, where, as we shall see, internationals were played in the 1930s and the first floodlit test in this country was staged in 1963, there has been just one other historic venue at which international rugby league has been played in the capital. This was the **White City Stadium,** which was built for the 1908 Olympics. It was derelict until Brigadier-General A. C. Critchley bought it in order to run greyhound racing, a sport which he introduced into this country in 1926. On 14 December, 1932 Leeds beat Wigan 18-9 in an exhibition game under White City's impressive floodlights, watched by 10,000 spectators. It preceded by a few days the first soccer game at the stadium, which became the home of British athletics until the development of Crystal Palace.

Wigan Highfield were given permission to move to the White City in 1933. Re-named London Highfield, although northern-based, they played under floodlights to avoid clashing with neighbouring Queens Park Rangers. On

22 November, 1933 they entertained the Australians, who were having their first experience of floodlights, before a crowd of 14,500. Attendances dropped dramatically during the winter evenings, however, and the White City Company decided not to continue with rugby league beyond this first season. At the same Rugby League meeting, in June, 1934, which heard this news, the offer to stage the Challenge Cup final at the White City was rejected.

The ground was considered following the postponed third Anglo-Australian test at Odsal in 1948. However, the game did not return to the White City until Friday, 3 November 1967, when Australia beat Great Britain 17-11 in a thrilling second test, under the lights, watched by a disappointing crowd of 17,445. Man-of-the-match Ron Coote marked his test debut by scoring a deserved try three minutes from the end. Due to the distance between the stands and the pitch, as well as the obstructions caused by the greyhound lighting, the stadium was not an ideal venue for rugby league. Demolished in the 1970s, the former stadium site, at the west end of the A40, now houses part of the B.B.C.'s new headquarters.

White City Stadium
1967 Great Britain 11 Australia 17 (Floodlit)   17,445

HULL Pre-1982, Hull City's **Boothferry Park** had hosted seven of Hull Kingston Rovers' numerous derby games, the first on the ground having been played on 3 April, 1953, when a club record crowd of 27,670 had attended. Boothferry Park, which was opened by City in 1946 and by 1951 possessed its own railway station behind the eastern terrace, had also staged Australian and New Zealand tour games against joint Hull sides in 1956, 1959 and 1963, and 1961 respectively. In 1980 Hull also played New Zealand there before a crowd of 15,945.

Nothing which had gone before, however, could possibly have approached Saturday, 30 October, 1982, when Max Krilitch's Invincibles humiliated Great Britain 40-4, scoring eight tries without reply. The lock-out crowd of 26,771 - the ground's capacity having been reduced from over 42,000 with the building, earlier that year, of a supermarket where the North Stand once stood - watched in awe as the Kangaroos, with Eric Grothe, Peter Sterling, Brett Kenny, and man-of-the-match, Wayne Pearce, making their test debuts, proved that they were light years ahead of Great Britain in terms of fitness, speed, and ability.

Keith Tindall looks to off load during Hull's game against the Kiwis at Boothferry Park in 1980. Current Wigan coach Graeme West is on the left - Mike Baxter.

Strange as it may now seem, only edited recorded highlights of this test were shown on B.B.C. television. But, with the national media having belatedly to acknowledge the fact that the Kangaroos were perhaps the finest international team in world sport, it became obvious, from the arrival of Wally Lewis' Australians in 1986, that larger stadiums were needed for the vital first tests. Therefore, that year the decision was taken to hire Manchester United's Old Trafford and Elland Road, Leeds; and inevitably, in 1990, to again stage internationals at Wembley.

Boothferry Park	
1982 Great Britain 4 Australia 40	26,771

MANCHESTER There has been a cricket ground at **Old Trafford**, half a mile away down Warwick Road, since 1857. However, the present home of Manchester United (*"The world's most famous football club"*, as they now modestly refer to themselves) was only opened in 1910, courtesy of the club's benefactor chairman, brewer John H. Davies.

What is believed to be the first game of rugby league at Old Trafford was played shortly after the Munich air tragedy, when Salford lost 22-17 to Leeds, on 5 November, 1958, under the ground's first floodlights. These had been officially switched on during March, 1957.

Old Trafford on that occasion bore little resemblance to today's fully-cantilevered, all-seater stadium. As with the neighbouring Salford ground, in 1941 Old Trafford suffered extensive war damage to its two stands. Subsequently, United had to play at Manchester City's Maine Road for eight years until their return home for the start of the 1949/50 season. At the 1939 FA Cup semi-final Old Trafford held 76,962 but its post-war capacity was originally limited to 55,000, and the main stand on the railway side was not completely re-roofed until 1951. However, from 1959, when the Stretford end was first covered, the capacity was raised to about 67,000.

From 1964 £350,000 was spent on the building of the first 10,000 capacity cantilever stand on the United Road side, which was opened in time for the 1966 World Cup. It incorporated the first hospitality boxes in English soccer and allowed for standing areas in front, as did each of the stands as they were progressively cantilevered. In 1973 the scoreboard end (Matt Busby Way) was completed, and by August, 1985 the main stand was finally finished, with new offices and executive suites covering the walkway at the rear. The Sir Matt Busby Suite and the Manchester United museum were also added on the Warwick Road corner.

When Great Britain lost 38-16 to Australia in the first test in 1986 the ground held 56,500 with 25,693 seated and 103 private boxes. The crowd of 50,583, a test record for this country, paid record receipts, outside of Wembley, of

Looking towards Old Trafford's scoreboard end during the Salford - Halifax Second Division Premiership final in 1991 - Mike Haddon.

Joe Lydon starts his run, supported by Henderson Gill and Garry Schofield, which led to his breathtaking try against Australia at Old Trafford in 1986 - Andrew Cudbertson.

£251,061. United did not ask for a cut of the gate as they were happy with ancillary revenue. That rain-swept day, winger Michael O'Connor's Anglo-Australian test record 22 points included a hat-trick of tries. The most memorable moment, however, was served up by full-back Joe Lydon whose 54th minute touchdown raised British hopes - only for them to be killed stone dead from the resultant kick-off when Wally Lewis put centre Gene Miles under the posts for the second of his three tries.

After the test success Old Trafford became the permanent home of the Premiership finals, with the innovation of the double-header staged there from 1987 and triple-header in 1993. New attendance and receipts records for this competition were immediately established, and also a record gate of £177,161 was taken at the 1990 Challenge Cup semi-final between Wigan and St. Helens. On the night of 4 October, 1989 Old Trafford also hosted the Fosters World Club Challenge when Widnes staged a remarkable come-back to beat Canberra Raiders 30-18 after trailing 12-0 after 11 minutes. A crowd of 30,786 paid £207,764, thus each club benefited to the tune of £68,000 on top of Widnes receiving the sponsor's prize of £50,000. In 1992 the demolition of the Stretford end limited the crowd at the Premiership finals to

33,157 but this still produced record receipts for the competition of £389,988 and this has been improved on each succeeding year.

From 1986 all the paddock areas have been seated, finishing at the Sir Matt Busby Way end of the ground at the start of the 1994/5 season. It had originally been proposed that the new Stretford end should be all-standing but following the Taylor Report the new Umbro Stand was made all-seater at a cost of £10.5 million. The new dressing rooms (first used against Benfica but officially opened on 4 August, 1993 against Celtic) are now located in this stand, and the players' tunnel is now in the corner where Joe Lydon scored the previously-mentioned try in 1986. However, the main stand's original tunnel has been retained, not only for posterity but as an integral part of the stadium tour, which attracts over 100,000 visitors each year.

In 1984 undersoil heating was installed but after teething troubles this was replaced in 1986. Only United's first team games are allowed on the pitch, which measures 69.5 metres by 105 metres, with training carried out at The Cliff (the former home of Broughton Rangers), and reserve games played at Bury's Gigg Lane, which is also shared with Swinton (see Manchester and Salford chapter).

Old Trafford's capacity will be raised from 44,508, including 174 executive boxes, to 55,300, with the redevelopment of

Old Trafford, Premiership final day 1994, looking towards the Umbro Stand (Stretford End) from the North Stand, which is currently being rebuilt - Henry Skrzypecki.

the North Stand into a triple-decker, seating 25,110, in time for soccer's European Championships in 1996. Costing an estimated £18.65 million, plus £9.2 million for the purchase on 20 acres of the adjacent Trafford Park trading estate on which it will encroach, the new stand, which will have a further 32 private boxes and 80,000 square feet of restaurant and other commercial facilities, will be the biggest at any soccer ground in England, with a drive through being necessary over United Road.

Although the ground's capacity will initially be reduced to around 31,000 thus affecting this year's Premiership final and the semi-final of the World Cup, in the long term the development is good news for the Rugby League as Old Trafford is now well established as the code's premier northern venue. And, having staged the classic second test in 1990 when Mal Meninga stole the game in the last twenty seconds, and the second test in 1994 when the Kangaroos ran riot, so far as the Australians are concerned, Old Trafford certainly lives up to its title, 'The Theatre of Dreams'.

Old Trafford	
1986 Great Britain 16 Australia 38	50,583
1989 Great Britain 16 New Zealand 24	18,273
1990 Great Britain 10 Australia 14	46,615
1994 Great Britain 4 Australia 23	43,930

LEEDS Until 1904 **Elland Road,** which then ran east to west rather than the present north to south, was the home of Holbeck Northern Union club. When Hunslet moved there in 1982 history had indeed come full circle as Leeds United's predecessor, Leeds City, had started life as the soccer section of Hunslet when the latter played at Parkside. In fact, the first ever soccer game on Elland Road involved Hunslet who beat Harrogate 1-0 in the West Yorkshire Cup final on 23 April, 1898.

When Holbeck went defunct Leeds City took over the lease, and during the summer of 1905, following their entry into the Second Division of the Football League, demolished both Holbeck's old stands, on the north and south (Elland Road) sides. The latter made way for a 4,500-seater costing £1,060. In Holbeck's days their pitch was usually devoid of grass, therefore it was necessary to raise the new 115 yards by 73 yards pitch fourteen inches and re-drain and re-turf. The derby game against Bradford City on 30 December, 1905 was watched by a crowd of over 22,000, a record for the ground during its east to west alignment.

In 1906, having acquired another five acres on Gelderd and Churwell Road from Monks Bridge Iron Works, Leeds City decided to adopt the major of three proposed schemes, which necessitated turning the ground round at right angles. The Elland Road grandstand therefore became the popular stand behind the goal. A double barrel-roofed main stand, holding 8,000, was built on the west (Morley) side. There were about thirty open terraces on the Lowfield Road side and slightly fewer behind the goal and the main stand paddock. The total cost of the scheme, which raised the ground' capacity to 45,000 and increased the field area to 125 x 85 yards, was estimated at £4,635.

On the newly acquired land was the old Beeston pit, which had been abandoned in December, 1880. Today Elland Road is unique in having its own underground water supply in the 36-foot well shaft (situated near the 20 metre line at the Kop end) which leads to these former mine workings.

In 1912 Leeds City and Elland Road fell into the hands of the receiver and the club, having almost finished up at Headingley under the Leeds C. A & F banner, was wound up in 1919 following allegations of illegal payments to players. A scheme in October, 1919 envisaged using the rich clay deposits under the playing surface and turning Elland Road into a brick works, but the ground was saved from this fate when Yorkshire Amateurs moved there prior to Leeds United being formed in 1920.

The dust flies at the 1938 Hunslet-Leeds Championship final at Elland Road.

On what is now partly covered by the training pitches (acquired by United after the Second World War) and partly by Fullerton Park industrial estate, stood the Kennels, Fullerton Park (also known as Leeds Speedway). This was opened for greyhound racing in 1927, and on 1 September, 1931 a record crowd of 28,000 watched speedway there.

During the 1920s a wooden barrel-roofed stand, later known as the 'Scratching Shed', was built behind the Elland Road goal, and the huge Kop at the north end gradually took shape. The old Lowfield Road stand (demolished in 1992), which was built in three stages from the late 1920s, was finally completed during 1934, and seating was added some time later.

On 30 April, 1938 a crowd of 54,112, a rugby league record at that time for this country, witnessed Hunslet's 8-2 victory over Leeds in the Championship final. Many thousands more were locked out. It was not until 1958 that rugby league was again played on the ground, when Hunslet beat Leeds 15-8 before a crowd of 19,289 in the first rugby league game to be played in the city under modern floodlights. These had been officially switched on for United's game against Hibs on 9 November, 1953.

During the early hours of Tuesday morning, 18 September, 1956 a blaze caused by an electrical fault totally destroyed the West Stand. A public appeal raised £60,000 towards the present £180,000 propped cantilever stand which was opened on 31 August, 1957 when Leeds United beat Leicester City 2-1. It originally had 4,963 seats and a standing paddock for 6,000, the latter being converted to seating in the 1970s.

The ground record of 57,892, with thousands more again locked out, was set on the evening of 15 March, 1967 when Leeds United met Sunderland in a hastily arranged FA Cup fifth round replay. The barriers at the Lowfield Road end gave way under the pressure with thousands spilling onto the pitch and 32 spectators being ferried to hospital, whilst such was the throng on the Kop that the writer recalls seeing very little of the play.

This huge expanse was cleared in 1968 when the new £250,000 North Stand was built with an all-standing capacity of 13,055. The pitch was then moved 30 feet towards that end which means that the players' tunnel is no longer on the centre line. In 1970 another £200,000 was spent on the 1,064-seater corner section which joined the North Stand

(then with electronic scoreboard) to the West Stand. A year later the north east corner stand (1,779 seats and standing below) was added at a further cost of £250,000. In 1974 the 'Scratching Shed' was demolished and the present South Stand, then with exactly 4,000 seats, was built for £400,000. Executive boxes were added in 1983 and it currently also houses the *Goal Line* restaurant. Seating was later added to both the main stand and South Stand paddocks, but due to supporters' pressure the lower section of the latter was later reinstated as a standing area.

When these new stands were built taller floodlights, costing £150,000, were needed. Three of the 260-foot pylons (the tallest in Europe at the time) were erected in 1974 and the other one in 1977. These have since been demolished with the building of East Stand in 1994 and the current £250,000 lighting system is now set on the stand roofs.

Elland Road, July, 1972, showing the new developments at the north and north-west corner, and the Fullerton Park training pitches. What was soon to be Hunslet's new ground, the Elland Road Greyhound Stadium, is in the foreground - Wood Visual Communications. Ref: A18953

Watched by referee Barry Gomersall, and the nonchalant assistant coach Phil Larder, Lee Crooks kicks the last-minute touchline penalty which squared the 1985 series against New Zealand - Mike Baxter.

Having thus spent £2.5 million between 1956 and 1982, in November, 1985 United, who were then heavily in debt, were forced to sell Elland Road to the Leeds City Council for a similar amount. The club were subsequently granted a 125 year lease, the terms of which were renegotiated in 1991 in order to limit the huge amounts of rent which United were liable to pay based on gate receipts. Hunslet signed a 20-year tenancy agreement with the Council in January, 1987 to play on the ground on Sundays.

When Hull beat Widnes on Wednesday, 19 May, 1982 in the Challenge Cup final replay under the lights there was a crowd of 41,171, of whom 19,626 were seated. This brought in record receipts, outside of Wembley, of £180,525. From that time Elland Road has staged seven Challenge Cup semi-

finals, four Yorkshire Cup finals, and the 1985 and 1986 Premiership finals. It is interesting to compare the small attendances of 15,518 and 13,683 at the latter two games with subsequent figures at Old Trafford.

However, because of its higher seating capacity, Elland Road had already started to outstrip Headingley as Yorkshire's premier test match ground. In 1985 a crowd of 22,209 (10,000 more than at the first test at Headingley) watched Lee Crooks slot over a pressure kick to draw the final test against New Zealand 6-6, and thus clinch what was arguably the best-ever series between the two sides. This bruising match was marred by a second half incident in which a couple of policemen stepped onto the pitch to separate a brawl, to which the Australian referee, Barry Gomersall, had turned a blind eye and allowed play to continue.

In 1989 there was more violence when Steve Hampson was sent-off, straight from the kick-off, for head butting Kiwi scrum-half Gary Freeman. Though on this occasion Britain still managed to pull off a famous victory, the first Anglo-Australian test on the ground, on 8 November, 1986, proved to be a nightmare for coach Maurice Bamford's flag-waving side as Wally Lewis' men ran in six breathtaking tries in their 34-4 Ashes-clinching victory. Britain's only points came in the 77th minute of the game through Gary Schofield's consolation touchdown.

Following the Taylor report seating was reinstated in the South Stand and the ground's capacity reduced to 32,500. This figure might well have been sold twice over for the deciding third test against Australia in 1990, when the Kangaroos again clinched the Ashes; and the same could have applied in 1994, when the same scenario was acted out, and by which time Elland Road had been transformed.

Having earlier spent £1 million on the south east corner and completed the banqueting suite at the rear of the West Stand, during the summer of 1992 Leeds United demolished the Lowfield Road Stand, the 2,600 seats from which were given to Bradford Park Avenue (see Bradford) to make way for the largest cantilever stand in Europe.

Financed by United, the Football Trust, and private sponsorship, the new two-tier 17,000-seater East Stand, in which there is ample room for a dining area and a number of shops, cost £10 million. It was not officially opened until 28 January, 1994 - by Lord Taylor of Gosforth, the Lord Chief

Elland Road, 1995, looking towards the new East Stand - Wood Visual Communications. Ref: AC 28288

Justice, whose report into the Hillsborough tragedy had recommended all-seater stadia - although the lower half was first used for the Bradford Northern-Wigan Challenge Cup semi-final in 1993. The 25 executive boxes on the second floor are set in hotel-style luxury and serviced by a lift - a facility which is much needed for patrons of the higher tier, whose fitness and tolerance to vertigo are well tested.

Due to Elland Road being chosen as one of the venues for the 1996 European Championships, and the poor state of the pitch being largely blamed on weekly rugby league, Hunslet were *"evicted"* at the end of the 1993/4 season. The Parksiders continued to use Elland Road for administrative and commercial purposes, but most of their games were played at Bramley before their planned move to the new £4.2 million South Leeds Stadium, which boasts a 2,500-seater grandstand and an athletics track.

The Kop was seated at a cost of £1.2 million for the start of the 1994/5 season, when a £150,000 electronic advertising board was also erected at the south west corner, and the stand named The Don Revie Stand in memory of United's famous manager.

At the time that Mal Meninga made his farewell appearance in this country in the final test in 1994, Elland Road was therefore a 39,500 all-seater stadium, but, politics permitting, this figure will be increased to over 55,000 when a second tier is added to the West Stand in time for the 1996 European Championships.

Elland Road	
1985 Great Britain 6 New Zealand 6	22,209
1986 Great Britain 4 Australia 34	30,808
1989 Great Britain 26 New Zealand 6	13,073
1990 Great Britain 0 Australia 14	32,500
1994 Great Britain 4 Australia 23	39,468

LONDON Despite its decrepit state, **Wembley Stadium** still manages to maintain an abiding appeal for most rugby league fans. The stadium, which is currently owned by Wembley plc, was originally financed by public subscription and built as the centre-piece of the British Empire Exhibition, being opened by the King on 28 April, 1923 at the Bolton-West Ham F.A. Cup final. Its central feature, the 126 feet high twin towers, has since become the stadium's trade mark, along with the motto *'Venue of Legends'*. Apart from the stadium, which cost £750,000 to build, the 75 acre complex also houses the Wembley Arena, which was opened as the Empire Pool in 1934, the £18 million Conference Centre which opened its doors in 1977, and the New Exhibition Hall.

Wembley's initial capacity was given as 126,500, including 25,000 seated under cover. With the stadium surrounded by

Wales halt an Australian attack during the game at Wembley in 1930 - The Hulton Deutsch Collection

153 turnstiles and over 600 police on duty this appeared more than adequate to deal with the anticipated crowd on that opening day. However, the authorities badly miscalculated the interest that the new stadium and the presence of the King would generate. In fact, the Empire Stadium was besieged by a crowd estimated at over 200,000, almost half of whom, *"more in the spirit of fun than any malicious intent"* obtained free admission (the official attendance was 126,047) once the low ornate turnstile walls had been breached. The efforts of the eleven mounted policemen to clear the pitch, particularly the one on the white horse, have since passed into English sporting folklore.

On the site of the present pitch once stood *'Watkins Folly'*, an abandoned tower which was built by Sir Edward Watkin with the intention of emulating the Eiffel Tower in Paris. However, because of the unstable foundations the precarious structure reached only one-sixth of its proposed height and was removed in 1908. The area was then used as a golf course and a became a haven for wildlife until it was chosen as the grounds for the above exhibition, which opened a year after the stadium, on 23 April, 1924. Many of

the former exhibition halls can be seen today on either side of Olympic Way in use as commercial premises.

Following the closure of the exhibition in October, 1925 the whole site, which was in danger of being demolished, was finally rescued by the Wembley Stadium and Greyhound Racecourse Co. Ltd., headed by (Sir) Arthur Elvin. They introduced greyhound racing in December, 1927 when 50,000 were at the first meeting, and this sport, with thrice-weekly meetings, has been the stadium's real lifeblood over the years. Speedway also proved popular although the team has since gone defunct and the World Speedway Championship was moved from Wembley to Odsal (see Bradford) in 1985 because the F.A., who signed a new 21-year lease in 1982, objected to the raising of the corners.

The decision to take the Challenge Cup final to Wembley in 1929 was perhaps the most important in the game's history. It stemmed from the proposal made by an exiled Yorkshireman, John Leake, who was then chairman of the Welsh Commission (see Wales), that this final should be played in London each year.

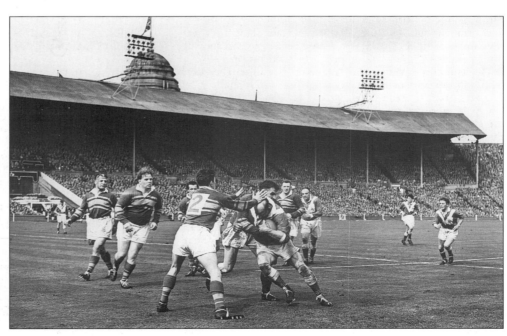

Wembley 1957, looking towards the Royal Box side. Barrow forward Jack Grundy is halted by the Leeds defence.

The Rugby League Council confirmed this course of action on 3 October, 1928 at the Griffin Hotel, Leeds, at which time Crystal Palace, Wembley and the White City Stadium had all offered their facilities. The latter was immediately rejected and secretary John Wilson and Rugby League chairman F. Kennedy (Broughton Rangers) were instructed to inspect the other two grounds. Subsequently - both men having climbed to the top of Wembley's towers to satisfy themselves that spectators would be able to see from the further points - on Wednesday, 24 October, 1928, at the Strafford Arms Hotel, Wakefield, the Emergency Committee unanimously decided to accept the offer of Sir Arthur Elvin, who wanted only 7.5% of the gate. By 1949 Wembley was taking 25% and today their rake-off is even higher.

Apart from 1932, during war-time, and the two replays in 1954 and 1982, Wembley has staged every Challenge Cup final since that opening game between Dewsbury and Wigan. In 1932, when the game was played at Central Park, it was impossible to find a suitable Wembley date due to the F.A. having priority, and the need for the cup final to be played before the departure of the tourists to Australasia.

Although the history of Wembley and the Challenge Cup is fairly familiar to most rugby league supporters, it is largely forgotten that the stadium also staged two inter-war internationals. On 18 January, 1930 Australia beat Wales 26-10 and were presented with a Challenge Bowl (donated by a London newspaper) by the Home Secretary. The game was kicked-off by Australian airman Bert Hinckler, who flew Harry Sunderland, the Australian manager, back home with the trophy. Although the crowd was only 15,000, it enabled the Australians to boost their record profits to over £7,000.

The 1933 Australians also ended their tour at Wembley, this time totally-outclassing what, on paper, looked like a powerful Welsh side, 51-19. Centre Dave Brown was easily the best man on the field, scoring 9 goals and a try to set a new individual points record (285) for a tourist. Jim Sullivan, whose record he had broken, was overworked at full-back as the Green and Golds ran in eleven tries, including hat-tricks for Sid Pearce and Jack Why. Early morning rain kept the gate down to about 11,000.

A ground plan for the scheduled Challenge Cup final on 20 April, 1940, which was played on club grounds over two legs because of the outbreak of war, shows Wembley to have had seating only in the upper (covered) level of the South Stand and on the whole of the North Stand (covered and uncovered), where in 1938 the 250-seater restaurant had been built behind the Royal Box. The dressing rooms at that time were at the western end but these were moved to their present position at the other end of the arena when Wembley staged the athletic events in the 1948 Olympics.

The first post-war international at Wembley, on 12 March, 1949, saw a sprightly French combination, two of whom were wearing plimsolls and short socks to help their speed, beat a highly fancied but *"Cup-tired"* English side, 12-5. France never looked like losing once they had equalised with a try in the fifth minute, and with full-back Puig-Aubert in great form, kicking a penalty and two drop goals, the visitors deservedly won a thrilling game on their one and only visit to the stadium. Following the precedent set at the 1948 Challenge Cup final, this game, which was considered a good advertisement, was also televised in the London area. The crowd of 12,382 was deemed satisfactory but, of course, hardly compared to the first 95,000 capacity crowd at the Challenge Cup final later that same season.

In 1963 the stadium's new owners spent £500,000 to make Wembley the only all-covered 100,000-capacity stadium in the world. This figure included 44,803 seats. At the same time the present 300-foot long press box was suspended from the roof of the North Stand and a television gantry from the South Stand. Wembley's first £22,000 floodlights, which had been installed on the stand roofs in 1955, were also re-aligned.

A waterlogged Wembley, 1968, Leeds versus Wakefield Trinity.

Wembley's twin towers, Challenge Cup final day in the late 1980s - Wembley Stadium Ltd.

However, it took more than a new roof and brilliant floodlights to entice southerners out on a wet Wednesday autumn evening, and the game's first-ever floodlit test match, played on 16 October, 1963, attracted a crowd of less than 14,000. Great Britain were handicapped with an 18th minute injury to stand-off Dave Bolton and their 5-man pack had no answer in the second half to the Australians' rampaging forwards. The result: a record winning margin, 28-2, for the Kangaroos, including a brilliant hat-trick of tries for centre Reg Gasnier.

Certainly the crowd at the famous Leeds-Wakefield Trinity 'watersplash final' in 1968 were grateful for the cover when a cloud burst minutes before the kick-off made playing conditions impossible. On any other day the game would

have been abandoned and we would all have been spared the now legendary missed goal on the final whistle by Lance Todd Trophy winner Don Fox.

Another came in November, 1973 when, at the insistence of the Australians, the live-televised first test was taken to Wembley and, with a crowd of less than 10,000, lost £500. However, those privileged to be in the vast empty stadium - and Prime-Minister Edward Heath was one of them - bore witness to one of the finest-ever tests - Hull Kingston Rovers' second-rower, Phil Lowe, crowning a magnificent two-try performance with a 30-yard run to the line to clinch the match. Another try-scorer that day - apart from future Australian coach Bobby Fulton - was Wigan hooker Colin Clarke.

He could hardly have envisaged at the time that his 2-year old son, Phil, would help steer Great Britain to another famous victory against Australia at Wembley in 1994, following the dismissal of captain Shaun Edwards. Some journalists likened the magnificent rearguard action, which followed Jonathan Davies' brilliant try just after half-time, to the Rorke's Drift test in 1914, although, of course, in terms of numbers and substitutions, there was no real comparison. The attendance of 57, 034 was a record for a test match in this country, eclipsing that at the corresponding fixture in 1990, but was some way short of the world record for an international, 73,631, which was set at the World Cup final in 1992 - figures which could only have been dreamed of back in 1973.

Wembley is now a 79,000 all-seater stadium, which includes 56 executive boxes and 4,000-seats in the Olympic Gallery, but the Rugby League are reluctant to sell many of the bucket seats on the lower tiers as they have such a restricted view.

In recent years Wembley plc has been the subject of intense speculation with a number of reported takeover bids. In 1991 the entire complex was valued at £172 million, including the stadium at £90 million, and the arena, a listed building, at £37.5 million. The fall in the property market, however, sent the Wembley plc's shares tumbling to 6p compared to a 1987 high of 157p, and until a refinancing package in April, 1995, the company had debts of more than £150 million.

Despite their increased bid of £100 million for the stadium being turned down, the Genesis Consortium, which includes the construction giant, John Laing, and architects, the Lobb Partnership, submitted plans in 1994 for Wembley's redevelopment. Retaining the twin towers, their proposals envisaged a new £250 million 100,00 all-seater stadium with a retractable roof. English Heritage, who had to be consulted because the stadium is a Grade 2 listed building, approved in principle the demolition of all but the famous twin towers, but they were apparently not impressed with the designs produced by Genesis, who went back to the drawing board confident that Wembley plc's heavy debts would eventually give then the opportunity to own the 'Venue of Legends'.

Wembley is among the short-listed sites, the others are at Birmingham, Manchester and Odsal (see Bradford), being currently considered by the Sports Council for development as the new national stadium. The decision is due to be

The capacity crowd stand for the national anthems prior to the World Cup final at Wembley in 1992 - Henry Skrzypecki.

announced later this year, and failure to secure this prize would almost inevitably result in Wembley's rapid decline once the new stadium is built towards the end of 1998 and Wembley's existing contracts with the F.A. and the Rugby League run out.

Wembley Stadium	
1930 Australia 26 Wales 10	16,000
1933 Australia 51 Wales 19	11,000
1949 England 5 France 12	12,382
1963 Great Britain 2 Australia 28 (Floodlit)	13,946
1973 Great Britain 21 Australia 12	9,874
1990 Great Britain 19 Australia 12	54,569
World Cup 1992 final Great Britain 6 Australia 10	73,631
1993 Great Britain 17 New Zealand 0	36,131
1994 Great Britain 8 Australia 4	57,037

BRADFORD

Park Avenue On amalgamation in 1879 the Bradford Football and Cricket Club moved to their new ground at (Horton) Park Avenue, which trustees had bought from Francis Sharp Powell, M.P. for £4,000. The multi-purpose ground, with its double-fronted stand, was officially opened with a cricket match on 20 July, 1880. As a founder member of the Northern Union, Bradford had the highest financial turnover of any rugby club in the country in 1895, and had made Park Avenue into one of the game's premier grounds. They regularly attracted five-figure crowds, the largest being 28,000, on 31 March, 1906, versus Halifax.

Just one international was played at Park Avenue, on Monday afternoon, 2 January, 1905, when England, trailing 11-0 at half-time, scored a 26-11 win over an Other Nationalities side containing an Irishman, two Scotsmen, and twelve Welshmen. Wigan's left-winger, James Leytham, scored, consecutively, four of England's six tries.

In May, 1907, following a loss of £600 on the previous season, Bradford decided to abandon the Northern Union and, after initially being rejected by the Football League, joined the Southern League. Bradford Northern were subsequently formed on 24 May, 1907 and before moving to Odsal Stadium played at Greenfield and Birch Lane.

Park Avenue in 1965 - Wood Visual Communications. Ref: A14216

Following the demise of the soccer club in 1974, Park Avenue was bought by the local council for £100,000, and it was agreed in principle that Northern should have moved there for the 1975/6 season. Had they done so they would have inherited a stadium with cover on three sides for 14,000 and a corner pavilion nicknamed the *"Doll's House"*. However, the cost of renovating the badly vandalised main stand, with its three pedimented gables and slate roof, proved to be the stumbling block.

Park Avenue	
1905 England 26 Other Nationalities 11	6,000

Part of the former rugby and soccer pitch now houses an indoor cricket school and nothing much remains of the football stadium apart from overgrown terracing at the Horton Park end. The cricket pavilion has also been demolished, but in recent years Park Avenue, which is now owned by the Yorkshire County Cricket Charitable Youth Trust and administered by Friends of Park Avenue, has been restored to county standard. Northern (now officially renamed the Bradford Bulls) may yet end up at Park Avenue, as in October, 1994 the club, mindful of the uncertainties surrounding the proposed development of Odsal Stadium, opened up discussions with Friends of Park Avenue over the possibilities of once again developing the ground for rugby.

Odsal Stadium Odsal Stadium was said by geologists in the 1950s to have been situated in a deep channel gouged out during the Fourth Ice Age! It is perhaps understandable therefore that the once-famous Odsal mud and freezing fogs, which can fill the huge bowl within seconds, have led to internationals being both postponed and transferred elsewhere. There has also been an occasion where a landslip threatened the cancellation of one international! Nonetheless, the ground held the attendance record, 43,500, for a test match in this country from 1949 until 1986, although this was small fry compared to its many other record gatherings.

Bradford Northern moved to Odsal, a former quarry, for the start of the 1934/5 season. It was Bradford's Director of Cleansing, Ernest Call, who put forward the idea of building a stadium by the controlled tipping of household waste, and at its opening it was estimated that some 140,000 cart-loads of material had helped form the stadium's huge two-tier ash bankings. Tipping continued for a couple more years, whilst most of the railway sleeper terracing, which only ever covered the bottom tier, was added much later.

A £2,000 Rugby League loan enabled Northern to erect what later became known as the Old Stand. This 1,500-seater on the present south-west terrace side proved to be a folly as it effectively reduced the ground's capacity by something like 40,000. Without it Odsal would easily have rivalled Hampden Park as the biggest stadium in Britain. It was the only stand on the ground when Sir Joseph Taylor, President of Huddersfield, officially opened Odsal on 1 September, 1934 when an estimated crowd of 20,000 saw Australian winger Ray Markham score four tries in Huddersfield's 31-16 victory. However, the honour of scoring the first try on the new ground went to Northern's left winger, R. E. Walker.

The club house and dressing rooms were officially opened by the Lord Mayor prior to the game against Hull on 2 February, 1935. The siting of these facilities, at the top of the steep banking, created a unique sight in British sport with players and officials having to make the descent to the pitch below. On rare occasions this created problems, as in 1952 when Northern were ordered to build dressing-rooms adjacent to the main stand following an attack on referee Syd Abram after a Yorkshire Cup-tie. It was not until 1985, however, that the old dressing-rooms ceased to be permanently used. During the war - when Odsal's capacity under air raid conditions was increased from 15-30,000 for its two war-time internationals - the lower floor of the clubhouse doubled as an Air Raid Precautions Centre.

In the 1980s the clubhouse was refurbished and renamed the Trevor Foster Lounge in honour of one of Wales' finest-ever players, who was the driving force in the club's reformation in 1964. Today he is President of the Welsh Rugby League Association and Odsal's greatest advocate. Few rugby league internationals can have played the role of Jesus Christ, as Trevor Foster did when the stadium held a floodlit pageant in 1956, this being just one of the many special events which the ground has accommodated over the years.

Odsal Stadium, 1938, with the clubhouse to the left and the Northern View hospital on the right - Wood Visual Communications. Ref: N2385

Odsal remained rectangular until the first speedway track was opened on the evening of 23 June, 1945, when a crowd of 20,000 watched the meeting for the A.J. Elvin Trophy, which had been donated by the owner of Wembley. The first stock car meeting outside of London was staged at Odsal during May, 1954 and attracted 38,212 spectators. Whilst most of the stadium's recent developments were a result of the World Speedway Final in 1985, and the stadium is currently shared with speedway and stock car racing, historically Odsal is principally identified with rugby league.

There were problems with Odsal's drainage from the outset and in 1937 the England versus France international was transferred to the neighbouring Thrum Hall, Halifax, because of eight inches of mud in the centre of the pitch. In Odsal's first international, on Saturday, 29 January, 1938, Wales maintained their unbeaten record in the European Championship with a 7-6 victory over England. On a windswept afternoon Cliff Evans scored in the corner after six minutes and Jim Sullivan's conversion proved to be the decisive score.

The original stand on the hospital side was in use for the Halifax versus Leeds Challenge Cup semi-final on 1 April, 1939 when the crowd (announced originally at 66,308 but since amended to 64,453) was a new record for English rugby league. In November, 1945 the stanchions on this stand moved out of plumb due to a serious land slip, and it was necessary to dismantle three-quarters of the roof to avoid further collapse. New tressel foundations were sunk forty feet deep through the yellow clay which had caused the problems, and both the spectator portion of the banking and that at the rear of the stand were regraded. Due to abnormally wet weather during Autumn, 1946 the work was delayed and only half the stand was in use for the final test against New Zealand on 20 December, 1947, in the first series after the war.

The crowd - reported as a record 45,150 but since corrected to 42,685 - were treated to a sparkling exhibition, with centre Ernest Ward, the only Yorkshire representative, giving a classic display on his home ground. He and full-back Martin Ryan, one of six Wiganers in the side, were the attacking force which swept Great Britain to victory in the first half-hour.

The following year the deciding third test against the Australians was postponed on 18 December, 1948 due to fog. The referee made his decision about 1.30 p.m. but half-an-hour later the fog had cleared sufficiently for the game to have been played. Wembley was considered as a likely venue on the tourists' return from France but the game eventually went ahead at Odsal, where, on 29 January, 1949, a record crowd for an international in this country of 43,500 saw Great Britain score 18 points in 13 exhilarating minutes to clinch the series 3-0. This attendance record was not eclipsed until the first test at Old Trafford in 1986.

The New Stand, with its 5,000 bench seats, was fully operational for the 1950 Warrington-Leeds Challenge Cup semi-final when a new ground record of 69,898 was established. This stand, which offered only part cover throughout its 43 year life, formed part of the first plan for the stadium, which was drawn up by the City Engineer S.G. Wardley in September, 1951. It was then envisaged that at a cost of £250,000 Odsal would have a capacity of 92,000 with potential to extend this to 100,000. Noticeably, the speedway track was to be increased to 440 yards in order to eliminate the need to lift the rugby turf at the corners.

Northern pioneered the use of modern floodlighting in the north of England, when on 31 October, 1951 they beat New Zealand 13-8 in front of 29,072 spectators. On that night an illuminated tram car scoreboard was in use. The Kiwis then requested an extra fixture under the lights, the result being that on Friday, 7 December, 1951 they beat Wales 15-3 in the first-ever floodlit international. Unfortunately, on a foul night, only 8,568 left their firesides.

However, when Other Nationalities beat Wales 30-5 in the first European championship game under floodlights, on 7 October, 1953, the game was rather better patronised (14,646) despite live television of the second half. Odsal's lights were used for only one other full international. This was on 11 April, 1956 when Great Britain, who were playing at night for the first time, gained surprise revenge over a French side who were handicapped by the dismissal of prop Berthomieu in the 65th minute. Storm damage in 1962 rendered the system useless. It was not until November, 1979 that Odsal was again lit up, since when there has been no mid-winter night crowd to equal that which attended the first experiment in 1951.

December 13th, 1952 was a day of shame for rugby league following events at the third test against Australia. In his official report, the Rugby League chairman thought that press reports of the incidents, *"which could only have covered 45 seconds"*, had been grossly exaggerated. But what became known as *"The Battle of Odsal"* was unanimously condemned by the critics, who rated it on a par with the

Carlson. By that time, however, most of the rain-drenched crowd were past caring, having had to endure a sickening spectacle of violence almost from the kick-off.

It was ironic that the second stage of the Wardley plan should commence after the demise of Bradford Northern in December, 1963, with most of the new 20,000 capacity terracing at the Rooley Avenue end in use for the reformed Northern's opening game against Hull K. R. on 22 August, 1964. The council then decided in 1965 to abandon the above plan, and a 35,000 police safety limit was placed on the ground in 1966 when Odsal first became a three-sided stadium. Northern signed a new 42-year lease of Odsal in November, 1975, under which the council have since taken over complete administration of the stadium.

Having staged, in 1967, one of this country's first professional rugby league match on a Sunday, Odsal has the distinction of being the venue for the first-ever Anglo-Australian test in England. This was on Guy Fawkes Night, 1978 when a Great Britain side, dubbed *"Dad's Army"* because of its veteran front-row of Jim Mills, Tony Fisher and Brian Lockwood, defeated the super-fit Australians 18-14 in a heart-warming contest watched by a crowd of 26,447. The last full-international at Odsal was on Sunday, 2 November, 1980, when New Zealand beat Great Britain for the first time on the ground, 12-8.

In the first Anglo-Australian test to be held in this country on a Sunday, in 1978, Britain's winger Stuart Wright scores from a kick by Roger Millward, with the beared Graham Eadie (right) and Chris Anderson arriving too late to stop him. - Mike Flynn

In many respects, the changes since then have done nothing to enhance the stadium's appeal as a rugby venue. After Odsal was chosen for the 1985 World Speedway Final (attendance 37,000) a £15-20 million plan was announced for a 60,000 capacity stadium. However, this scheme was dropped after over £3 million had been spent on what, in terms of spectator comforts, amounts to little more than open terracing (where the demolished Old Stand had stood) and 6,000 plastic seats for the New Stand. At this stage the latter remained half-covered, but was completely re-roofed for the start of the 1993/4 season at a further cost of £250,000. Following the Taylor Report Bradford Council also had to spend £370,000 on new perimeter walls and electronic turnstiles to allow the contracted 1990 World Speedway Final to be staged.

Despite this vast expenditure the cavernous stadium still has only very basic social facilities, and a glaring lack of cover on the exposed terraces; whilst the recent covering of the New Stand has been cancelled out by track debris being deposited on the front dozen rows of seats. The once full-sized pitch has also been much reduced by the demands of motor sport, whilst the heavily banked track also means that the touch-in-goals curl ludicrously at the corners - a factor, alone, which should rule out Odsal, in its present state, from ever again staging internationals.

However, all these deficiencies will be remedied should a 70-80,000-seater £200 million National Superdome, be build in time for the city's centenary in 1997. Complete with a retractable roof, it is described by the developers, Gleyson, Stewart, as a *"multi-functional, sports, entertainment, convention and exhibition multiplex"*. By taking in the adjacent Richard Dunn Sports Centre, the site of the former Northern View hospital, and the former tip at the Low Moor end, the proposed scheme covers an area of 100,500 square metres with parking space for 7,500 vehicles.

Bradford Council chose the Superdome, which is currently short-listed by the the Sports Council for national stadium monies, ahead of more modest schemes early in 1994, but it was not until May, 1995 that they finally granted planning permission, with a recommendation to the Ministry of the Environment that the huge project should proceed. If central government's decision is favourable the developers claim that work will start in October this year, which will mean the temporary rehousing of Bradford for the start of the Super League.

Odsal Stadium	
1938 England 6 Wales 7	8,637
1939 England 3 Wales 16	15,257
1941 England 9 Wales 9	4,339
1943 England 9 Wales 9	16,028
1947 Great Britain 25 New Zealand 9	42,680
1949 Great Britain 23 Australia 9	43,500
1951 Great Britain 21 New Zealand 15	37,475
1951 Wales 3 New Zealand 15 (Floodlit)	8,568
1952 Great Britain 7 Australia 27	30,509
1953 Other Nats. 30 Wales 5 (Floodlit)	14,646
1953 England 7 France 5	10,659
1954 Great Britain 17 France 8 (Evening)	14,153
1955 Great Britain 27 New Zealand 12	24,443
1956 Great Britain 18 France 10 (Floodlit)	10,229
1956 Great Britain 9 Australia 22	23,634
World Cup 1960 Great Britain 23 New Zealand 8	20,577
World Cup 1960 Great Britain 3 Australia 10	32,773
1961 Great Britain 23 New Zealand 10	19,980
1965 Great Britain 15 New Zealand 9	15,970
1968 Great Britain 19 France 8	13,992
World Cup 1970 Australia 15 France 17	6,215
1972 Great Britain 45 France 10	7,313
World Champ. 1975 Gt. Britain 27 New Zealand 12	5,937
1978 Great Britain 18 Australia 14	26,447
1980 Great Britain 8 New Zealand 12	10,946

Odsal 1995. The Richard Dunn Sports Centre (top) will be linked to the stadium by a footbridge should the Superdome reach fruition.
The site of the former Northern View hospital and the old tip (right) will be used for car parking - Wood Visual Communications. Ref: AC - 28714

CASTLEFORD

Situated in the heart of the Yorkshire coalfield, Castleford has long been renowned as one of the finest breeding grounds for international rugby league players and coaches. This highly-successful club, however, has been allocated only two full internationals during its 69-year history as a senior organisation, which is perhaps understandable in view of the town's small population. At one time Castleford had three mines, but since the miners' strike of 1984 and the abandonment of deep mining in the area, the old cliché about mine-shafts and rugby league players no longer has any meaning.

Following a split in the town's first rugby club (founded in 1877), a Northern Union club was formed on 12 May, 1896. Mr. Hunt's field, off Lock Lane, which was popularly referred to as *"The Sandy Desert"*, was rented, Castleford playing their first match there on 2 September, 1896 against Radcliffe. In Roman times Castleford (Legiolium-Lagentium) occupied one of the most strategic positions in Roman Britain, and the military road, Ermine Street, ran through one corner of this particular field. Castleford disbanded in 1907 but were reconstituted in 1912, when they continued to use *"The Sandy Desert"*, which is now an open recreational area, near to Hunt Street, used by the local amateur side, Lock Lane.

At their second attempt to join the Rugby League, on 17 February, 1926, Castleford headed their submission *"Distinction or Extinction"*, and they duly became the last junior club to be elected to full membership. The 1926/7 season was their last at *"The Sandy Desert"*, where two ex-army huts acted as dressing rooms, and an old double-decker tram, which they later took with them, was used as a press box and refreshment room.

Wheldon Road On acquiring their new status Castleford were in desperate need of a better ground, so when Wheldon Road, the home of ailing soccer club Castleford Town, became available, Castleford were loaned £800 by the Rugby League towards its purchase . They had lost to St. Helens Recs at Wheldon Road in a 1926 Challenge Cup tie, but Castleford's first senior game on their new ground was the 3-0 defeat by Huddersfield on 27 August, 1927, when Fartown's Australian winger Ernie Mills scored the game's only points.

Castleford inherited just one small wooden stand (behind which were some leaky dressing rooms) which they extended in 1933 to seat about 500. On Wednesday morning, 7 November, 1934, this structure was swiftly gutted by fire. Gale force winds prevented the official opening of the present replacement - originally a 1,400-seater with a paddock area. But it was ready for the third round Challenge Cup-tie against

The opening of Wheldon Road's floodlights on 20 September, 1965 at Yorkshire's game against New Zealand - Les Hoole Collection.

Hunslet on 9 March, 1935, when the present ground record of 25,449 (greater than the town's population at the time) was set during Castleford's first successful march on Wembley. Future tourist and club captain in 1935, Arthur Atkinson, has the entrance gates to Wheldon Road named in his honour.

Having repaid all outstanding loans to the Rugby League, Castleford announced plans in August, 1947 to use the land behind the main stand, previously rented to allotment holders, for the present car park and training pitch, the latter which is today used by Lock Lane ARLC.

The Minister of Sport, Mr. Denis Howell, switched on the first Wheldon Road floodlights prior to Yorkshire's 15-9 victory over New Zealand on 20 September, 1965 watched by a crowd of 15,063; the present upgraded lights, which cost £17,430, being first used against Hull K. R. on 15 March, 1985. For the Challenge Cup second round replay on Wednesday, 1 March, 1967, when Castleford beat the Robins 13-6, the official attendance was given as 22,582, but it was estimated that nearly 10,000 spectators broke in without paying.

Shortly after that game the Wheldon Road end was covered with the present propped cantilever roof. And for the start of the 1968/9 season, during which Castleford made their second successive visit to Wembley, and Great Britain U24s beat France 42-2, a new frontage on Wheldon Road replaced the original wooden fencing. The Princess Street stand was also rebuilt and extended to full pitch length.

Castleford also improved Wheldon Road's social facilities to coincide with the first full international on the ground, the International Bar being opened on 15 August, 1970 as part of improvements to the main stand. These included tip-up seats being added to the paddock area for the 1970 World Cup floodlit game between Great Britain and France, when all the 8,958 hardy spectators sought cover from the continuous drizzle. That night referee Fred Lindop awarded

Wheldon Road, looking towards the main stand, on 7 May, 1995 at the Premiership game against Warrington - Malcolm Billingham.

nearly 40 penalties as Great Britain plodded through the mud and rain to book a place in the World Cup final. Through their solid defence, France limited Britain to just five penalty attempts, three of which, all from difficult angles, were converted by Widnes full-back Ray Dutton.

There was also a leaden sky when Wheldon Road staged its first, and only, test match on Saturday, 16 October, 1971. The depressing afternoon, with little or no atmosphere from a crowd of only 4,108, was brightened though by the magnificent performance of the Kiwis, whose 17-14 victory allowed them to celebrate their first test series success in Great Britain for 63 years. Great Britain led 11-0 at half-time and looked certain to have squared the series, but in the second half they totally collapsed once Bob Haigh broke his arm - powerful right-winger Phil Orchard sealing the game with a hotly-disputed try in the final minutes.

Following the Popplewell Report in 1985 £35,000 was spent on fireproofing and tin cladding the main stand, which now allows it to be fully used, seating 1,500. In terms of other spectator comforts, however, Wheldon Road has seen few changes since that historic test match in 1971. True enough, eight executive boxes, catering for 80 VIPs, were erected at the railway end (south terrace) in 1989, the same year the adjacent scoreboard was first used; and a new restaurant, behind the main stand, was opened with a New Year's Eve party in 1992. But Wheldon's Road's general appearance is still much as it was during that halcyon period of the late 60s and early 70s, although nowadays the ground's capacity is much reduced from those days - the crowd which turned up to see the night game against the Australians in October, 1994 being near to the present permitted limit of 11,735.

In response to the Rugby League's *Framing the Future* report, however, Castleford have drawn up plans for a £2.1 million improvement scheme, £1.75 million of which is allocated to a new, fully cantilevered, main (east) stand. This will run the full length of the pitch and seat 2,500, including 130 in ten executive boxes, whilst the floodlights on that side of the ground will be set into the roof. Should funding be obtained and the scheme go ahead Wheldon's Road's capacity will be reduced slightly, to 10,687, with cover for all but 2,605 on the south terrace.

Wheldon Road		
World Cup 1970 Great Britain 6 France 0		8,958
1971 Great Britain 14 New Zealand 17		4,108

CUMBRIA

WORKINGTON

Cumbria's leading rugby league ground, Derwent Park at Workington, has yet to stage a full international, and after originally being earmarked for one of the Centenary World Cup games was inexplicably overlooked when the revised schedule was announced. This therefore leaves Cumbria without a game in this competition, which is an appalling oversight for a region steeped in rugby league history.

Lonsdale Park On 17 March, 1898, the first Workington club, the Zebras (formed in 1877), became the second Cumberland club to join the Northern Union. Their Lonsdale Park ground was used for county fixtures from the early part of the century until after the Second World War. Cumberland beat the All Golds 21-9 in 1907/8, and the ground was also used for fixtures against touring sides in 1921/2, 1926/7 and 1929/30. Workington *"Reds"* AFC (formed 1884) also played there before 1913 and from 1921 until 1937. In 1926 the ground was bought from Lord Lonsdale by Harry Hurrell, and later the Cumberland Greyhound Company became the sole lessee. The oval was also used for speedway in the 1930s.

As the Northern Union club had disbanded in 1909, the staging of the England versus Other Nationalities game on Saturday, 5 February, 1921, which drew a record West Cumberland crowd of 10,000, raised hopes that the game might be revived in the town. Having been scheduled for the 1914/5 season, the game must rank as the longest postponed fixture in the history of the code! Other Nationalities were, in fact, all Welsh and they proudly wore their national jersey. The crowd were fully entertained but the loss of forward Jack Beames after 15 minutes proved too much for the *"Welsh"*, who went down 33-16 and by seven tries to two. The grass was apparently so thick around the edges that it interfered with the goalkickers' run-ups.

It is not known what length the grass was on 7 February, 1925, but something certainly affected the great Jim Sullivan, who missed three easy conversions which effectively cost Wales the match. Playing on a heavy pitch, England were 13 points up in the first 15 minutes, but the result was in doubt until the 75th minute, when, appropriately, Huddersfield's Cumbrian forward, Douglas Clark, scored the 13th try of the match to ensure England's 27-22 victory.

Londsdale Park 1995, an unpretentious flapping track.

Because the ground did not have a scoreboard there was much confusion at the England-Other Nationalities match on Thursday afternoon, 30 March, 1933, when the wrong result was circulated by the press. Shortly after half-time England led 21-10, and there then followed what most people thought was an obstruction try to the New Zealander, left-winger Hardgrave (St. Helens), which Jim Sullivan appeared to convert. From that point onwards the crowd were enthralled at the Other Nationalities' remarkable come-back, which appeared to give them a 30-29 lead with only a minute remaining. And judging by the response to the try by the Warrington centre Dingsdale, and the goal by Leeds' Cumbrian full-back Jim Brough, there seemed little doubt that this wonderful exhibition had ended with England winning 34-30.

However, when Jim Sullivan casually mentioned the obstruction incident to journalists on the return train journey they were astonished to find that the referee had not awarded a penalty try to Hardgrave but only a penalty, and that the final score was really 34-27!

That day there was an attendance of 11,000, which was improved on slightly when 11,300 watched Cumberland's fixture with Yorkshire on 26 September, 1946. Having played the original Workington club there in the Challenge Cup in 1907, Wakefield Trinity also met local amateurs Broughton Moor at Londsdale Park in 1950.

Londsdale Park greyhound stadium now consists mostly of rusting corrugated iron shelters along the finishing straight, with the old football pavilion surviving as a licensed bar. The original small stand, on the back straight, has long since gone.

Lonsdale Park	
1921 England 33 Other Nats. 16	10,000
1925 England 27 Wales 22	14,000
1933 England 34 Other Nats. 27	11,000

Borough Park The first rugby league game at the council-owned Borough Park, the new home of the *"Reds"*, was on 18 September, 1937 when Cumberland lost 23-17 to Lancashire before a crowd of 10,200. However, it was not until December, 1944 that Workington Town, with a large majority of *"Reds"* directors, were registered as a company. The soccer club agreed for Town to share the ground, which was formerly used for school football until the soccer club moved there in 1937 as sub-tenants. Although a representative side played an exhibition at Borough Park prior to Town's first league game on 25 August, 1945, when they sensationally beat Broughton Rangers 27-5, there was only one full international ever staged there.

This was on Monday evening, 19 September, 1949 when a poor England side lost 13-7 to Other Nationalities in front of a hugely disappointed crowd of 17,576. The Other Nationalities' superiority can be judged by the fact that George Wilson, Huddersfield's Scottish wing who was playing out of position at full-back, did not have to kick the ball once throughout the match. It was he who scored the first try after supporting a break by his club colleague and fellow Scot,

Workington's Eppie Gibson passes the ball to Albert Pepperell during the game against Australia at Borough Park in 1948.

Dave Valentine. Although England rallied to 8-7 after 55 minutes, they faded badly, with Brian Bevan scoring his second try and Huddersfield's Pat Devery, who outshone Barrow's Willie Horne at stand-off, adding a penalty before the final whistle.

The club's record attendance of 20,403 was established on 8 March, 1952 against St. Helens in the second round of Town's Challenge Cup winning campaign under captain Gus Risman. Ground-sharing created unprecedented problems a week later for the third round tie against Warrington, when soccer and rugby were played on the same afternoon. It was finally agreed that the *"Reds"* should kick-off their game against Oldham Athletic at 2.p.m. to be followed by Town's 20,000 all-ticket tie at 4.45 p.m. This left only one hour to clear and prepare the ground for rugby, an arrangement which emphasised the need for Town to complete the development of Derwent Park, on which they had taken out a 199-year lease from the local council.

Town erected a popular side cover at Borough Park in 1951 at a cost of £5,000, and this, along with another old shelter behind one goal, still survives. The floodlight pylons, which are now half their original height, were bought from Manchester United in 1976, the year before the *"Reds"* were voted out of the Football League. Faced with safety restrictions, in 1987 the *"Reds"* demolished the wooden seating and roof of the main stand, thus leaving only the social facilities underneath intact. A shelter has since been provided for the faithful on this side but there is still no seating in the ground.

Borough Park
1949 England 7 Other Nats. 13   17,576

Derwent Park Although Town's "A" team played at Derwent Park during the 1947/8 season, because of problems with the drainage pitch and a scarcity of building permits, the first team did not play there until Monday, 27 August, 1956, when they lost 24-0 to Wigan.

Town's legendary director, and Great Britain tour manager in 1958, Tom Mitchell, had overall responsibility for the building of Derwent Park, which is on the site of a former rubbish tip and what was previously, in part, a tidal estuary. The original bankings were composed of thousands of tons of shale from the Siddick Colliery. In 1954 a start was made on the present full-length popular side cover but it was not

Derwent Park's present popular side - Mike Haddon.

until March, 1956 that the 1,700-seater main stand took shape. The ends of this stand, which are set at an angle of 45 degrees to enable for viewing of the corners of the pitch, were not completed at that opening game.

A record attendance of 17,741 was set on 3 March, 1965, against Wigan in the third round of the Challenge Cup, but following the Popplewell Report Derwent Park's capacity was reduced to an unbelievable 986. Because of such ridiculous restrictions the Challenge Cup-tie against Wigan on 6 February, 1986 was transferred to Borough Park. Having spent over £100,000 on safety work Town received a £450,000 lifeline in January, 1989 with the sale of their training pitch for what is now a Tesco supermarket. Town, however, have simply moved their training ground to an adjacent field. This windfall enabled Town to install their first £72,000 floodlights, which were officially switched on when Cumbria entertained the Australians on 17 October, 1990, the fixture having been transferred from Whitehaven's Recreation Ground.

Although there was a disappointing crowd of only 4,277 at Derwent Park for the opening game of the 1994 Australian tour, it is at present the only suitable rugby ground in West Cumbria capable of staging representative fixtures. There was obvious disappointment at being denied an international during the centenary celebrations, but

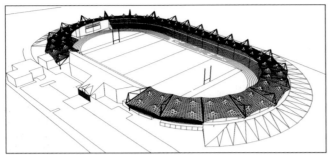

The proposed Allerdale Stadium -
© Tim Britton / Richard Lindsay Associates, 1995.

undeterred by this rebuff, early in 1995 Town's directors unveiled plans for a £6.5 million redevelopment of the ground with the support of Allerdale Council.

Under the proposed scheme Derwent Park will be re-named the New Allerdale Stadium, and its capacity raised from 10,000 to 15,000, with seating increased from 1,200 to 2,900. Fully covered by a glass-fibre roof supported by steel tension rods and a cantilevered frame, the stadium have potential to seat 12,000. Other features would include a 6-lane athletics track, computerised scoreboard, hospitality boxes, and undersoil heating. Funding, of at least some of the stages, is anticipated through the Sports Council's Lottery Fund before the start of the 1995/6 season.

WHITEHAVEN

Recreation Ground Formerly marshlands, the Whitehaven Recreation Ground has been used for organised sport since about 1895, when it was the home of junior club Whitehaven Recreation. The ground was the venue for many of the early county fixtures, including the visit of the first Australians in 1908/9 when Cumberland lost 52-10. However, in 1924 and 1925 such games were played on the nearby Playground, officially opened for cricket and other summer sports by Lord Londsdale on 1 May, 1838, and enlarged in 1877 to accommodate the town's first rugby club.

The Recreation Ground's original pavilion, which was situated, inconveniently for players and harassed referees, just outside the main gates, was built circa 1898. At that time a small open stand stood on the site of its replacement, which survived until Christmas 1994.

Originally seating just less than 750, this wooden structure, which was no more than 30 yards in length, was officially opened on 4 February, 1926 by the renamed (Whitehaven Colliery) Recreation Club on the occasion of the Recreation Ground's only international. That Thursday afternoon England easily beat Other Nationalities before an excellent crowd estimated at 7,000. The ground conditions suited England's heavier forwards and Other Nationalities trailed 16-0 shortly after half-time. They drew back to 19-11 at one stage but four English tries, three of which were converted by Burgess via the crossbar, took the final score to 37-11. Leeds and England full-back Jim Brough was in outstanding form in this match, and it was his last minute goal which gave Cumberland victory over the 1933 Australians on the same ground.

Prior to being voted into the Rugby League in March, 1948 Whitehaven had agreed a lease of the Recreation Ground with the Whitehaven Miners' Welfare, their present landlords under another name, who had acquired it in 1944 from the Earl of Lonsdale. Thousands of tons of waste pit slag were used to increase the re-aligned bankings in anticipation of a record crowd for the official opening against Hull on 21 August, 1948. Unfortunately, with no shelter because the old stand was in need of repair, the appalling conditions kept the crowd down to 8,982. Home loose-forward Joe Flanagan had the honour of registering the first points with a penalty goal.

Australian half-back Cyril Connell scores a try during the tourists' 14-11 defeat against Whitehaven at the Recreation Ground in 1956.

By the end of that year the Supporters' Club had completely terraced the popular side with railway sleepers, but it was not until May, 1950 that this was covered, only for the roof to be severely damaged in 1952 by gale force winds. This cover had been repaired and two tin shelters (all since demolished) erected either side of the main stand by the time that Whitehaven scored their famous 14-11 victory over the 1956 Australians. Included in that Whitehaven side was the future Great Britain tearaway forward, Dick Huddart.

The Recreation Ground's old main stand (right) has now been replaced - John Story, Whitehaven News.

On 19 March, 1960 the record attendance, officially returned at 18,500 but considered by many experienced supporters to have been many thousands more, provided unprecedented scenes at the third round Challenge Cup-tie against eventual winners, Wakefield Trinity. The following year the Kells end was covered at a cost of £9,000, and on Thursday, 21 September, 1973 the first floodlights were officially switched on for the league game against St. Helens. The £100,000 dressing room complex, sponsored by British Nuclear Fuels, was opened in September, 1986.

Its modern design contrasted sharply with the adjacent wooden stand, which was closed for a time in 1989 and 1990 on safety grounds. This stand later acquired a steel frame but its antiquated condition, and the fact that it seated only 460, was the principle reason why Cumbria's game against the Australians was transferred to Derwent Park in 1990. It was finally demolished in December, 1994 to make way for a £500,000 improvement scheme, financed by the Sports Aid Foundation and regeneration grants. This will include the erection of a 500-seater cantilever stand, the reinstatement of cover over the adjacent standing areas, and the re-roofing of the popular side, in time for the opening of the 1995/6 season.

In the longer term, Whitehaven hope to raise another £2 million to build a new main stand on the popular side, and also install new corner floodlights. The new stand is designed to hold 3,000, including 2,000 seated, with eight executive boxes, to bring the ground up to the minimum requirements of the *Framing the Future* report.

Recreation Ground
1926 England 37 Other Nats. 11   7,000

HALIFAX

It was an advertisement in the local newspaper placed by members of the Fourth West Yorkshire Rifle Volunteers which brought about the formation of the present Halifax club in late 1873, although their first home fixture, against Wakefield Trinity, was not played until Boxing Day, 1974. This was on the Halifax Trinity Cricket Club field, which is now Norfolk Place. Their third move in as many seasons then resulted in Halifax sharing the Hanson Lane cricket field with the above Trinity C. C., with whom it was decided to amalgamate, in May, 1878, shortly after winning the inaugural Yorkshire Cup.

Unable to make improvements to Hanson Lane because of their short lease, in 1886 the Halifax Cricket, Football and Athletic Club purchased the freehold on the neighbouring Thrum Hall farm for £3,000. The Hanson Lane ground, which had hosted several representative games in its time, was partly used as hen runs until 1931, when the filter house and offices of what became Yorkshire Water, opposite the main drive way to Thrum Hall, was built on the site. In recent years this land has been taken for housing. In exchange for land, with which they widened the country lanes of Thrum Hall Lane, Spring Hall Lane and Gibbet Street, Halifax Corporation built the boundary walls to the new ground. Other land was also exchanged to assist in the design of the multi-purpose arena, which is the highest above sea-level (776 feet) in the whole of the Rugby League.

Thrum Hall After the grounds had earlier been opened with a cricket match between a Yorkshire XI versus 18 of the District, the rugby ground's official opening took place on 18 September, 1886 - Alderman Riley kicking off before the defeat of Hull. A crowd of 8,000 saw forward Ernest Williamson make the first score on the ground with his one and only try for the club.

The original rugby enclosure (150 yards by 90 yards) was slightly oval in shape. It was not until 1953 that the picket fencing was replaced by the present concrete walls. The ground, as today, sloped nearly twelve feet from touch-line to touch-line. On the site of today's main stand was a 60-yard long, seven-row 2,000-seater brick and timber open stand, in front of which was a standing enclosure, and a press box which was situated inside the rails. The old 95-yard long open stand from Hanson Lane was placed on the Thrum Hall Lane side. Its four rows apparently held 1,800, and a sloping *"promenade of wood grating"* increased its capacity to around 3,000.

This was replaced during the 1894/5 season by another open wooden structure, a mere 39 yards in length, which, with certain structural alterations, was covered in 1934 and still exists today. The original boundary at the Gibbet Street end, where there was additional terracing, was far narrower than today, with the pitch being subsequently shortened with the building of Newstead Terrace. The present double-fronted pavilion, which cost £1,900, then housed the first scoreboard.

Because of the rugby field being frost bound, the games against Leigh on 5 March, 1904 (won 8-5) and against Warrington on 28 February, 1911 (won 44-0) were played on the cricket field, which was last used for county championship cricket in 1897 when Yorkshire beat Kent. The now redundant track around the cricket ground, which in 1889 was 480 yards in circumference and banked for cycling, has also been used for both speedway and greyhound racing from the 1930s.

On the evening of 17 November, 1907, after a defeat at Bradford, a stray black cat wandered into the pavilion, and apparently brought the club such good luck, with a run of 16 successive wins and one draw, that it was granted celebrity status. Subsequently named Smut, a figure of this mascot is still to be found on the roof of the pavilion, which in the 1930s was handed over to the cricket section in exchange for the writing-off of a £750 debt. Subsequently, the rugby club, which became a limited liability company in 1936, has to this day been left with just the end wing comprising of changing rooms, board room, and the secretary's office.

The 1930 Other Nationalities side, with the then roofless Thrum Hall Lane stand in the background.

The first cover at Thrum Hall came with the erection of the present main stand. Costing £987/5/0d, the corrugated-roofed brick and wooden stand was designed to seat approximately 1,800 with a paddock for 1,000. It was officially opened by the club President, J. H. Bromwich, before the kick-off against Rochdale Hornets on 16 September, 1911. Room was allowed for dressing rooms to be added later and the press were now accommodated at the rear of the stand. Thrum Hall was subsequently given its first Championship final at the end of that season when Huddersfield beat Wigan in front of a crowd of 15,000.

A new ground record of 29,122 was established in 1913/14, when Halifax lost 39-0 to Huddersfield in the Yorkshire Cup second round, and during that same season Thrum Hall hosted, not only the Yorkshire Cup final but its one and only Challenge Cup final when Hull beat Wakefield Trinity 6-0 in front of a crowd of 19,000.

The estate's trustees, having managed to stave off the threats from builders during the First World War, then set about making the necessary post-war repairs and much-needed improvements. For example, in 1921, the year that the first deed was set up between the bowling, cricket, and rugby clubs, to guarantee Thrum Hall's future as a sports ground, £2,000 was spent on covering the Gibbet Street end.

The new stand (the cause of many future postponements due to it cutting out the sun) was first used for the Infirmary Cup charity match on 22 August, 1921, when a crowd of 12,000 saw Halifax lose 36-12 to a British Lions side captained by Harold Wagstaff. By the end of the decade the Supporters' Club had helped pay for new terracing at this end, as well as the erection of an Omega scoreboard at the pavilion end, and, in November, 1930, the modernisation of the pavilion.

Earlier that year Thrum Hall had hosted the first of its two internationals, when on Monday evening, 7 April, Other Nationalities beat England 35-19, despite trailing by 13 points at one stage in the first half. The turning point came in the 26th minute when Jim Sullivan joined in an attack from full-back to put his outstanding Wigan colleague, New Zealand forward Mason, over for a try. From that point the Other Nationalities never looked back, and although Warrington centre Dingsdale scored a first half hat-trick of tries, he was still to find his side badly-outclassed in a game containing 14 tries.

On 1 September, 1934, the present shelter on the Thrum Hall Lane side was officially opened by Alderman A. L. Whitaker prior to Halifax's 20-nil victory over Barrow. It was the opening of nearby Odsal Stadium on that same afternoon, however, which proved to be much more significant, as it virtually ended Thrum Hall's claims to big-match status. Having staged the Challenge Cup semi-finals in 1924 and 1926, and the Championship final in 1929 and 1930 (replay), thereafter Thrum Hall was only allocated two Yorkshire Cup finals, in 1935 and 1945 (when Bradford Northern were involved), and the Roses match in 1949. Ironically, however, it was Odsal's notorious pitch which provided the opportunity for Thrum Hall to stage its second international.

Because of problems with mud in the centre of the Odsal pitch it was decided, after an inspection of both grounds on the Friday, to transfer the England-France game to Thrum Hall on the scheduled date of Saturday, 10 April, 1937. Considering the last-minute arrangements, and the fact that Wales had already won the championship, the crowd of 7,024, which did not appreciate the unnecessary rough tactics of several of the home forwards, was considered satisfactory.

It was only in the last quarter that England wore down the French, who were handicapped by the loss of right-winger Samatan, to finish 23-9 winners. Swinton's goal-kicking forward Martin Hodgson, who literally and metaphorically towered above his colleagues, not only kicked three goals but saved a certain try when he carried left winger Cussac over the touch-in-goal. Although the left-wing pair of Tom Winnard (Bradford Northern) and J. H. Cumberbatch (Broughton Rangers) shared four tries it was Liverpool Stanley full-back Billy Belshaw who was the best of the English backs. However, it was the French threequarters who really caught the eye, captain Max Rousie's magnificent drop goal being the real highlight of the afternoon.

A new ground record of 28,150 was established in 1950 at the top four Championship replay when Halifax lost 18-2 to Wigan. The following season the main stand was re-roofed, and a press box, which survived until 1984, built into it. From 1957 until 1959 the Supporters' Club donated almost £20,000 for both ends to be completely re-terraced, with the Hanson Lane end, complete with the present scoreboard but then minus the present hospitality boxes, being reconstructed to its present design. This enabled the present ground record of 29,153 to be set at the all-ticket third round Challenge Cup-tie against Wigan on 21 March, 1959.

England's centre Tom Winnard kicks ahead against France in 1937.

In 1962 the licensed Supporters' Club (re-named the Taverners Bar in 1982) was opened at the Newstead corner, and this currently houses the Halifax Hall of Fame. The first floodlights were officially switched on by the Rugby League secretary, Bill Fallowfield, during the half-time interval of the game against Widnes on 25, August, 1967. They cost £8,524 and have since been upgraded on the same ten parallel pylons.

Following the Valley Parade fire, the 75-year old wooden main stand was finally passed fit for use after it was *"fire-proofed"* and 1,200 plastic seats installed for the start of the 1988/9 season. Thrum Hall's capacity was then reduced from 11,313 to 9,832 following the Taylor Report recommendations, but, for some reason, the provision of new crush barriers was only considered necessary in 1994.

Prior to a new consortium taking over the club in 1990, Halifax were in the hands of administrators with debts conservatively estimated at £650,000. Unlike some other rugby league clubs, who have been in financial difficulties in recent years, Halifax did not have the easy option open to them of selling their ground. Under and agreement made in June, 1934 the estate is vested in trustees *("to hold in perpetuity for the purpose of sport for the benefit of the public of Halifax")* appointed by the Thrum Hall Estate Joint Committee, which consists of members of the bowling, cricket and rugby club. No structural alterations or additional building can be made without the consent of the trustees, and, furthermore, no association football can be played for profit, so long as rugby is played on the estate.

However, in February, 1994 the trustees apparently agreed in principle to waive this agreement, subject to certain safeguards in relocating the bowling and cricket clubs, when plans were announced for Halifax Town to ground-share with Halifax at a redeveloped Thrum Hall. The expectations were that a £6.3 million 15,000 capacity stadium, which would have been sited on the Thrum Hall cricket pitch and have retained the renovated pavilion, would have been mostly financed by the sale of the soccer club's council-owned Shay ground.

This scheme, however, now appears to have been abandoned following the refusal of planning permission for retail development at the Shay, a decision which threatened the very future of professional sport in the town. At the time of writing, Halifax, having done a rapid U-turn on their decision to reject £1 million of Super League money and merge with Bradford Northern at Odsal, were taking a leaf out of Town's book by appealing to the public for help in meeting essential safety work at Thrum Hall. It now seems likely that piecemeal development will take place, starting with the pavilion end.

Thrum Hall	
1930 England 19 Other Nats. 35	2,300
1937 England 23 France 9	7,024

Thrum Hall, June 1995. The former Hanson Lane ground is now covered in housing (top left) - Wood Visual Communications. Ref: AC28566

HUDDERSFIELD

Fartown Despite its age and size, and the fact that it hosted over 25 cup semi-finals and finals, Fartown was allocated only a handful of internationals, including just one fully-fledged test match. This was mainly due to competition in Yorkshire from both Headingley and Odsal. The past tense is accurate as Fartown is no longer a first-class rugby league stadium following the Claret and Golds departure, firstly to ground-share with Huddersfield Town at Leeds Road, and last season to do likewise at the new Alfred McAlpine Stadium. Even in its present state, however, Fartown can claim to be the oldest surviving ground in Yorkshire where international rugby has been staged, Dewsbury's Crown Flatt having relinquished this title in 1991 when it was enveloped in housing.

The first six acres of the present Fartown grounds, a field then owned by a Mr Rutter of the George Hotel, were officially opened on 4 April, 1868 for use by St. John's Cricket Club. Their amalgamation with the local Athletic Club on 27 November, 1875 eventually led to Fartown's enlargement courtesy of the Ramsden Estate, which owned the grounds until the Huddersfield and Kirklees Councils inherited them. The first game of rugby was on 2 November, 1878 against Manchester Rangers.

In those days there was a tennis ground and a line of trees in the middle of the present pitch. An *"unsightly wooden structure"* was the only spectator comfort on the rugby ground, but, nonetheless, Fartown was chosen by the F. A. for one of their Cup semi-finals in 1882, when the soccer authorities were trying, unsuccessfully, to gain a foothold in the rugby-dominated West Riding. It is perhaps worth bearing this in mind when we consider rugby league's present dependence on soccer grounds for many of its internationals.

Huddersfield's headquarters and dressing rooms were then a short ride away at the George Hotel, where, of course, the Northern Union was formed in 1895. The problem of violence towards referees and visiting teams was not overcome until the pavilion (opened in 1884) was later used. As a means of evading the mob outside the George, a referee once took to wearing a policeman's uniform but when his disguise was uncovered he was pelted mercilessly!

In 1890 radical changes were made at a cost of £8,600. The first stage was the building of terraces for the cricket field,

which was levelled and a cycle track laid around in time for the annual Athletic Festival on 20 June, 1891, when the Manhattan (New York) Athletic Club attracted over 15,000 spectators. Work then commenced on the rugby ground where, on 31 October, 1891, in their first home game of the season, Huddersfield defeated Cardiff 14-7. Many of the 10,000 crowd were sat on the fifteen Roman amphitheatre-type steps of the new north terrace, a corner of which has survived to this day. At this first match the new main stand was roofless but still usable.

A month later, on a dreadful day, 23,250 watched the Roses match. Although an illustration of this record crowd shows the ground to have been well developed, for the Challenge Cup semi-final in 1903 *"hundreds of wagonettes"* were said to have been needed for vantage points. By 1905, however, there was terracing, of sorts, at both the pavilion and Netheroyd Hill ends, the latter which also had a schoolboys' pen.

It is more than likely that the legendary Harold Wagstaff stood there in the years preceding his signing for Huddersfield in 1906 as a 15-year old. On 2 January, 1909, however, he entered the field as the youngest player, at that time, to represent his country. Two of the 17-year old's superb dribbles resulted in tries for England as they defeated Australia 14-9. This was just one of seven internationals played on that first tour by Australia, and for many years it was considered to be the first ever test against the two countries. Historian Stanley Chadwick said that the tour committee minutes referred to it as such, however this is now only recognised as an additional international, the first test at Park Royal, London (see Soccer chapter).

Harold Wagstaff

The attendance at the Fartown international was only 5,569, which contrasted sharply with the new ground record of 28,053 at the drawn third round Challenge Cup tie against Wigan on 27 March, 1909. At the start of the following season there were seven Internationals on the club's books and the facilities were improved to coincide with the emergence of Wagstaff's *"Team of All the Talents"*.

A standing-only barrel-roofed stand, the last of its kind in the game, was opened at the pavilion end on 9 September, 1909, when Huddersfield beat Leeds 31-0 in front of 14,242 spectators. A new ground record of 30,125 was set on 21 February, 1914 for the visit of Wigan, and during that summer work commenced on a new main stand. Complete with a central gable, it was finished during the 1914/15 season, with its twenty rows of wooden seats being slightly curved to allow for optimum viewing. This stand was extended towards the pavilion end for the start of the 1930/1 season, taking Fartown's seating capacity to 3,200, which at that time was certainly on a par with any other ground in the league.

Despite these improvements, however, there were only two internationals played at Fartown during this period. On Monday afternoon, 1 October, 1923, England beat Wales 18-11, scoring all their points in the first half. Halifax half-back Frank Todd, who was drafted in to replace Jonty Parkin, was a revelation but no Welshmen enhanced his position for a likely tour place. In 1931, however, with a spectacular try from Gus Risman, Wales were definitely the better side for the first hour, although most of the thrills were confined to the last ten minutes with England stealing the game 23-18. The casual approach up to half-time made *The Yorkshire Post* correspondent remark: *"There is not the sternness...to make these games really worth while; chiefly they are looked upon to provide a demonstration on exhibition lines of the finer points of the game."*

If indeed he was correct, he had not long to wait for some genuine European rivalry following France's entry onto the international scene in 1934. Before Puig-Aubert's Chanticleers graced this famous turf, however, Fartown was to stage its one and only test match. Unfortunately, with Great Britain having retained the Ashes and with thick fog in most other neighbouring towns, there was a crowd of only 9,093, on 18 December, 1937, to see a surprise Australian 13-3 victory. This was to be the last international before the war, following which Fartown, which was used for fitness training and drilling in 1940, was allocated its first European Championship game. This too was something of an historic occasion as the England-France encounter on 25 October, 1947, when the French were unlucky to lose 20-15, was the first occasion that a French referee had controlled a game in England - Monsieur Guidicelli's performance being hailed by everyone present.

The ground record of 35,136 had been set at the Challenge Cup semi-final on 19 April, 1947 between Leeds and

The 1948 Australians perform their war cry before a then record crowd, 26,053, for the opening game of a tour in this country.

Wakefield Trinity, whilst on 18 September, 1948 a new record attendance (26,053) for the opening game of a tour was established against the Australians. Because of such support, the north terrace was reconstructed for the start of the 1951/2 season, adding about 7,000 to its capacity.

Huddersfield had five players in the Championship-winning Other Nationalities side which beat England 31-12 at Fartown in 1952. The policy of playing internationals and league games on the same Saturday afternoon also affected Warrington, who had four players on duty and suffered their heaviest home defeat for several seasons. England led 11-5 before injuries and the loss of possession at the play-the-ball took its toll. Brian Bevan helped himself to four tries with some bewildering running, and Fartowners Peter Henderson (2) and Lionel Cooper also scored tries, watched by a crowd of 20,459. Strange as it may seem, this was to be the last international on the ground.

The only other major ground development since the 1950s was the opening of the present Supporters' Social Club on 25 September, 1965, on land which was formerly terracing and an access point to the barrel-roofed stand. The first parallel floodlights were then opened on 18 October, 1967.

One of the last surviving members' clubs, Huddersfield became a limited company in 1977, in time for the ground's centenary game against Wakefield Trinity on 29 October, 1978, with 82-year old Hubert Pogson, the last surviving

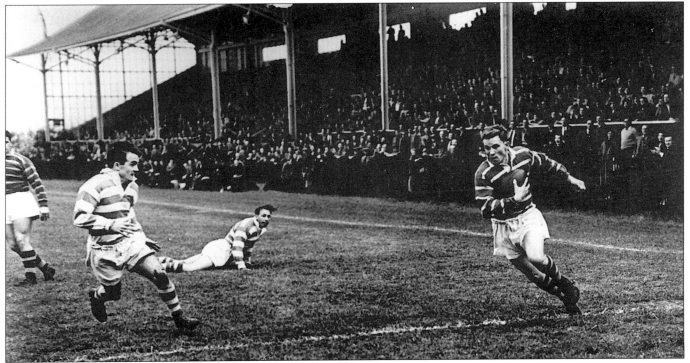

Great Britain's most capped player, Mike Sullivan, scores against Batley at Fartown in front of a packed main stand. - Kirklees Cultural Services.

member of Huddersfield's 1920 Challenge Cup-winning side, ceremoniously kicking off.

In August, 1983 the new club owner, Mr John Bailey, controversially renamed the historic grounds *"Arena 84"* as part of the club's new image. However, safety measures imposed after the Valley Parade fire caused the main stand to be closed and the ground, like the once-famous team, continued its sad decline. In November, 1989 a new board reinstated the ground's historic name, and with the help from Kirklees Council, again opened up the stand and upgraded the floodlights. At the same time, the score-board, originally erected in memory of Great Britain's 1954 World Cup captain Dave Valentine, was also renovated. It was not until November, 1991, however, that problems were resolved with the lease, which has allowed Mr Bailey to retain the mock Tudor pavilion as a nightclub, and for the adjacent Supporters' Club to remain on the site.

By this stage the debt-ridden Fartowners had been invited to join in Huddersfield Town's proposed new multi-million pound stadium, following their sale of Leeds Road - where the 1951 Rugby League Championship final was staged - for the building of a B&Q retail depot. This involved them vacating the near-derelict Fartown - £50,000 compensation was paid by Kirklees Council for them to do so - and ground-sharing with Town throughout the 1992/3 and 1993/4 seasons whilst the new stadium took shape.

Apart from the sale of Leeds Road for £4.7 million and major sponsorships, the new ground, just a few hundred yards away, was also financed by the Football Trust, Kirklees Council, and the Foundation for Sports and the Arts, the latter grant being dependent on the Fartowners' involvement in the scheme. A joint holding company, Kirklees Stadium Development Ltd., was formed with both Town and the council having 40% of the shares and the rugby club 20%.

Oldham's captain, the ex-Huddersfield and Great Britain full-back Frank "Spanky" Dyson, is brought to ground by Hull K.R.'s Blackmore during the Challenge Cup semi-final second replay at Fartown in 1964 - NMPFT/Science and Society Picture Library.

There were doubts, however, that the Fartowners would survive to play in the new stadium, as during October, 1993 they were placed in the hands of an administrator with debts of £460,000. Former club directors, who were the majority creditors, threatened legal action to stop the administrators acceptance of only £30,000 from a new consortium. Only when the KSDL put their weight behind an increased bid of £140,000 in May, 1994, and agreed to meet the administration costs of £80,000, was the takeover battle resolved and the rugby club able to become part of the new development.

Although no one was to know it, and the historic event therefore went unheralded, the Claret and Golds last senior game at Fartown was a Yorkshire Cup tie against York on August, 1992. In marked contrast to this low key departure, Town's final game at Leeds Road against Blackpool on 30 April, 1994, before a 16,000-plus all-ticket crowd, was expertly marketed with a range of souvenirs available and an auction of parts of Leeds Road. In some respects this was a reflection on the respective running of the two clubs at the time, although the circumstances at Fartown were slightly different in so far as the ground, which is now administered by the council's Leisure Services, has continued to be used for second team and Academy games.

Ironically, the week that Huddersfield played their opening match at the new stadium, on 28 August, 1994, the bulldozers moved in to demolish Fartown's main stand where vandals had earlier set fire to the dressing rooms.

Fartown	
1909 England 14 Australia 9	5,569
1923 England 18 Wales 11	11,066
1931 England 23 Wales 18	6,000
1937 Great Britain 3 Australia 13	9,093
1947 England 20 France 15	14,175
1952 England 12 Other Nats. 31	20,459

The Alfred McAlpine Stadium Although it has yet to stage a rugby league international, the Alfred McAlpine Stadium is due to figure prominently in the Rugby League centenary celebrations. As well as staging the opening ceremony to the 1995 World Cup, it has not only been allocated Australia's match against Fiji but the tournament's second semi-final, beating off competition from Elland Road.

Built on the site of a 100-year old dye works and bounded by the River Colne and the wooded Kilner Bank, the former Kirklees Stadium was renamed after a ten-year £2 million sponsorship deal was struck with the ground's main contractors, Alfred McAlpine. The same company had also built the previously mentioned B&Q depot on the Leeds Road ground.

Work commenced in June, 1993 with the laying of the £368,000 undersoil-heated pitch; and the stadium was officially opened on Saturday, 20 August, 1994, when Huddersfield Town lost 1-0 to Wycombe Wanderers before an all-ticket crowd of 13,334. The Fartowners played their first game there on 28 August, when a crowd of 4,300 watched them score a 50-12 win over Barrow, captain Neil Flanagan scoring the first senior points on the ground with a try. A parade of former players included 86-year old Gwyn Parker who had made his debut in the 1920s.

Because all the funding was not yet in place, at the opening there were only two stands in operation - the two-tier 8,500-seater Riverside Stand, now called the Lawrence Batley Stand following a £250,000 10-year sponsorship by one of the town's leading businessmen, and the 7,250-seater John Smith's Stand on the Kilner Bank side. The Lawrence Batley Stand includes 26 executive boxes, the administration block, and a 500-seater banqueting and conference suite, the latter

Looking towards the (Kilner Bank) John Smith's Stand at Huddersfield's opening game against Barrow - Mike Haddon.

which was officially opened on 15 September, 1994 by Sir Stanley Matthews, CBE. The South Stand, which is now called the Gardner Merchant Stand after the stadium's catering company, was still being built. When completed in November, 1994 it lifted the ground's capacity to just over 20,000 and the ground's total cost to £16 million, most of which has been offset by grants and sponsorships. Completion of the two-tier North Stand within the next few years will eventually bring the stadium's all-seater capacity up to 25,000, which was the brief given to the architects, Lobb Partnership.

Their winning scheme was based on a prototype, *Stadium for the Nineties*, which they had developed for the Sports Council. The four *"orange-segment"* shaped stands are the result of the plan to have a maximum viewing distance of 150 metres from the four corners of the pitch - 3D computer software being used to check the view from every seat. The blue sheet roofs are supported by arches consisting of white tubular-steel prismatic trusses, the largest stretching 140 metres and weighing 78 tonnes. From a distance these can easily be mistaken for a bridge. These arches, which should not require painting for another 20 years, are held in place at each corner by huge reinforced concrete legs, which also hold the 40-metre high £299,000 floodlights (172 2kw lamps) and the stadium control box.

The 51-acre complex also includes a floodlit golf driving range; whilst a dry ski slope is planned down the Kilner Bank at the northern end, where it is likely that a multiplex cinema will be built at some stage. Proposals for the stadium to house a rugby league museum, however, have received little encouragement from the Rugby League, despite its officials clearly viewing the Alfred McAlpine Stadium, situated in the birthplace of the game, as a model venue for some of its most prestigious games.

The only criticism of the stadium has been the traffic conjestion caused by poor road access. Rather than pandering to the motorist, however, stadium officials could perhaps inform potential visitors that the Alfred McAlpine Stadium is within reasonable walking distance of Huddersfield railway station and the adjacent George Hotel. It was the trans-Pennine rail link, in fact, which was the main reason why the Lancashire and Yorkshire clubs chose the George for their meeting in 1895 when the Northern Union was formed.

Wigan's Dennis Betts on his way to scoring a try against Oldham in the 1995 Challenge Cup semi-final at the Alfred McAlpine Stadium - Nick Fairhurst, Rugby Leaguer Newspaper.

KEIGHLEY

Cougar Park (formerly **Lawkholme Lane**)   Looking at it objectively, rather than being influenced by the hype of *"Cougarmania"*, Cougar Park is an unlikely setting for the staging of a full rugby league international. The forthcoming Centenary World Cup game there between Fiji and South Africa was perhaps granted, not because of Cougar Park's obvious suitability, but more as a recognition of the Keighley Cougars' recent playing successes and their innovative work within the local community.

In fact, throughout the world, apart from Greymouth's Wingham Park in 1954, there has been no smaller ground used for international rugby league. Since the sale of the ground to the West Yorkshire Motor Group in 1987 and the building of the filling station on what was the site of the Kop, the pitch has been slightly shortened (97 metres post to post by 67 metres) and new terracing laid at both ends. Although its record attendance stands at 14,500, Cougar Park's present capacity is a mere 5,800, including 1,150 seated, a figure which is only likely to be increased to around 6,700 by the time of the international in October.

Keighley have played at what was formerly Lawkholme Lane since 1885. Up to 1933, on the western side the rugby pitch had more or less a common boundary with the cricket field. In those early days there was just one small open wooden members' stand, known as the *"henpen"*, which was demolished following the game against Swinton on Easter Tuesday, 1933 and replaced by the sunken terraces of what, after being covered in 1937, became known as the *"scrattin shed"*.   This was due to be demolished at the end of last season to allow for the extension of the terracing on that eastern side where 22 hospitality boxes are to be installed.

For the present, however, the only public cover on the ground is the main stand, the original section of which was officially opened on 9 September, 1933.   This was extended to its current length, including new dressing rooms, for the visit of Oldham in December, 1954.   The tip-up seating which once graced the central members' area has long since disappeared and overseas VIPs for the World Cup game may be less than overjoyed by the primitive wooden seating.   They are more likely to be impressed by the new £250,000 Sponsor's Lounge, adjoining the stand, which was opened following the Cougar's Third Division Championship success in 1993, and also the atmosphere generated at this compact arena.

Australia on the rampage during their 54-4 win over Keighley in 1952.

On that score, and on the promotion of the international generally, the club will have few worries, although there will doubtless be many sleepless nights over the likely state of the playing surface. This cost Keighley the Academy international against France in February, 1994 and after the club spent £22,000 on levelling and re-draining last season the pitch was waterlogged in parts. The responsibility for this, however, was laid firmly at the door of the contractor and this problem should be addressed in time for Cougar Park's big day. In the longer term, there are proposals for a 1,800-seater cantilever east stand which will raise the ground's capacity to 8,500, whilst, with the club only having a short lease, the option is currently being considered of buying back the cricket ground in order to develop a new stadium which will meet the requirements for any subsequent entry to the Super League.

Cougar Park at the 1995 Premiership game against London Broncos.

KINGSTON-UPON-HULL

HULL F.C. Formed in 1865, Hull were the first northern club to join the London-based Rugby Union. During the 30 years up to their arrival at the Boulevard the club played on six grounds, including one at Selby, where they stayed for one season as a means of enticing the leading West Riding clubs to travel east. As we shall see, 100 years later Hull was still regarded as an *"outpost"* area of the Rugby League.

In 1881/2 Hull merged with Hull White Star F.C. and moved to the latter's small ground at Hall's Field on Holderness Road. Here they remained until they made the controversial decision to rent the home of their junior neighbours, Hull Kingston Rovers, who were formed in 1883 by a group of apprentice boilermakers under the title of Kingston Amateurs.

The Boulevard Rovers had played on the Hull Athletic Company's ground, off the Boulevard, from February, 1892. But, before the end of The Robins' 3-year tenancy, Hull agreed a 10-year lease on the ground at three times Rovers' rent. Consequently, Rovers crossed to the east side of the Humber to settle at Craven Street. Hull's *"unsportsmanlike action"* later proved to be justified, as Holderness Road was soon sold off for the building of Mersey Street and Severn Street. Having bought the ground in 1899 for £6,500 Hull named it The Boulevard. The club later took the nickname The Airlie Birds from the street on which the main entrance is situated.

As a founder member of the Northern Union, Hull played their first home game on 21 September, 1895, when they beat Liversedge by a try from Jacketts before a local record crowd of 8,000. Hull inherited the Athletic Company's timber-framed covered grandstand, and prior to this historic match the first stage of the now famous Threepenny Stand had been built. 75 yards in length, with room for about 2,000 spectators *"The Thrummer Stand"* (as one journalist referred to it) was made of Russian pine and had over 20 roof supports. The existing 130-foot section was added before 1906. Since its renovation in 1989 it has retained its original ornate cornice, but many of its wooden beams have been removed for safety purposes, and it is now completely clad in corrugated sheeting.

At that opening match the dressing rooms were behind the Airlie Street goal, and there was a sectional stand at the Gordon Street end. This could well have been a temporary measure, as fifty wagons were placed at this end for the game against Bradford in March, 1898 when there was a record crowd of 20,000.

The Athletic Ground's cycle track, which ran on the site of the present end terraces, disappeared in the 1920s, but was re-laid for greyhound racing in 1927 and also during the 1950s. Speedway also made a brief appearance in the 1970s before being dispensed with due to its detrimental effect on the pitch. The Boulevard has still retained its original oval shape, however.

A terrace extension was added to the main stand for the start of the 1914/5 season, thus making it full pitch length, and tip-up seats were also installed in the original stand section. However, there was still only seating for about 500 at the time that Australia won the second test, 16-2, on 5 November, 1921. For this game 400 seats were placed on the main stand terraces and another 500 around the track.

An early injury to Leeds winger Squire Stockwell proved decisive, and after the scores were level 2-all at half-time, the Australians had a field day, with left centre Dick Vest and Norths' wingers, Harold Horder and Cecil Blinkhorn (2), each scoring tries due to pathetic tackling and sloppy British handling. The worst culprit was Hull's right winger, Billy Stone, who, after dropping an easy pass, simply watched as Blinkhorn raced in for his second try. All in all, it was a poor birthday present for Wakefield Trinity's Jonty Parkin, who was captaining the side for the first time.

A view of the famous Threepenny Stand - Andrew Cudbertson.

The crowd in 1921 was 21,504, but there were less than a third of that number in 1926 when Great Britain gained the upperhand in the last few minutes to beat an impressive New Zealand side, 21-11. The present ground record was established on 7 March, 1936 when 28,798 saw Hull lose 5-4 to Leeds in the third round of the Challenge Cup. Such was the crush that the players were lifted bodily from the dressing rooms onto the pitch!

During 1941 enemy bombing seriously damaged the original Athletic Company stand, and it was not until August, 1949 that the New Stand was built on much the same site. Well into the 1950s its 240 bench seats accounted for the ground's total seating capacity. Because of building restrictions the present steel framed roof was not erected until March, 1954; and the previous standing area at the Gordon Street end was not seated until Hull's Wembley season of 1979/80. The stand presently seats about 1,500 with perhaps a similar number accommodated in the sunken paddock, from where you get a poor view of the play.

However, the entrance where the players and officials step up onto the pitch would certainly have been an interesting place to have witnessed The Boulevard's first post-war international in November, 1951, when a crowd of 18,000 saw Other Nationalities (ten Australians, two Scots, and a New Zealander) beat France 17-14. The game was an astonishing mixture of superb open rugby and rank brutality, the Carcassonne forward Edouard Poncinet finally receiving his marching orders in the 70th minute after rendering unconscious his third Australian victim - namely, Leeds forward Arthur Clues, who was stretchered off with concussion after only four minutes; Lionel Cooper, who, in the mayhem, somehow managed to score a brilliant hat-trick of tries; and then the Leigh forward Jeff Burke, whose broken nose finally prompted referee George Phillips to act.

When Hull won the Challenge Cup in 1914 for the first time in their history their captain, Bert Gilbert, buried a horseshoe under the once notoriously heavy pitch to bring the club even more luck. This was only rediscovered in May, 1969, when the

Man-of-the-Match Maurice Brereton (right) is served by his Kiwi colleague Gary Woollard during the World Cup game against France at The Boulevard in 1970. Note the length of the grass which caused comment - Yorkshire Post Newspapers.

playing surface was re-levelled prior to The Boulevard being allocated the France-New Zealand 1970 World Cup fixture, which New Zealand won 16-15 after trailing by six points. The highlight of this exciting game was a length-of-the-field try by the French right-winger Serge Marsolan.

Hull won few friends in high places due to the bumpy state of the pitch and the disappointing attendance, one leading Rugby League Council member believing that it would be *"some considerable time"* before Hull, which was then seen as *"a rugby league outpost"*, would be granted another international.

Of course, it only took the Humberside resurgence during the late 1970s and early 1980s to alter this opinion, with the Boulevard playing host to the Great Britain-France internationals in 1981 and 1983. In the former game Great Britain came within two points of a record score (37-0) with Hull loose-forward Steve *"Knocker"* Norton and Hull K. R. stand-off Steve Hartley, until the latter's retirement before half-time, causing the French most problems. Five of the seven tries went to the West Indian wingers, Leigh's Des Drummond and Wigan's 19-year old Henderson Gill, the latter who was an instant hit with the Threepenny Stand patrons in the 13,000 crowd as he raced in for a hat-trick.

Sadly, the match in 1983, which a disappointing home side won 17-5, was almost a repeat of the game at The Boulevard three decades earlier, only on this occasion New Zealand referee Don Wilson had the easy option of sin-binning three

players for kicking and brawling. The last international on the ground was on 7 March, 1992, when Hull right-winger Paul Eastwood scored a try and converted each of his side's six tries as Great Britain beat France 36-0 in a World Cup rated game.

In July, 1990, the club had made the monumental decision to demolish the original Threepenny Stand, even before they could guarantee finding the cash to replace it. It was only when brewers Joshua Tetley's came forward with a £50,000 three-year sponsorship deal that work commenced on the 840-seater, fully cantilevered Joshua Tetley Three Penny Stand (since renamed the ABI Caravans Three Penny Stand). There is also standing room for 480 and 14 hospitality boxes at the rear of the stand.

The stand was officially opened on 14 November, 1990 by the Tetley's sales director before Hull's visit by Australia, which also marked the official opening of two 30 metre high corner floodlight towers, which replaced the parallel system on that side dating from 1967. The crowd in 1990 was 13,500, slightly above The Boulevard's present permitted limit.

The Boulevard	
1921 Great Britain 2 Australia 16	21,504
1926 Great Britain 21 New Zealand 11	7,000
1951 Other Nats. 17 France 14	18,000
World Cup 1970 France 15 New Zealand 16	3,824
1981 Great Britain 37 France 0	13,173
1983 Great Britain 17 France 5	6,055
1992 Great Britain 36 France 0	5,250

HULL KINGSTON ROVERS When Hull K.R. (who joined the Northern Union in June, 1897) moved to their present Craven Park ground in 1989 it was their ninth home since their formation. After leaving the Boulevard they moved to Craven Street (capacity 18,000), the former home of the old Southcoates club. Due to its limitations, and the closure of the best stand during the 1920/1 season when Rovers were beaten by Hull in the Championship final, it was finally decided to purchase the site adjacent to the tram/bus depot on the eastern end of Holderness Road at a total cost of £13,411.

2 September, 1922 (the first day under the game's new title of Rugby League) marked the start of Rovers' Championship season, and was also the day on which the The Robins opened their new **Craven Park** ground. The visitors were Wakefield Trinity, for whom the legendary Albert Rosenfeld scored the

The contrast between the original Threepenny Stand (left) and the new structure, viewed from the main stand - Henry Skrzypecki.

The old Craven Park ground, which since its closure in 1989 has been covered by a retail superstore - Aerofilms.

only try of the match in front of an estimated crowd of 15,000. The official opening, however, took place before the match against Featherstone Rovers on Thursday evening, 21 September, 1922, with the club chairman, E. W. Brown, performing the ceremony in the afternoon. On 7 October, 1922 a record crowd of 22,282 watched the local derby.

The 2,500-seater main stand, which survived until the ground's demolition, was only partly roofed on that opening day. The original east stand, which at that time housed the stadium club, together with the greyhound totaliser offices, was destroyed by a fire on Monday afternoon, 8 July, 1946. Its replacement had three railway carriages at the rear, which served for the tote's use, one of which was rescued at the ground's closure by the Great Central Railway based at Loughborough.

Craven Park hosted its one and only test match on 5 October, 1929 when a crowd of 20,000 saw Great Britain soundly thrashed by Australia, 31-8, despite having a 5-1 pull in the scrums. Australia, who put on a brilliant exhibition in scoring

seven tries, gained most of their possession at the play-the-balls. Stand-off Eric Weissel (see Australia chapter), with a try and five conversions, equalled the then record points in an Anglo-Australian test.

The ground's other post-war international, in February, 1936, saw Wales beat England 17-14, the first time in 13 years, to take the European Championship. The Welsh forwards, of whom Hal Jones of Keighley was outstanding, surprisingly lasted the pace better in the ankle deep mud, and they were well supported by brilliant half-backs in George Bennett and Billy Watkins. The crowd of 17,000 was testimony to the revival of interest in the code in the city.

At the outbreak of war Rovers struggled to the end of the 1939/40 season before closing down. They sold Craven Park to a greyhound syndicate - the first race meeting had been held on 5 May, 1928 - for £10,750 and took out a 21-year lease with the option of renting the ground should they ever return, which seemed doubtful at the time. The pre-war capacity was drastically reduced by the opening, on 2 September, 1939, of the totaliser at the Holderness Road end.

The ground was therefore unable to accommodate the derby games, which were transferred to Hull City's ground at

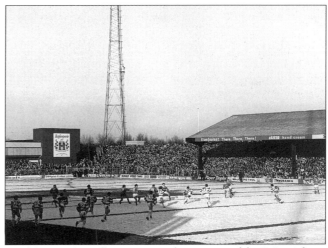

Boothferry Park (Hull City AFC) on the occasion of the JP Special Trophy final in 1985 between Rovers and Hull - Mike Haddon.

Boothferry Park (see chapter one), where, on Good Friday, 3 April, 1953, the club record attendance of 27,670 was set. The irony in this, of course, is that in 1896/7 Hull City were only a minor section of the Rovers club. When the Football League stopped the playing of rugby league on their club grounds in the mid-1960s there was an urgency for Rovers to develop a new stadium.

In fact, for the start of the 1967/8 campaign Rovers had planned to move to a site at Winchester Avenue, which they had originally bought in 1958 as a training ground. However, by selling Winchester Avenue in January, 1971 to a developer Rovers were able to buy back Craven Park for £65,000 and run greyhound racing as a subsidiary - a sport which they incorporated into the new Craven Park.

England easily beat a moderate Welsh side at Craven Park in March, 1980, with Rovers' forwards Len Casey and try-scorer Roy Holdstock starring in the 25-9 victory. Also Wigan full-back George Fairbairn scored a try and six goals, and St. Helens loose-forward Harry Pinner celebrated his full international debut by dropping two goals.

In Rovers' Wembley year there had been a post-war record

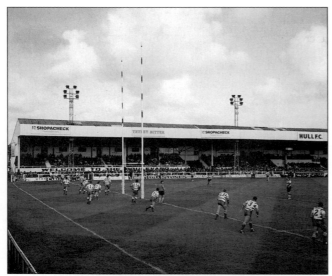

The Boulevard's main east stand, which is due to be replaced by a £2.2 million double decker stand - Henry Skrzypecki.

crowd of 14,315 against Salford on 15 March, 1981. But following the Popplewell Report Craven Park's capacity was reduced to a mere 7,227, even after Rovers had spent over £100,000 on safety work. With the club having liabilities of £500,000, Rovers therefore sold Craven Park to the Wright Group of Companies for £4 million and they developed Rovers' present ground at Preston Road for £3 million, thus enabling Rovers to clear off their debts. Rovers played their last game at Craven Park on 9 April, 1989, when they lost 16-13 to the champions Widnes, for whom full-back Alan Tait scored the last points on the old ground with a 67th minute try. Craven Park is today covered by the Co-operative Retail Services superstore, which also took in the adjacent bus depot. In the move Rovers lost much of their traditional support.

Craven Park	
1929 Great Britain 31 Australia 8	20,000
1936 England 14 Wales 17	17,000
1980 England 26 Wales 9	7,557

At a time when professional rugby league in Hull is at a very low-ebb, there has been a great deal of speculation, further fueled by the now abortive Super League merger between Rovers and The Airlie Birds, over the possible building of a *"super-stadium"*, which both rugby clubs could share with Hull City. Although talks have taken place, such a prospect seems to be more on the agenda of local councillors than the clubs themselves, with all three having development plans for their own grounds.

Although the Boulevard has been allocated one of the preliminary games, Papua New Guinea versus Tonga, in the Centenary World Cup, neither of Hull's rugby grounds are really suitable venues for representative fixtures, with Boothferry Park having far more to offer. This is likely to change, however, if Hull FC's plans to redevelop The Boulevard over the next two to three years at a cost of £6.6 million reach fruition.

The first phase, a new £2.2 million double-decker East Stand, has received planning permission and should be under construction during the truncated 1995/6 season. It is envisaged that the ground will eventually have covered seating on three sides with the building of a North Stand and an extension to the new Threepenny Stand, which will mean, of course, the demolition of The Boulevard's 100-year old relic.

LEEDS

Headingley Although the Northern Union was formed at the George Hotel in Huddersfield, the fact remains that Headingley is still widely perceived as rugby league's true spiritual home.

Leeds was the last of West Yorkshire's major cities to form a multi-purpose sports club with adjoining first-class facilities. But by learning from the earlier developments at Sheffield (Bramall Lane), Bradford, and Huddersfield, its leading citizens were able to build the finest football and cricket enclosure in the British Isles. The Vicar of Leeds, the Reverend J. F. Jayne, announced in November, 1887 that the Leeds, Cricket, Football and Athletic (Sports Co.) Ltd was to be formed, and subsequently Yorkshire's cricket captain, Lord Hawke, became the company's first chairman, and Charles Francis Tetley, of the brewing family, its first vice-chairman. £25,000 was then quickly raised to buy the 22 acres (Lot 17a) from the Cardigan Estates' trustees during January, 1889. Leeds St. John's (formed 1870) decided to become the rugby section of the new club when their ground at Cardigan Fields, which had staged the England-Wales international in 1884 and several of the early Yorkshire Cup finals, was needed for housing. Their headquarters were opposite the ground at the present Cardigan Arms.

Headingley was informally opened on Whit Tuesday 1890 with a cricket match against Scarborough; and on 2 August,

Batley (left) and St. Helens pose for the camera before the first Challenge Cup final, which was played at Headingley in 1897.

1890 the first athletics and cycling meeting took place on the one-third of a mile banked track, parts of which still survive today around the cricket field. Yorkshire have been tenants since their match against Derbyshire on 8-10 June, 1891 whilst test cricket was first played in June, 1899 when England drew with Australia. The first game of rugby at Headingley was on 20 September, 1890 when Leeds defeated Manningham, G. B. Naylor having the honour of scoring the first try and points on his new home ground.

The double-fronted, partly covered, main stand held approximately 2,000 spectators, only a few of whom were actually seated. A large room in the roof, which was later used as the press box, overlooked both fields. This stand survived until the fire in 1932. Later during that first season a 40-yard long open wooden stand was built on the south side. Its covering during 1911 with a galvanised iron barrel roof was the only improvement on the rugby side of the ground until after the First World War. The estate also included a bowling green and eleven tennis courts, the latter being situated on the site of the present training pitch. The estate's initial cost, including that of the corner pavilion, was £30,300.

Before Leeds became a founder member of the Northern Union Headingley hosted several major rugby union occasions, including the 1890 North versus South game; Scotland's victory over England on 4 March, 1893 watched by a crowd of 20,000; and Yorkshire's tussles, as champion county, with Rest of England sides in 1892, 1894 and 1895. Although the ground was also the venue for the Yorkshire Cup finals whenever Leeds were not involved, the highest attendance for a rugby union match at Headingley was 27,654 for a third round Yorkshire Cup-tie against Halifax on 2 April, 1892.

Headingley was therefore the natural choice for the inaugural Northern Union Challenge Cup final in 1897 between Batley and St. Helens, and the ground staged the greatest number of such finals prior to the game being taken to Wembley in 1929. Headingley has also been the most popular venue for other major rugby league play-offs and Challenge Cup semi-finals. At the Halifax-Salford final in 1903 a new ground record was established of 32,507.

Despite the Rugby Union's draconian professional rules, which steadfastly forbade the playing of rugby union on Northern Union grounds, it was found expedient to hire Headingley for Yorkshire's 40-0 defeat by the All Blacks on

Wednesday, 12 December, 1905, when 23,683 paid for admission (not surpassed for a rugby union game in the north until 1993 at Anfield). A New Zealand Parliamentary report later showed that the New Zealand government subsidised the first All Blacks' visit to this country to the tune of £1,963. But this did not stop opponents of New Zealand's first openly-professional side from labelling the party the All Golds.

The Northern Union's first-ever test match (as distinct from international) was played at Headingley on Saturday, 25 January, 1908 when, with Dally Messenger absent and double admission charges being asked, the crowd was 8,182. The 14-6 scoreline to England flattered the All Golds who were totally outplayed in a disappointing match. Both sets of

backs had difficulty in catching the narrow, over-inflated ball, which may also have partly explained why none of the six tries were converted.

There was added public interest at the England-Wales international, played on Wednesday 19 January, 1921, through the appearance of the French heavyweight boxer, Georges Carpentier, and other ring personalities. The diminutive Jimmy Wilde kicked off whilst Joe Beckett, the British heavyweight champion, started the second half. The game was so one-sided, 35-9 that *The Yorkshire Post* wondered why *"in face of the disparity in skill and vigour, it should be thought necessary to go to Wales for football players. The native Northern Union talent has always been*

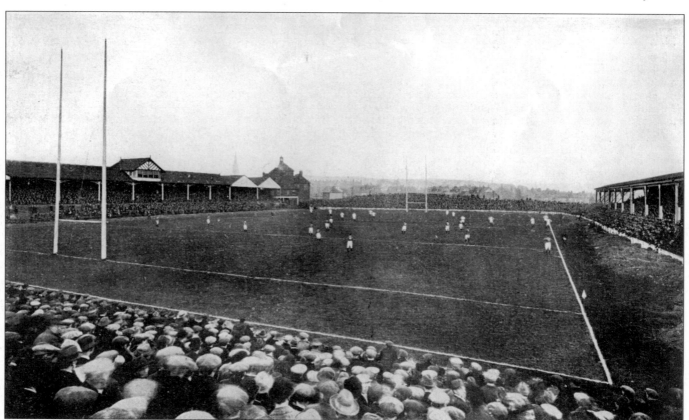

The new bays of the main stand, next to the pavilion, are prominent in this picture of Headingley (1921-26) - Dave Makin Collection.

superior in these official tests in the past, and on yesterday's showing it is immeasurably so today." One highlight was the sight of Huddersfield's champion wrestler-cum-forward, Douglas Clark, running half the length of the field for a try with the fastest Welsh back unable to catch him.

For the start of the 1921/22 boom season twin-span bays were added to each end of the main stand, and the extra seating helped create a British receipts record of £3,959 at the first test on 1 October, 1921. The game ended dramatically with Great Britain pulling off a 6-5 victory over Australia thanks to a 77th minute try by the Leeds left-winger Squire Stockwell, but not before winger Harold Horder had almost snatched a try at the other end with only seconds remaining. Later that season the attendance of 34,827 at the Rochdale Hornets-Hull Challenge Cup final set a new record for the game in this country.

In order to add 1,000 extra seats for the cricket test against Australia in 1926 the barrel-roofed Lady Airey Stand (so named as it was the brain-child of the wife of the club chairman and builder, Sir Edwin Airey) was built on top of the original section of the main stand. Its rear wall on the rugby side was a blot on the landscape, under which shadow both the 1926 New Zealanders and the 1929 Australians played. By the time the 1933 Australians arrived, however, Headingley had changed immeasurably for the better.

The strike-hit tour of the 1926 Kiwis ended on a bitter note at Headingley, where the final test was delayed for about ten minutes due to a sudden press conference called by the New Zealand party. The players were aggrieved at a statement made by the Rugby League chairman, Mr. E. Osborne, in which he appeared to have sided with the six striking players who had been sent home. Several of the test players demanded a similar £10 fee to that given to the suspended players as travelling expenses, and only the wise counsel of their captain H. Avery averted a cancellation of the test. As it was, with the series already decided, there was very little public interest in the game, which produced 11 tries and a vain rally by the Kiwis before they went down 32-17.

During the summer of 1931 the barrel-roofed south stand was demolished to make way for the present 128 yard long South Stand. At its opening on 29 August, 1931 for the game against York the new stand's capacity was given as 13,000, but it was not until at least 1957 that its second pitched roof offered complete cover.

On Good Friday, 25 March, 1932, the main stand opposite was gutted by a fire, which was started in a bay at the pavilion end, during the match against Halifax. All 2,000 spectators who were in the stand at the time managed to make their escape, many by clambering into the paddock and onto the field. It appears to have been almost identical to the Valley Parade fire in 1985 except for the horrific loss of life.

William Airey & Sons erected the present £20,000 double-fronted main stand, which was first used on 27 May, 1933 for Yorkshire's game against Kent. Surprisingly, for such a major undertaking, there appears to have been no official opening ceremony. The 116 yard long rugby stand then had seating for 3,800 (since reduced by a few hundred due to sponsor's boxes) and a paddock for about 3,000. Despite the new stand having a central tunnel, and a vast amount of room available for dressing rooms, the players still marched out from the pavilion, as they would until 1991, for the second Anglo-Australian test of 1933. This ended with Barrow's left-winger *"Tank"* Woods scoring the winning try to make the score 7-5, ninety seconds from the end.

At the Keighley-Wakefield Trinity Challenge Cup semi-final in 1937 a new ground record of 40,034 was recorded. This was beaten at a vital league game against Bradford Northern on the evening of Wednesday, 21 May, 1947, when the present record of 40,175 was established in the season of the first *"big freeze"*. The previous Saturday England had beaten France 5-2, in a game which had been transferred from Odsal in March and had been postponed on several occasions. England thereby took the championship, but the crowd's cheers were still for the Frenchmen, whose play was brilliant compared to the *"creeping barrage"* methods of the English forwards.

On 4 October, 1947 Headingley also staged the first test in this country for ten years. This ended with an ill-prepared Great Britain side snatching a 72nd minute 11-10 victory from New Zealand. A try by Warrington left-winger Albert Johnson, after a kick through by his St. Helens centre Jimmy Stott, settled matters. Dewsbury's full-back Jim Ledgard was man-of-the-match despite giving away an interception try from half-way to the West Coast winger J. A. Forrest.

In this game Great Britain were well below their best form, but they helped serve up a record 12-try treat for the 36,529 all-ticket crowd at Headingley on 11 November, 1948, when they beat Australia 23-21. The receipts at this enthralling first test were a record for this country of £8,020, a figure which was broken (£8,601) at the first test in 1952, despite the latter game being the first Anglo-Australian test to be televised live.

Each member of their front-row (Blanchard, Butterfield and Maxwell) scored a try in the surprise 28-13 defeat of Great Britain in the final test in 1955, and against Australia in 1959 another prop, Don Robinson of Leeds, wrote his name into the record books with a try after only 55 seconds. Until then this was almost certainly the fastest try in an international on home soil.

During the second big freeze of modern times the Leeds board decided in January, 1963 to install a £10,000 underground electric blanket, a first for rugby league. There would therefore be no repeat in future of having to use the cricket field, as happened on 24 December, 1938 against Salford, when the rugby pitch was frost-bound. The first game saved by the blanket was the Loiners' defeat by Dewsbury on 21 December, 1963.

Kiwi forward Mel Cooke breaks a Dick Huddart tackle to race in for a try at the pavilion end in the first test in 1961 - Hulton Deutsch Collection.

A month earlier the final test against Australia had generated sufficient heat of its own. Australia had two men sent off and another, winger Ken Irvine, carried off, whilst St. Helens prop Cliff Watson also received his marching orders from *"Sergeant Major"* Eric Clay, as Britain salvaged an undignified victory after losing the series by a record margin at Swinton. Headingley, in fact, has had its fair share of international rough houses over the years.

In 1967 Dennis Manteit, the Australian prop, was sent-off for a challenge on Roger Millward in a test which marked the end of the great Reg Gasnier's international career. This game, however, was kindergarten stuff compared to the World Cup final play-off between the old enemies on 7 November, 1970, which marked Australia's first victory at Headingley. Whilst the classic between Australia and New Zealand in the 1960 World Cup tournament was hailed as one of the finest internationals to be played on the ground, the 1970 final ended in shame as players continued trading blows long after the final whistle.

Australia's first victory in a test at Headingley came three years later, on 24 November, 1973, in another torrid encounter in which Brian Lockwood, hero of the Wembley test, was sent-off, and Australian captain, Bob McCarthy, scored the only try of the game. The Australians' second victory at a packed Headingley in 1978, saw Bobby Fulton's panzer division sweep away the challenge of the Dad's Army side. By so doing they started a sequence of 15 unbeaten tests, which only ended in Sydney in 1988.

With Great Britain trailing 6-4 at half-time in the ferocious third test at Headingley in 1982 there did appear to be an outside chance of a long-overdue home victory. However, when Hull's Lee Crooks, who had earlier dropped a magnificent goal, was sent-off after 53 minutes, all hopes disappeared. In the end, the Australians, who were brilliantly led by their ball-playing captain Max Krilitch, who helped himself to one of their six second half tries, ran out easy 32-8 winners. Remarkably, Great Britain's only try in four tests against the Kangaroos was scored by Hull centre Steve Evans when it was eleven men against twelve, four players having been sent to the sin-bin by the excellent French referee J. Rascagneres.

Monsieur Rascagneres refereed all three tests of that series and firmly established the usefulness of having neutral referees for internationals. He also helped erase the memory of the performance by his compatriot Guy Cattaneo, who, at Headingley on 21 February, 1981, gave one of the most bizarre performances in the history of the game, as France beat England by the equally bizarre 5-1 scoreline.

Whilst Monsieur Cattaneo needed a police escort from the field that day, at the 1975 England versus France World Championship game leading Sydney referee, Keith Page, was given a rather more sympathetic reception by the Headingley crowd, when he had to retire only minutes into the game after suffering an attack of vaccine fever.

Not only Monsieur Cattaneo, but Frenchmen generally, must be haunted by the thoughts of Headingley. Including the defeat in 1947, and another unlucky set-back in 1950 - the latter in which the legendary full-back Puig-Aubert was both hero and villain, by dropping an incredible goal one minute and then costing his team the match the next - French sides have lost in 13 of their 15 appearances on the historic ground. Furthermore, on five of those occasions a half century of points has been conceded.

On 16 February, 1991 Martin Offiah broke Alec Murphy's record of four tries set in the first official test between the two countries in 1957, by scoring five in the 60-4 annihilation. This helped restore the status quo after Britain's 25-18 shock defeat at Headingley the previous year. Then, on 2 April, 1993 Great Britain's 17 man squad re-wrote the record books with a then world record 72-6 win over the brave but hapless Frenchmen, in a game in which Jonathan Davies equalled Bernard Ganley's tally of ten goals against the French in 1957.

The above game was the first wholly floodlit international to be played at Headingley, the present £115,000 system being first used on 28 September, 1988 when Leeds met Wakefield Trinity in the Yorkshire Cup quarter final. These had replaced the first set which had been officially switched on for the Roses match on 21 September, 1966.

Leeds were the first rugby league club in this country to have an electronic scoreboard (since updated), which was erected in March, 1981 at the Kirkstall end. This made redundant the scoreboard built in 1963 at the St. Michael's Lane end, which is now fronted by a row of hospitality boxes.

Headingley's centenary in 1990 passed with little or no pomp although on the evening of 4 May there was the surprising appearance of the Moscow Magicians side which played the Leeds "A" team, and during the centenary season a major improvement programme commenced with the installation of 1,670 tip-up seats in the paddock thereby making the main stand all-seater.

Underneath this stand £1.2 million was also spent on a gymnasium, medical rooms, and dressing rooms, which were officially opened by the Lord Mayor on 11 February, 1991, after the latter were first used for a match on 22 December, 1990. As these facilities are now shared with Yorkshire cricket, the advent of summer rugby will necessitate Leeds having to improve the existing Academy dressing rooms under the South Stand. Radio Headingley (1413 AM), who share the same box as the BBC ball-by-ball commentary team, will also need to be relocated next summer.

Ever mindful of the possible loss of cricket test match status, Leeds had planned to add a third tier banqueting suite to the main stand but they were refused permission after objections from local residents. Undaunted, in September, 1992 Leeds turned their attention to the pavilion on which they spent £2.2 million. Officially opened by HRH The Duchess of Kent on 26 July, 1993, since modernisation the pavilion now has nine hospitality rooms. Past players will be interested to note that Headingley's old dressing rooms have been converted into what is now known as The Museum Suite.

As the finest joint football and cricket ground in the United Kingdom, Headingley appears to have kept pace with the demands of top-flight cricket. But with the Anglo-Australian tests having outgrown all the traditional rugby league venues, since 1982 the ground has only staged internationals against France and New Zealand, the Kiwis' 24-22 victory in 1985 proving to be one of the most exciting tests to be played on the hallowed turf. Also, whatever the future of international rugby league may be, Headingley now faces stiff competition from Huddersfield's all-seater McAlpine Stadium for tests and other major games.

Taking up this challenge, in May this year Leeds, in consultation with Yorkshire, unveiled a £30 million 10-year masterplan for Headingley's 17.6 acres (see colour section). Under the proposals it is envisaged that the rugby side will finally have an all-covered, all-seater capacity of 25,000 (present capacity 27,500). The first phase, which is not likely to start until 1996 at the earliest, will be the building of a new two-tier South Stand providing 7,500 seats and 30 executive suites, plus restaurants and bars. As well as retaining the relocated dressing rooms, underneath this stand there will be housed the supporters' club, a gymnasium, a sports injury clinic, and a range of rooms for community activities. On this side, part of the present training pitch will become a floodlit all-weather area for hockey and 5-a-side.

The proposed North Stand will also be two-tiered, whilst the South and West Stands will both be single-tiered. In the proposed changes the pitch will be moved about six metres towards the pavilion end. The architects, David Lyons and Associates, have opted for an open plan approach to the stadium's boundaries in order to enhance their appearance and to help increase on-site parking and reduce queuing on public roads. Another aspect of the scheme which is aimed at pleasing local residents is the removal of the floodlit towers in favour of less obtrusive roof edge lighting.

Although there is provision for a Yorkshire cricket museum in the first phase which is to start in August, no mention is made of a similar facility on the rugby side. A pity, because rugby league is in desperate need of a permanent site whereby supporters can cherish the game's heritage. Such an asset at the game's true spiritual home would also provide the opportunity for Leeds to organise money-spinning tours of the complex, similar to those at Old Trafford, Wembley, Twickenham, and the Sydney Cricket Ground and Football Stadium, where nostalgia certainly does help pay the bills.

French referee J. Rascagneres intervenes as Australian forward Les Boyd threatens the prostrate Tony Myler during the test at Headingley in 1982 - Rugby Leaguer Newspaper.

Headingley

1908 Great Britain 14 New Zealand 6	8,182
1921 England 35 Wales 9	13,000
1921 Great Britain 6 Australia 5	31,303
1924 England 17 Other Nats. 23	3,000
1927 Great Britain 32 New Zealand 17	6,000
1929 England 27 Other Nats. 20	5,000
1929 Great Britain 9 Australia 3	31,402
1932 England 14 Wales 13	4,000
1933 Great Britain 7 Australia 5	29,618
1937 Great Britain 5 Australia 4	31,949
1947 England 5 France 2	21,000
1947 Great Britain 11 New Zealand 10	28,445
1948 Great Britain 23 Australia 21	36,529
1950 England 14 France 9	22,000
1951 Great Britain 16 New Zealand 12	18,649
1952 Great Britain 19 Australia 6	34,505
1952 Wales 22 France 16	10,380
1955 Great Britain 13 New Zealand 28	10,438
1957 Great Britain 45 France 12	20,221
1959 Great Britain 50 France 15	21,948
1959 Great Britain 11 Australia 10	30,184
World Cup 1960 Australia 21 New Zealand 15	10,736
1961 Great Britain 11 New Zealand 29	16,540
1962 England 18 France 6	11,099
1963 Great Britain 16 Australia 5	20,497
1967 Great Britain 16 Australia 11	22,293
1969 England 40 Wales 23	8,355
1970 England 26 Wales 7	9,393
World Cup 1970 Great Britain 11 Australia 4	15,169
World Cup 1970 final Great Britain 7 Australia 12	18,776
1971 Great Britain 12 New Zealand 3	5,479
1973 Great Britain 6 Australia 14	16,674
World Champ. 1975 England 20 France 2	10,842
1977 England 2 Wales 6	6,472
1978 Great Britain 6 Australia 23	29,627
1981 England 1 France 5	3,229
1980 Great Britain 10 New Zealand 2	8,210
1982 Great Britain 8 Australia 32	17,318
1984 Great Britain 10 France 0	7,646
1985 Great Britain 50 France 4	6,491
1985 Great Britain 22 New Zealand 24	12,591
1987 Great Britain 52 France 4	6,567
1988 Great Britain 30 France 12	7,007
1990 Great Britain 18 France 25	6,554
1991 Great Britain 60 France 4	5,284
1993 Great Britain 72 France 6 (Floodlit)	8,196
1993 Great Britain 29 New Zealand 10	15,139

LEIGH

Kirkhall Lane/Hilton Park Formed in 1878, Leigh played on two grounds prior to moving to Mather Lane in 1889. It was here that the club were suspended, from September until the end of November, 1894, for alleged breaches of the professional rules; and where they played their first game as founder members of the Northern Union on 7 September, 1895 against Leeds.

In 1940 Mather Lane was purchased by the Callender's Cable and Construction Company for use by its employees, and the Siddow Common Works 2 was later built on the ground. Consequently, Leigh played all their fixtures away from home during the 1940/1 season, and were forced to close down for the remainder of the war. However, the club remained solvent, and in January, 1946, as a new company, bought the site of the present ground on Kirkhall Lane, which was then called Church Fields. Whilst the new ground was being developed, a temporary home was found at the Leigh Harriers and Athletic Club ground at Charles Street/Holden Road.

The cable works donated the old stand, which was first erected at Mather Lane in 1928, and this was dismantled and its framework used to build the present main stand at Hilton Park. On 12 July, 1947 Mr. Jack Harding, the future club chairman and Great Britain tour manager in 1970, won the auction to lay the last pieces of turf. However, he generously passed these to Tommy Sale for the club captain to complete the job which he had so expertly supervised.

It was the St. Helens' captain, Jimmy Stott, however, who scored the first points on the ground, when he kicked a 4th minute penalty in a Lancashire Cup-tie on 30 August, 1947. The crowd of 17,000 helped take Leigh's average attendance during that first season to 11,500. A new club record of 29,500 was then set on 26 February, 1949 at the Challenge Cup second round replay against Wigan.

The ground was re-named Hilton Park in June, 1959 as a tribute to James Hilton, the club chairman who had died earlier that year.

Most of the major developments at the ground have either been carried out, or financed by, the Supporters' Club. For example, the present Supporters' Club stand was opened for the game against Leeds on 11 February, 1950, although seats were only added in 1963. The Mick Martyn Bar, which was

Hilton Park's popular side in December, 1949 as spectators buy raffle tickets for a rugby ball - Hulton Deutsch Collection.

opened underneath this stand in 1987, is named after Leigh's all-time record try scorer, who still holds the record of 23 tries for a forward on tour. The Supporters' Club also financed the building of the present scoreboard during the 1955/6 season.

Leigh's centre Kitchen finds Australians, Flannery (left) and Paul, barring his way during the 34-5 home defeat in 1952.
The recently opened Supporters' Club stand is in the background.

The current ground record of 31,326 was accommodated at the third round Challenge Cup-tie against St Helens on 14 March, 1953.

Later that year Leigh followed Bradford Northern in installing floodlights - these two clubs being the only ones in the Rugby League to have such a facility prior to the mid-1960s. These were erected on the present four corner pylons, and gantries on both stand roofs were added for the visit of the 1965 Kiwis. At the official opening of the £4,100 lights, on 14 October, a crowd of 12,870 saw Lancashire beat Yorkshire 18-10 in the second of seven Roses matches to be staged on the ground. Leigh's first experience of their own lights came a week later when they entertained Northern.

McDonald Bailey

It was under these lights that the world 100 metre record holder, 32-year old McDonald Bailey, made his much-publicised debut in Leigh's 11-3 defeat of Wigan in a friendly match on 16 December, 1953. Watched by a crowd of 14,996 and seventeen photographers Bailey did manage to score a try just after half-time despite carrying an injury. But it was to be his only appearance in rugby league, having signed for a reputed sum of £1,000 in July of that year.

As well as the Australians' fixture in 1956 against a Rugby League XIII, each of Hilton Park's three senior internationals have also been floodlit events. The first was on 19 November, 1954 when Australia beat New Zealand 18-5 in a friendly following the World Cup in France. With both sides playing exhibition rugby, New Zealand led twice but succumbed to a late rally which resulted in centre Harry Wells scoring two converted tries in the dying minutes. Other Nationalities clinched the 1955 European Championship by defeating France 32-19, but it was the French stand-off, Gilbert Benausse, who was the star of the match with five goals and an opportunist try. On that occasion there was little to choose between the sides in the

first half and the French played fast, attractive rugby. In 1964, however, France were a shadow of this side, and Great Britain ran out easy winners in Hilton Park's one and only test match. Although Neil Fox scored 21 points with 9 goals and a try, the architect of the 39-0 victory was Huddersfield's mercurial scrum-half Tommy Smales.

Since the 1960s there have been significant and regular changes to Hilton Park's immediate surrounding area. For example, a B&Q superstore now stands on what was the

Hilton Park's distinctive scoreboard - Henry Skrzypecki.

training pitch behind the Supporters' Club Stand; the allotments behind the main stand have been taken over for the Leigh East ARLC's pitches and clubhouse; and the former trackbed of the Bolton-Leigh railway has been used for the town's by-pass. The landscape has further altered in recent years with the demolition of both the Victoria Mill and the Parsonage Pit for an Asda development. Inside the ground, however, apart from essential safety work to the old main stand in 1986, little of any consequence has taken place since the concrete terracing was completed in 1963.

Nevertheless, the possible loss of Hilton Park to the bulldozers galvanised local opinion and saw an unprecedented campaign to save both the ground and the club. When Leigh were placed in administration in April, 1991 with debts of £1.1 million the title deeds were held by the club's former chairman, who turned down several offers which fell below his asking price of £650,000. The three-and-a-half year saga was only resolved when Grundy Estates, the owners of Horwich RMI AFC, bought Hilton Park, having sold their own ground for housing, and agreed a 50-year lease with Leigh for them to ground-share. This was signed before Leigh's game against Barrow on 5 March, 1995.

Hilton Park

1954 Australia 18 New Zealand 5 (friendly)	6,000
1955 Other Nationalities 32 France 19	7,289
1964 Great Britain 39 France 0	4,750

A view of Hilton Park, looking towards the main stand and scoreboard end, in April, 1993, at a time when the ground was threatened with closure - Harold Troughton, Rugby Leaguer Newspaper.

MANCHESTER and SALFORD

Noticing the popularity of soccer in Manchester today, it should perhaps be borne in mind that in the early days of *"football"* the city was a rugby stronghold. Before the 1930s, however, the rugby league authorities were always faced with the problem of finding a suitable big-match ground in the Manchester area on a par with Headingley.

The Fallowfield ground, off Old Hall Lane, which was later renamed the Harris Stadium after it was bought by the world professional cycling champion Reg Harris, was used as a compromise for the 1899 and 1900 Challenge Cup finals. Admittedly, there were no chaotic scenes to match those at that grounds staging of the 1893 FA Cup final, nor those at the 1899 Liverpool-Sheffield United FA Cup semi-final replay, when the game was abandoned at half-time because of crowd encroachment. Nevertheless, Fallowfield's poor spectator facilities, and the expense of hiring the ground and erecting temporary stands made it an unsuitable venue for Northern Union internationals. And, unfortunately, until the opening of Swinton's Station Road in 1929 the rugby club grounds in and around Manchester had neither the capacity nor the seating for the game's major events.

Of Salford, Swinton and Broughton Rangers, each of whom had been formed in the mid to late 1870s, only Rangers were a founder member of the Northern Union, although it did not take long for both its neighbours to realise their mistake in initially opposing the split. Salford, of which Broughton is a district, is, of course, an entirely separate entity from Manchester, but Salfordians will hopefully forgive me for including them in this particular chapter, the format of which was decided on long before the original Super League proposals merged Salford with Oldham and miraculously placed both of them under the Manchester banner.

BROUGHTON RANGERS/BELLE VUE RANGERS Founded in 1877, Broughton Rangers had moved to **Wheater's Field** by 1895. Today the streets built on the site of the ground are appropriately named Wheaters Crescent and Wheaters Street. Although it staged the 1907 Challenge Cup final between Warrington and Oldham, and held 20,000 at several semi-finals, an inspection by the Cup committee in 1900 found the ground to be not up to standard.

Just one international was staged on Wheater's Field, namely, England's overwhelming 31-7 defeat of Wales on Wednesday afternoon, 29 December, 1908. The frosty weather, coupled with a glut of fixtures over Christmas, partly accounted for the attendance of only 4,000. All but four of the Welsh side were from northern clubs, but Wales were so weak that the atmosphere was more in keeping with an exhibition game. However, despite conceding seven tries, Wales had the consolation of scoring the game's best try when Halifax's right-winger Dai Thomas intercepted and raced 75 yards on the treacherous surface. The best three-quarter on view, however, was James Lomas, who later that evening was chosen to lead his country against the Australians at Huddersfield.

Wheater's Field	
1908 England 31 Wales 7	4,000

In 1913 Rangers moved to **The Cliff,** Lower Broughton Road, a former cricket and tennis field on the opposite bank of the River Irwell to the site of the old Manchester racecourse. In 1921 21,000 were in the ground for the Leigh-Halifax Challenge Cup final, a figure which was surpassed at the Salford-Swinton Lancashire Cup final in 1931/2 when there was an attendance of 26,471. The Cliff's only full international was played on Wednesday 6 April, 1927, when England won 11-8. The Welshmen, however, deserved at least a draw, the scores being level until St. Helens winger Alf Ellaby scored the winning try 15 minutes from the end of an highly enjoyable game.

The Cliff	
1927 England 11 Wales 8	6,500

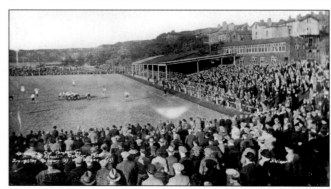

The Cliff, at the first round Lancashire Cup-tie between Broughton Rangers and Wigan in October, 1931. The stand and bankings are now covered by Manchester United's indoor training facilities.

In July, 1933 a new company was formed and the club transferred its first team games to the Belle Vue Zoological Gardens, although the club did not change its name to Belle Vue Rangers until the 1946/7 season.

The Cliff was sold to Manchester United in 1951, since when it has been used as their training ground. United came to the rescue of the Rugby League by agreeing to stage the England-France amateur international under floodlights at The Cliff on Thursday, 7 February, 1952. These lights were later sold to Workington *"Reds"* soccer club at Borough Park (see Cumbria chapter).

Belle Vue could seat nearly 20,000 under cover, and in 1933 a capacity crowd of 34,000 paid a British record of £4,659 at the first test against Australia. However, large numbers of spectators encroached onto the speedway track despite the efforts of mounted police, and therefore, with the opening of the more spacious Station Road, this proved to be Belle Vue's only major rugby league event. The attacking flair of the previously unbeaten tourists was neutralised by incessant rain - Jim Sullivan's brilliant tactical kicking, and his two goals, which were the only points of the match, being the decisive factors of the forward-dominated game.

After receiving a notice to quit in June, 1955, Rangers were later excluded from the Rugby League. The stadium was used for stock car and speedway racing up to the early 1980s but the whole site was then sold to the car dealers, BOC.

Belle Vue
1933 Great Britain 4 Australia 0   34,000

A packed Belle Vue at the test against Australia in 1933.

SALFORD Salford, who were formed in 1873 as Cavendish F.C., joined the Northern Union for the 1896/7 season. They then played at New Barns, from where they had to move because the land, including the adjoining Manchester racecourse, was swallowed up by the new Number 9 Dock, which marked the terminus of the Manchester Ship Canal. Since the Salford Quays development it is now possible to walk on the site of New Barnes, this being the car park to Batley's Cash and Carry on Broadway.

Salford's present ground, **The Willows,** Weaste, was opened at the 37th Salford-Swinton derby on 21 December, 1901, when James Lomas' drop goal was the only score. There was a crowd of 16,981 that day, accommodated on the three stands and the corner bankings. The ground was elliptical shaped for cycling and athletics until developments in the 1930s. The dressing rooms were situated on the ground floor of the two storey corner pavilion at the cricket ground end until they were damaged by bombing during the Second World War.

When Salford won the Championship final in 1914 the ground and their assets were actually in the hands of the receiver. However, during the post-war boom season of 1921/2, they were able to build a new grandstand, and The Willows was controversially allocated the deciding test against Australia in 1922. Although 2,000 tons of cinders were added to the bankings to help accommodate the anticipated record crowd, many considered that The Willows, which had previously hosted the Challenge Cup finals and Championship finals, was quite unsuitable for such an important occasion.

"The Tackler" in *Football Special,* for one, did not mince his words.:
There is not the slightest doubt that the Northern Union authorities have erred in their decision of choosing Weaste as the venue, for although many improvements have been made the reserved seating is totally inadequate. The authorities ought, by exercising more foresight, to have granted Lancashire the second, played the first at Hull, and the last at Leeds, the only enclosure in the game capable of doing justice befitting an occasion such as the game has never known in its history.

Snow made the surface better suited to the home side's footrush tactics, but the Australians, who lost their full-back and captain *"Chook"* Fraser with a broken leg shortly before the interval, attempted to play their usual brand of open rugby. Whilst this made for a terrific contest it cost Australia both the match, 6-0, and the Ashes Trophy, which they did not regain until 1950. The occasion was a personal triumph for Harold Wagstaff, who ended his brilliant test career by being carried shoulder high to the pavilion, in the process of which his jersey was ripped from his back by discerning souvenir hunters. Allowing for the climatic conditions, those critics of The Willows were perhaps vindicated, as only 21,000 witnessed this titanic struggle.

In Salford's defence, it has to be said that the club were handicapped by the fact that they only leased the ground on a yearly tenancy. However, they managed to build a new embankment, to hold 8,000, at the Willows Road end - the ground thereby losing its oval shape - for the start of the 1931/2 season, during which The Willows hosted its second international.

On that occasion Salford were commended for getting the pitch, which had a reputation as a mud-bath, into reasonable condition. Visibility, however, was extremely poor for the 8,000 crowd on Wednesday afternoon, 27 January, 1932, when England beat Wales 19-2. All but one of the English side were chosen to tour Australasia, whilst five of the Welsh side, including Jim Sullivan, the Lions captain, were also selected. This was perhaps a fair reflection of the day's play, with a general lack of understanding among the Welsh, and flashes of brilliant play from the English backs.

When Salford purchased the ground from the brewers, Groves and Whitnall Ltd, on 9 December, 1933, further improvements were placed high on the agenda, and in 1935/6 the present popular side stand was erected at a cost of £4,000. The following season, on 13 February, 1937, the ground's record attendance of 26,470 was set against Warrington in the first round of the Challenge Cup.

During the war enemy bombs landed on the pitch and damaged the pavilion, resulting in improvised dressing rooms being built under the popular stand, where they have remained ever since. Fund-raising for ground reconstruction in 1949 resulted in the re-roofing of both stands, the provision of new entrances at the Willows Road end, and an increase in seating, but it was not until the 1960s that The Willows underwent major change.

Salford were one of the first eight clubs to enter the BBC2 Floodlit Competition, the original lighting being first used for the league match against Widnes on Friday, 11 March, 1966. Later that year The Willows' appearance was dramatically altered with the building of the present social complex, which meant the demolition of the open terracing at the Willows Road end. This was completed in June, 1966, and the first extensions opened on the night of 11 October, 1967 when the Australians beat Lancashire 14-2. A casino and restaurant was then added in October, 1968.

It was the revenue from these palatial social facilities, at one time sold but now back in the club's hands, which helped pay for the record signing, in October, 1967, of Welsh stand-off David Watkins. He captained Salford at Wembley in 1969, and led them to the First Division Championship in 1974 and 1976. Such enterprise also resulted in The Willows being allocated five internationals during this halcyon period.

In October 1968 Wales, with the Salford half-back pairing of Watkins and Bob Prosser, beat England, for the first time since 1950, 24-17. Goal-kicking was the decisive factor as, although England scored five tries to four, Bradford

The Welsh left-winger Gwyn Parker races through the mist during the game against England at The Willows in 1932.

The Willows from the North Stand, looking towards the popular side, at Salford's game against Halifax in September, 1992 - Henry Skrzypecki.

Northern full-back Terry Price kicked six goals, whilst his opposite number, Brian Jefferson of Keighley, landed only one. Another Welsh star that night was Halifax's barn-storming second-rower, Colin Dixon, who had become a Red Devil by the time that he played in the Welsh side, also containing clubmates Bob Prosser and Maurice Richards, which lost 8-2 to France at The Willows in 1969. The Welsh cause was not helped by the late arrival of Terry Price, whose car had broken down on the journey over the Pennines.

By the time, in September, 1971, that The Willows staged its second, and last, test match the new 1,600-seater North Stand was in use. Not that it was needed, as only 3,764 turned up to see the televised first test against New Zealand, which the Kiwis surprisingly won 18-13. Local officials blamed the Salford public's love of Friday night rugby for the poor turn-out, but the reasons were much more complex.

The fact that this series drew the lowest-ever aggregate crowds in this country was a reflection, not so much on the chosen venues, but on the general apathy towards international rugby and the game's low self-esteem, as a result of which the Rugby League employed a firm of Manchester marketing consultants, Caine Associates, to advise on the game's image. Ironically, a marketing man's dream was the fact that the Kiwis were captained by Roy Christian, a direct descendant of Fletcher Christian of

Mutiny on the Bounty fame, but nothing was done to exploit this.

No sooner had Great Britain licked their wounds after losing this series than the main wooden stand was partly gutted by fire on the evening of 26 November, 1972, following the game against Workington Town. The stand was later reconstructed and the present high level central tier added.

Since that time The Willows has hosted two floodlit internationals involving Wales. In 1975 the dismissal of Widnes prop Jim Mills appeared to inspire his Welsh team mates, who staged an exhilarating fightback with a try and a goal from David Watkins, before England finished on top, 12-8; and later that year Wales beat France 23-2 in the final match of the eight-month long World Championship. Only 2,247, the lowest-ever for an international in Britain, turned up to see who would take the wooden spoon.

With almost £100,000 having been spent on new crush barriers alone, from 1985 *"yo-yo club"* Salford have found it difficult to keep pace with both the safety regulations and the work of young arsonists. After the end wooden sections of the main stand were temporarily closed in 1989, the area in disuse at the social club end was destroyed by fire during the summer of 1990.

It has taken rather longer than expected to start work on rebuilding, but with help from the Sports Aid Foundation a £160,000 500-seater section, with room for 30 disabled supporters, should be in place by the start of next season. Shortly before they thought they would be bidding against Oldham for the *"Manchester"* Super League spot, the Red Devils also announced plans to build, with the support of the local council, a new 10,000 capacity, 2,000-seater, stand on the popular side. This proposal would have increased the ground's capacity from 12,000 to 20,000, but it would now appear that it is unlikely to proceed within the near future.

The Willows	
1922 Great Britain 6 Australia 0	21,000
1932 England 19 Wales 2	8,000
1968 England 17 Wales 24	6,002
1969 Wales 2 France 8	5,610
1971 Great Britain 13 New Zealand 18	3,764
1975 England 12 Wales 8	8,494
World Champ. 1975 Wales 23 France 2	2,247

SWINTON Founded in 1871, Swinton (and Pendlebury) Football Club joined the Northern Union for the start of the 1896/7 season. They then played at Chorley Road (the site of which is now covered in housing on Victoria Avenue, Hazel Avenue, and Lilac Avenue), where in 1901 the main stand was destroyed by fire. Its immediate replacement and Chorley Road's popular side cover dating from 1925 were to give good service at **Station Road** - a former part-allotments site adjacent to the L. M. & S. main line, which Swinton bought for £2,000 from the profits of winning all four cups in 1927/8.

The 1,750-seater main stand from Chorley Road became the Townsend Road Stand, whilst the old shelter was erected at the Wolseley Street end. The only new structure was the 60-yard long elevated grandstand, which originally seated 1,800. Until the early 1960s, when work commenced on concreting them, the terraces were made of ash and railway sleepers.

Initially costing £11,665, Station Road was officially opened by the club chairman, Sir Edwin F. Stockton, on 2 March, 1929, when a crowd of 22,000 saw Swinton beat Wigan 9-3. The first points came from the boot of Swinton's second-row forward, Martin Hodgson, who was also a member of Great Britain's pack in the first of Station Road's three pre-war tests against Australia.

This was on 4 January, 1930, when a then record crowd of 34,709 for a test match in England saw the one and only scoreless draw in the history of rugby league tests. For most of this heart-stopping game Australia were on top, but in the dying minutes they were robbed of victory, in one of the sport's most controversial incidents.

"Chimpy" Busch, had dived for the corner for what the tourists, and the referee, Bob Robinson, thought was the winning score. However, as the touch-judge believed that the Australian scrum-half, and not the covering Swinton forward, Butters, had flattened the corner flag first, he had no hesitation in raising his flag. Mr Robinson therefore had no alternative, under the rules, but to disallow the try, for Britain to retain the Ashes.

Despite the fog, which threatened a cancellation and reduced the crowd to only 10,990, the third test against Australia in 1933 was easily the best of the series, with no more than two points separating the teams from the 30th to the 78th minute. Castleford's centre, Arthur Atkinson, saved the match, 19-16, mid-way through the second half, when he crash-tackled Vic Hey on the line as the elusive Australian half-back looked a certain scorer.

In 1937 Australia offered nothing like the same resistance. With a more mobile pack Great Britain wrapped up the series in the second test. All the points in the 13-3 win came from Salford men, with tries from wingers Alan Edwards (2) and Barney Hudson, and two goals from centre Gus Risman.

During the war Station Road was requisitioned by the local Home Guard and all Swinton's seven home fixtures in 1940/1 season were played at The Willows. The Ministry of Works had possession of Station Road until December, 1945, the club's major source of war-time income being government payments for storage and damage to the ground.

Station Road's record attendance of 44,621 was set at the Wigan-Warrington Challenge Cup semi-final in 1951, but plans to increase the ground's capacity to 60,000 never materialised.

Hosting tests against Australia and New Zealand in every series from 1948 until 1967 meant that, apart from the 1960 World Cup, Station Road was allocated only two French internationals, in 1946 and 1965; and only one Anglo-Welsh game, again in 1946.

Welsh prop Frank Whitcombe passes the ball whilst under pressure during the game against England at Station Road in 1946.

In February of that year England beat France, 16-6, after the visitors, who had erred in playing against the wind, trailed by 16 points at half-time, thanks to a hat-trick of tries by Warrington winger Johnson. The Frenchmen's crisp handling thrilled the 20,000 crowd but Calixte, a loose-forward playing on the wing, lacked the pace to finish. Seventeen of the 26 players on view in Wales' 13-10 win over England in 1946 had toured Australasia during the summer, but, nevertheless, the game was mediocre until the last ten minutes when Wales just managed to hold out.

Although Wigan's Joe Egan gave Britain a staggering 63-16 pull in the scrums, the 1947 New Zealanders were the first overseas side to win an international at Station Road, with their 10-7 victory levelling the series.

The thrill-a-minute, nine try, second test against the Kiwis in 1951, which Great Britain won 20-19, was the first outside sporting event to be screened by the BBC from the north of England and broadcast in full to a nationwide audience. The opening of the Holme Moss transmitter had made this possible, although for technical reasons such broadcasts had to be within a two mile radius of Manchester, hence the choice of the Station Road test. Alan Dixon was the commentator, assisted by Eddie Waring and Harry Sunderland, and, surprisingly, the Beeb even managed to fit in half-time interviews with both captains. Although only 28,246 attended the match, the entertainment provided was the finest possible advertisement for the code, and was certainly not equalled in subsequent tests against New Zealand at Station Road.

So inadequate were the 1955 Kiwis that they allowed Great Britain to score five tries when the home side were reduced to only twelve men. Whilst in 1961 it was Britain's superiority in and around the scrum that largely contributed to them posting the highest score against New Zealand in this country, 35-19 - scrum-half Alex Murphy scoring a hat-trick of tries direct from the set-piece, and Workington Town prop Norman Herbert also touching down on his international debut. In 1965 New Zealand lost what Alfred Drewry of *The Yorkshire Post* described as *"the most boring test of all time"*. An unopposed try by Halifax's Scottish loose-forward Charlie Renilson, from a favourite blind-side move of Bradford Northern scrum-half Tommy Smales, was the only highlight in the 7-2 home win.

Equally, from the 1950s, the history of tests against Australia at Station Road is also like the curate's egg. For example, the

50th Anglo-Australian encounter, in 1952, which ended with Britain retaining the Ashes, would have been totally forgettable but for the virtuoso performance by Ernest Ward, who, along with skipper Willie Horne, was chaired off the field by his colleagues. That day the pitch was described as being *"no better than a recreation field"*, and, likewise, the decider in 1956, was also played on a mud heap. Even though it was Britain's highest winning margin on home soil, 19-0, the game was a total let-down because of the feeble Kangaroos.

In contrast, their successors in 1959 achieved Australia's first-ever test victory in Manchester, when their charismatic young centre, Reg Gasnier, scored a hat-trick of breathtaking tries. However, it was his balding St. George teammate, loose-forward Brian Clay, who was the real star of the show. Similarly, St. George number 13, Johnny Raper, mesmerised Britain in 1963, when he had a hand in nine of the record twelve tries, as Australia became the first side in a series to score 50 points, which included 20 from centre Graeme Langlands. Britain therefore relinquished the Ashes at home for the first time in over 50 years.

Only three members of that great side, Langlands, Raper and hooker Noel Kelly, played in the deciding third test in 1967, when the blizzard conditions made Station Road a place for none but the brave. And there was none braver than the Hull's full-back, Arthur Keegan, whose heroic defence kept the Australian's winning margin down to only 11-3. The game, which perhaps should never have been played, ended with Noel Kelly being sent-off for a high tackle on Roger Millward as the Hull K. R. stand-off followed up his own kick.

Unfortunately, the long walk for the *"early bath"* was all too familiar a scene at internationals at Station Road. In Great Britain's 33-7 victory over France in the 1960 World Cup the St. Helens loose-forward, Vince *"The Wild Bull of the Pampas"* Karalius, and the French captain, Barthe, became the first players to be sent-off in the competition; whilst in 1965 another French captain created a further unwanted landmark. Leading 7-4 at half-time, the French effectively beat themselves with a series of infringements, which not only allowed Neil Fox to kick seven goals from eight attempts but led to the dismissal of prop Marcel *"The Bear"* Bescos in the 61st minute.

There was a sensational hold-up to the live televised game, when referee Dennis Davies marched off the field after his French touch-judge had failed to persuade Bescos to take his

punishment; and, having followed the referee to the dressing-rooms, it was several minutes before the depleted French side returned to complete the match. All this created dramatic viewing, but did little for rugby league's image.

Station Road's final international was in the 1970 World Cup, when Great Britain beat New Zealand 27-17 to qualify for the final play-off. Shortly after this game part of the Wolseley Street end was taken for the building of the Swinton Squash Club and Lynton Suite, and, with these improved social facilities from 1971 until 1980 Station Road staged six Championship and Premiership finals. Also, up to 1984, it was still considered to be a suitable venue for Challenge Cup semi-finals. Since then, however, a brief history of Station Road, and that of the once-proud Swinton club, makes painful reading.

The Popplewell Report, in August, 1985, resulted in the demolition of the Townsend Road Stand, and a drastic effect on the main stand's seating capacity. A ground, which since 1929 had hosted 22 major finals, 30 Challenge Cup semi-finals, and 19 tests and internationals, with crowds of over 30,000 at 22 of these, including 40,000-plus on four occasions, was now given a safety limit of no more than 4,000! By 1991 this figure had risen to 11,000, but, with the club in debt to the tune of £1.1 million, Station Road's days were numbered.

In May, 1992 came the news that Swinton had signed a 4-year lease to ground-share with Bury F.C. at Gigg Lane. At the same time, with the Pendlebury Road car park already having been earmarked for housing Swinton were granted planning permission for housing (now called Lowery Park) to be built on their abandoned ground, where arsonists had partly gutted the main stand during the summer. Station Road's subsequent sale for £995,000 helped pay off most of the club's debts prior to the old company being liquidated.

Swinton's 24-16 defeat against neighbours Salford on 20 April, 1992 was therefore the last professional game of rugby league played at Station Road, although the following week Irlam Hornets beat Folly Lane in the Valentine Cup final, and an amateur sevens tournament was also played before the close-season.

Before the bulldozers moved in on Station Road - where now the streets of Lowery Park make no mention of famous past players or the significance of the site - groundsman Gary Lewis had two difficult tasks to perform. One was to take down the 67-foot posts, which, because they had been sunk 15 feet into the ground, could only be removed by sawing them off at the base. What must have been the tallest and finest rugby league posts in this country were subsequently given to Eccles ALFC and now grace their ground near junction 4 of the M63. The second task was even more problematical, for it meant locating the urns, containing the ashes of former Swinton supporters, which had been buried on the pitch since 1929.

Station Road		
1930 Great Britain 0 Australia 0		34,709
1933 Great Britain 19 Australia 16		10,990
1937 Great Britain 13 Australia 3		31,724
1946 England 16 France 6		20,000
1946 England 10 Wales 13		20,213
1947 Great Britain 7 New Zealand 10		29,031
1948 Great Britain 16 Australia 7		36,354
1951 Great Britain 20 New Zealand 19		29,938
1952 Great Britain 21 Australia 5		32,421
1955 Great Britain 25 New Zealand 6		21,937
1956 Great Britain 19 Australia 0		17,542
1959 Great Britain 14 Australia 22		35,224
World Cup 1960 Great Britain 33 France 7		22,923
1961 Great Britain 35 New Zealand 19		22,536
1963 Great Britain 12 Australia 50		30,843
1965 Great Britain 17 France 7		9,959
1965 Great Britain 7 New Zealand 2		8,541
1967 Great Britain 3 Australia 11		13,615
World Cup 1970 Great Britain 27 New Zealand 17		5,513

OLDHAM

Watersheddings Watersheddings was always considered to be the highest ground in the English Rugby League until research by architect and ground-expert Henry Skrzypecki revealed that Halifax's neighbouring Thrum Hall is slightly higher - 776 feet above sea level to Watersheddings' 761 feet. It is perhaps because of its elevated position on the Pennines that Watersheddings, like Thrum Hall, has been granted only two internationals in its 106-year history.

From their formation in 1876 Oldham played at the rear of the Glodwick Spinning Company mill, Gartside Street, Glodwick Lows, and later shared part of Oldham cricket club's sloping pitch at Clarksfield, both grounds which are now covered by housing.

Oldham's opening match at Watersheddings took place on 28 September, 1889 when a crowd of 7,000 saw them lose to Swinton, for whom centre Jim Valentine scored the first points on the new ground with a try. He was directly opposed by Welshman Bill McCutcheon (see Wales), who was destined to referee the first international on the ground in 1912. Along with forward Jack Armstrong, who also played for Oldham on that opening day, McCutcheon took part in a brief ceremony in 1939 to mark the ground's 50th anniversary.

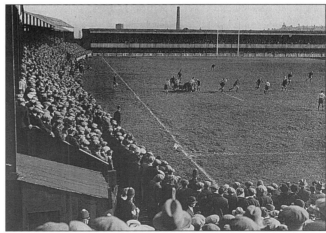

Watersheddings' curved main stand and original "penny rush" on the occasion of Australia's visit in 1933.

Originally a sub-tenant of the cricket club, the rugby section later bought the grounds and appointed trustees, who were entrusted to see that Watersheddings *"should remain as an open space for sport for all time"*.

At its opening Watersheddings had a 40-yard long open main stand, and wooden planking on the full length of the Herbert Street side. The boundary fencing came almost to the dead balls lines and until about 1909 there were tennis courts where the Kop now stands, making it possible to watch games from the hillside at that end. The present pavilion overlooked the cricket field, which was turned into a greyhound stadium/baseball field from 1930. The adjacent bowling green became part of the training pitch in the 1950s. In the 1960s a half-time retreat was added to the main stand but the players and officials still change in the pavilion.

The skyline was dominated by the chimney of the Ruby Mill, which was also opened in 1889. Its reservoir, into which the pitch drained, bounded the Herbert Street side of the ground. Superstition had it that demolition of this chimney in 1935 acted as a bad omen, causing the club, who had appeared in four consecutive Challenge Cup finals from 1924, to enter a period of decline.

It was reported in September, 1893 that a new stand had been built, thereby making the ground as good as any in the county. This could well have been the original double-decker stand, later known as the *"penny rush"*, which originally ran the full width of the pitch.

A record crowd of 20,000 could be accommodated against Salford on 20 September, 1897 as a result of developments the previous season, which included the erection of the present main stand. Its end sections were added no later than 1909. The popular side was also covered in three stages, between 1920 and 1930, and became known as the E Stand.

Watersheddings from the G. F. Hutchins Stand end, showing the pavilion (centre) and the greyhound stadium - Oldham Evening Chronicle. Ref: 94J1047

Refereed by Bill McCutcheon, Watersheddings' first international was on Saturday, 20 January, 1912, when England adapted more easily to the heavy conditions to score a 31-5 victory over Wales. The Welsh were on the defensive throughout the first half when England, dominated by their Huddersfield contingent, Wagstaff, Moorhouse, and Clark, scored six of their nine tries. When it looked as if this poor Welsh side would never cross the England line, Evan Davies, the Oldham left centre, broke clear to put W. T. (Will) Davies, the Halifax right winger, over for a consolation try in the closing minutes.

Although only 8,000 braved the elements that day, the following month the present ground record of 28,000 was established at the league game against Huddersfield. However, when Huddersfield beat St Helens by a record 37-3 in the 1915 Challenge Cup final, the first time a major final had been played on the ground, again there were only 8,000 present.

During the First World War - which claimed the lives of six Oldham players who are remembered on a Roll of Honour in the pavilion - it was decided to sell a wooden stand, which had been hurriedly erected, for a game with Wigan, at the Watersheddings end. Due to the scarcity and value of wood, this sale enabled the club to clear their debts.

Watersheddings' only other international came during wartime, when on 9 November, 1940, England beat Wales 8-5 in a thrilling game. Added to the excitement was the fact that an air-raid warning interrupted the game during the first half. Although, for some reason, the incident was not reported in the local match report, Welsh captain Trevor Foster recalls that the players took shelter under the stand for about twenty minutes until the all-clear was given. Wales were unfortunate to lose after staging a late rally, during which Salford winger Williams was held inches short of the line in the closing minutes, and then hurled into touch at the corner flag with the last tackle of the match. Mid-way through the second half the English forwards had to fight tenaciously to repel the Welsh attacks. Fortunately for the home side, full-back Belshaw was on top form with his long touch-finding. He also converted the winning try by St. Helens centre Waring, who took full advantage of a rebound following a dribble to score from close range.

Most league games that day failed to cover expenses. For example, Leeds took only £17 at their game against Keighley. In the circumstances, the receipts for the international of £234 from a crowd of 5,000 were considered to be highly satisfactory. During the war German Prisoners of War, including the future Manchester City goal-keeper, Bert Trautmann, helped build many of the present boundary walls.

In 1946 the ground underwent extensive reconstruction. The present main stand was partly rebuilt using a steel frame, and 1,059 tip-up seats were added. However, the top deck of the wooden *"penny rush"* stand was not made safe until the start of the 1954/5 season when it was re-opened and re-named the G.F. Hutchins Stand in memory of George Frederick Hutchins, a great servant to the club who was one of the original trustees and joint Great Britain tour manager in 1928 and 1932. His ashes were scattered on the ground on 10 July, 1947. After Oldham's success in winning the League Championship in 1957 the present Watersheddings end cover was erected for the start of the 1958/9 season at a cost of £12,000.

The floodlights were officially opened on 20 October, 1965 when Great Britain Under 24s beat France 12-5 in front of a crowd of 6,333. One of the original parallel lattice towers was blown down prior to game against Leeds on 31 August, 1986.

Following the Valley Parade fire, in August, 1985 Oldham demolished the E Stand, and the ground's capacity was reduced to about 7,000. At this stage they were also ordered to demolish the main stand, the wooden end sections of which were derelict. However, the central seated section and the paddock area were reopened in time for the first round Challenge Cup-tie on 4 February, 1987 when a crowd of 11,906 saw Oldham beat Wigan 10-8 - the last occasion on which Wigan suffered defeat in this competition.

When Oldham became the Rugby League's first plc in January, 1989 - as an attempt to clear off debts of £1.4 million - the share prospectus spoke of *"fully maximising the potential of the Watersheddings site"*. One imagines that the founding fathers would have interpreted this aim rather differently than the present generation. But, faced with their cash crisis, and the failure to secure a grant from the Foundation for Sports and the Arts for the rebuilding of the main stand, which was again closed in 1995, the directors had very little choice but to sell the club's main assets.

Approximately £400,000 was raised in 1991 by the sale of the training pitch for housing and then in March, 1994 the club agreed to sell the rest of the Watersheddings site for £1.2 million in an arrangement worked out by the local council and

Oldham may play some of their Super League games at Boundary Park (background) whilst their new stadium is being built on the Westwood athletics track (left) - Oldham Evening Chronicle. Ref: 92K1026

a private developer. Under the terms of the rescue package a joint venture company was set up with the investor paying £300,000 for two club houses and the greyhound stadium, and also providing the club with a £425,000 sponsorship grant and a 3-year loan of £500,000, plus £25,000 for immediate ground safety work. The company has the choice of either building houses on the ground, outline planning permission for which has already been granted, subject to them finding the club an alternative site for a new stadium, or redeveloping Watersheddings (current capacity 8,250) for rugby.

The former option is the one favoured by Oldham, and in March, 1995 plans were announced for a new £5 million 10,000 capacity stadium, meeting all the requirements of the *Framing the Future* report, to be built on the Westwood athletics track, which will be resited. The planned stadium, which rapidly doubled in size when it was known Oldham were vying with Salford for a Super League place, will run parallel with Oldham Athletic's Boundary Park - earlier plans to build a back-to-back rugby and soccer having been scrapped. It forms part of a £20 million development for the area, under which the 100 yards or so which separate Boundary Park from the proposed stadium will be filled with housing, and there will also be room for a supermarket, leisure centre, and a filling station, with a new road providing motorway access to the site. Provided planning permission is granted, following the example of the McAlpine Stadium, the pitch will laid first in order to give it two years to get established before the anticipated opening in 1997.

Watersheddings	
1912 England 31 Wales 5	8,000
1940 England 8 Wales 5	5,000

ROCHDALE

Athletic Grounds Following the scoreless draw at Swinton, which left the 1930 series against Australia also drawn, there was clamour for a deciding test to be played. The chosen venue was Rochdale Hornets' Athletic Grounds on 15 January. It was the only international ever to be staged there, although the ground once held the attendance record for rugby league in this country.

As far as the home officials were concerned the mythical Ashes were not at stake. However, the public and the Australians thought otherwise. Fortunately, there was to be no further argument as Great Britain finally came out on top, 3-0, in this defence-dominated game. It was not until Australia had lost centre Cec Fifield with a broken ankle in the 65th minute that the deadlock was broken, with Leeds left-winger Stanley Smith scoring the only points of the match with a controversial sliding try six minutes from the end. Four of the Australians later returned to play in England, including Fifield and forward Vic Armbruster who both joined Hornets.

Stanley Smith

Formed in 1871, Hornets first played on the Old Athletic Grounds, which covered the same site on Milnrow Road. After using four other venues, principally sharing with the local cricket club, Hornets returned occasionally to the new Athletic Grounds following its opening in June, 1894. They moved there permanently in 1900 before purchasing them from Councillor William Watson on 5 February, 1913.

Around the pitch was an outer banked cycling circuit, inside which was a quarter-mile ash track. On the latter F. E. Bacon set a new world record in June, 1897 by covering 11 miles 1,170 yards in the hour, watched by a crowd estimated at 25,000 spectators; and in 1924 the Northern Counties AAA held their Olympic trials. On the railway side was an uncovered stand which had seen service at the 1894 England-Wales rugby international at Birkenhead. This was demolished in 1902. The main stand opposite seated 1,200. After being extended in 1911/2 it was gutted by fire in 1935. Hornets first game at the Athletic Grounds was on 8 September, 1894 when they beat Crompton 11-0. That day, some of the 7,000 spectators surged onto the cycle track when the perimeter fencing gave way - an omen of future disaster on the ground.

In Hornets' Challenge Cup-winning year a new ground record of 26,664 was established at the third round tie against Oldham on 25 March, 1922. The bulk of the spectators in those days were accommodated on the unterraced mound of ashes where the scoreboard stood at the town end.

It was chiefly due to this expanse, later referred to as *"Hill 60"* after some war-time exploit, that the Athletic Grounds accommodated the record attendance for this country of 41,831 at the 1924 Challenge Cup final.

This game is famous for the pitch invasion and the incident involving Van Heerden, Wigan's South African winger, who avoided a police horse to score one of Wigan's tries in their 21-4 victory over Oldham. With the ground already full, the police wisely allowed a number of spectators to climb onto the cycle track, but the crowd simply lost control and thousands rushed across to the main stand side, with some even climbing onto the stand roof. When it was decided to kick off the police were still driving spectators out of one of the in-goal areas, whilst six mounted policemen patrolled the touch-lines during the whole match. Van Heerden scored the most memorable try when he picked up a cross-kick *"almost from underneath the feet of a prancing horse"*, or *"rounded a mounted policeman"* (depending on which report you believe) to score under the posts. Parker is said to have "dived right into the feet of the crowd in the in-goal" for the third try, and for the fourth Price *"forced a way through the ranks of spectators to find the in-goal"*. The crowd had to be moved back to enable Jim Sullivan to attempt to convert after the fifth and final try.

The decision to stage the Challenge Cup finals at Wembley from 1929 ensured that there were fewer incidents of this nature at future finals. However, the Athletic Grounds were again chosen in 1926, when 27,000 saw Swinton beat

Spectators cling to the roof tops and straddle the touch-line as a casualty is carried away following the collapse of the Railway Stand at the Challenge Cup semi-final on 1 April, 1939 - Rochdale Library.

Oldham, and, of course, for the previously-mentioned international in 1930, whilst on 1 April, 1939, at the Wigan-Salford Challenge Cup semi-final, there was a repeat of the 1924 invasion. This time, however, there were tragic consequences

On that fateful day for rugby league, many thousands gained illegal entry and did not register in the official attendance of 31,212. Five minutes into the game, after an earlier crowd invasion had been restored to order, the roof of the wooden Railway Stand, which had been built in 1911/12, collapsed under the weight of spectators who had climbed on top. Scores were trapped underneath resulting in one fatality and seventeen injuries. At another part of the ground a woman also died from what was believed to be shock. Nonetheless, the game, which was to be the last major event staged there, was played to its conclusion with thousands of spectators lining the touch-lines.

The ashes of *"Hill 60"* were bought during the 1970s by the Hornets' chairman, haulier Jack Grindrod, who loaned the club £5,000 which was paid back at the rate of £11 per wagon load! The hill made way for a pit area for stock cars, which were introduced in 1969 but ceased in 1987 following complaints from local residents. Speedway racing, which was first held on 4 August, 1928, was also staged in the 1970s. From the 1930s greyhound racing also shared the ground, the totaliser dominating the Kingsway end until its demolition in the 1950s.

Hornets' perilous financial position in the 1930s was not helped by the fire which gutted the main stand on the morning of Wednesday, 18 September, 1935. Its £4,725 replacement was officially opened on 7 March, 1936 by the Mayor prior to the game against Liverpool Stanley.

At its opening in 1894 the Athletic Grounds was favourably compared with Headingley, but long before closure the ground was showing many signs of neglect. The wide track always made rugby viewing difficult, and underfoot conditions for the majority of spectators were among the most primitive in the Rugby League.

In 1987 Hornets had debts of £350,000, and after Rochdale Council abandoned their £3 million plan to turn the ground into a modern athletics stadium, Hornets accepted the Wright Group of Companies' offer of £2.4 million for the site. After playing their last game at the Athletic Grounds on 16 April, 1988 against Carlisle, Hornets entered into a ground-sharing arrangement with Rochdale FC at Spotland, which the rugby club now own jointly, the soccer club and the local council being minority shareholders in the ground company.

Rochdale's former Athletic Grounds is now the site of a Morrisons Supermarket, which has a rugby league-themed entrance, and garage. The only question that remains for rugby league historians to answer is where exactly did Stanley Smith score his match-winning test try in 1930 - near the delicatessen or in the car wash?.

Athletic Grounds	
1930 Great Britain 3 Australia 0	16,743

ST. HELENS

Knowsley Road St. Helens have played on the same ground for over 100 years, and are one of the most successful clubs in the modern era. Why then have Saints never hosted a test against Australia or New Zealand, and only a handful of other internationals and major play-off games? The answer to this rhetorical question is mostly related to the fact that, in south-east Lancashire, Central Park has ruled that particular roost.

What is often forgotten, however, is that for long periods of their history St. Helens (as Alex Service reminds us in the first of his two-part definitive history of the club, *Saints in Their Glory*) also had to play second fiddle to their local rivals St. Helens Recreation, who were formed in 1879 by the Pilkington Crown Glass Works.

The first St. Helens club had been formed in November, 1873 after William Douglas Herman, an English chemist of German descent who worked at the glass works, had advertised in the local newspaper. Their opening game against Liverpool Royal Infirmary was played on 31 January, 1874 at the Recreation Cricket Ground, Boundary Road, which is now the Queens Recreation ground. In 1879 St. Helens moved to Queens Park, St. Annes, a ground which the original club members, on hanging up their boots, forfeited to a youth team, who called themselves both Eccleston Rangers and St. Helens Rangers before dropping their suffix in 1885. At that time St. Helens, as they now became, shared the present local cricket club ground at Denton's Green Lane, which they were forced to vacate at the end of the 1889/90 season.

Pilkington Brothers then agreed to rent St. Helens a field off Eccleston Lane, as Knowsley Road was then called, and adjacent to the L.M.S.R. branch line near to Ravenhead Junction. Subsequently, on 6 September, 1890, the club chairman, Lt. Colonel Wilcock, kicked off the first game on the new ground, with Billy Cross' drop goal being the first score in Saints' victory over Manchester Rangers. With the building of a small open stand the club's assets at the end of that first season were valued at £190; and until four turnstiles were installed around 1893, spectators paid at pigeon holes in the fencing at the town end.

As founder members of the Northern Union St. Helens had their headquarters at the Duke of Cambridge, Duke Street. It was from there that the teams were taken to the ground by waggonette, and where Saints doubtless drowned their sorrows after being defeated by Batley in the inaugural Challenge Cup final in 1897.

Around 1902/3 Saints built a 1,000-seater wooden reserved stand on the Knowsley Road side, which had no fewer than 29 Y-shaped supports. But it was not until after the First World War that other developments took place, with the opening of the present pavilion on Boxing Day, 1920 by the late Lord Derby. This ceremony was performed prior to St. Helens, who that day wore his Lordship's racing colours of white (shirts) and black (shorts), losing 22-4 to Wigan, watched by a crowd of 24,000. In 1925 Saints bought the ground and pavilion from Pilkington Brothers, and, thanks to the Supporters' Club, a popular side cover was erected in two stages by 1927.

An estimated 20,000 had watched the 1926 Championship final between Warrington and Wigan and when Saints met Wigan in the third round of the Challenge Cup in 1929 a new ground record of 27,305 was established. There were to be no other play-offs at Knowsley Road, however, until the mid-1960s

In January, 1930 the allotments, on the site of the present car park and training pitch, together with extra land at the Eccleston Lane end, were also purchased from Pilkington Brothers for under £1,000. The following year the Supporters' Club erected a large wooden members' clubhouse which was placed next to the pavilion. The plan to stage greyhounds at Knowsley Road in 1933 was dropped at an advanced stage after opposition from the clergy and supporters, but principally because such a development contravened the deed of covenant under which the ground was purchased.

Saints staged their first international on Saturday, 25 February, 1939, when France gained an unexpected first-ever victory over England, 12-9, to win the European Championship. Rarely, if ever, had such handling been seen on an English ground. After giving away an early try to Stan Brogden, Max Rousie's side trailed 6-3 at half-time. However, the rearrangement of their three-quarters, which included Rousie moving from full-back to centre, eventually brought results, with a magnificent try for his partner Dauger, who had started the game at stand-off. The visitors' open style earned the backing of the 10,000 crowd and they had much to cheer when, following a forward dribble, Cougnenc gave France the lead after an amazing pick-up and a spectacular leap over the line. Then Brunetaud, who was arguably the best loose-forward in the world on this performance, shot away from a scrum to register the fourth try.

It was in July of that year, incidentally, shortly before the outbreak of war, that St. Helens Recreation resigned from the Rugby League. During hostilities Knowsley Road was designated as an air raid warden's post and the Home Office approved the possible use of the pavilion as a first-aid station. The pitch was used in 1941 for grazing cattle and after the war players returned to find the ground not only vandalised but a health hazard!

With the terracing having been extended, the immediate post-war period saw the Knowsley Road attendance record progressively raised. In 1947/8 28,765 cheered Saints and Wigan in the Lancashire Cup, and a league record of 28,000 was also set at the traditional Boxing Day derby. During October, 1948 29,500 were at the game against Warrington, and in February, 1949 a crowd of 30,276 watched the first round, second leg, Challenge Cup-tie against Bradford Northern.

Also during the 1948/9 season work started on the first stage of the Eccleston Kop terracing. Building approval to extend and cover what became the Edington Stand (in memory of the late George Edington, the former chairman of the Supporters' Club) was given shortly before the present ground record of 35,695 was set against Wigan on Boxing Day, 1949, when it was estimated that the attendance was nearer 38,000 as the gates had been rushed. The Edington Stand was officially opened by Mr Bert Hughes, the

Skipper Len Aston welcomes the Turin captain, Vincenzo Bertolotto, to Knowsley Road before the Italians' 74-38 defeat by St. Helens in 1950.

Saints South African winger Jan Prinsloo finishes in style against Dewsbury. The popular stand (right) was given to Liverpool City in 1962.

Supporters' Club treasurer and match announcer, before the first round, second leg, Challenge Cup-tie on 17 February, 1951 against Bradford Northern.

Knowsley Road's second international, on Wednesday evening, 19 September, 1951, was all over after 30 minutes following injuries to Gwyther and Harrison when Wales led England 8-5. Reduced to eleven men and a 3-man pack the Welsh battled courageously, with the sporting crowd of 20,918 cheering their every move. Although England added 20 points in the last 15 minutes to run out 35-11 winners, the night still belonged to Wales.

Unlike the internationals played in Wales this game yielded a profit of £1,492; and a similar crowd, 19,357, was also at Knowsley Road for the evening game in September, 1953 when England inflicted a more convincing defeat on a full-strength Wales, 24-5. Although John Henderson (Workington Town) did enough on his international debut to win a tour place in 1954, the game was marked by a general lack of understanding between the forwards.

The evening of 10 April, 1957, when Great Britain beat an injury-hit French side, was filled with mixed emotions for two famous Sullivans. Jim Sullivan could only watch as Lewis Jones (who registered 17 points) broke what was then considered to be Sullivan's points in a season record (since amended) which was set in 1933/4. Whilst for Huddersfield's Mick Sullivan, after moving from wing to right centre, the night was one of triumph after bagging two tries and setting up a walk-in Jones' try.

Apart from the Central Park factor, the main reason why, up to that time, Knowsley Road had staged so few major games, was the ground's lack of seating. During the 1957/8 close season, however, the old stand was demolished, and Saints' six Great Britain tourists returned to find the present 75-yard long main stand erected in its place. Costing £32,000 and seating 2,372 it was officially opened by Sir Harry Pilkington on 23 August, 1958 against Featherstone Rovers. Its striking feature is the rear elevation, which overhangs what is now the car park, but until the 1960s, when it fell into disuse, was the L.M.S.R.

Saints centre Ken Large cuts through against New Zealand in 1961 with Tom Van Vollenhoven (left) moving inside - Geoff Sutcliffe.

Eccleston branch line. The old stand's seats finished their days at Rochdale Hornets' Athletic Grounds.

Compared to Saints' free-for-all against the 1959 Australians, when a crowd of 29,000 saw the Kangaroos win 15-2, Great Britain's return engagement against the French, in March, 1960, was a tame affair. After the torrid Toulouse game three weeks earlier, the British pack put in a spiritless performance, which allowed France to deservedly draw the match 17-all after trailing by ten points up to the 69th minute.

Britain made no mistake in 1961 when, despite the muddy conditions, they gave a brilliant display of handling and support play in their 27-8 win. Saints' light-footed scrum-half Alex Murphy took full advantage of an injury to his French opposite number to strike up a telling relationship around the scrum with his clubmate Vince Karalius, and the home side led 20-8 at half-time. All but one of the game's seven tries, including the first to Swinton winger John Stopford who was making his international debut, were scored in this first

period - the try of the match coming after a 75-yard 8-man move by the visitors. Sadly, such Gallic flair was sadly lacking in the future French sides who visited Knowsley Road.

Following their Wembley victory over Wigan in 1961 St. Helens embarked on a number of ground and social improvements. With Saints about to record a seasonal average of nearly 12,000 per match, there was clearly a need for the present full-length popular side cover, which was completed for the start of the 1962/3 season at a cost of £15,000. The wooden structure from the 1920s which it replaced was given to Liverpool City for their new ground at Knotty Ash. During November, 1962, the present social club, to which an extension was added in 1967/8, was opened courtesy of the Supporters' Club. Also in the 1960s Knowsley Road's first floodlighting system, since upgraded on the same roof gantries, costing £10,923 was officially switched on by Sir Harry Pilkington before the St. Helens versus Other Nationalities game on Wednesday, 27 January, 1965. Later that year Knowsley Road staged its sole Challenge Cup semi-final when Wigan beat Swinton 25-10 before a crowd of 26,658, and also the first of its seven Lancashire Cup finals.

Knowsley Road hosted its first Sunday international on 30 November, 1968, when Saints' scrum-half and captain Tommy Bishop sparkled throughout Britain's 34-10 win over France. Halifax's Colin Dixon was the outstanding forward on his international debut, although Saints John Warlow twice started moves in the first half which resulted in tries.

This poor French display was repeated in the first international to be played under the Knowsley Road lights, on Wednesday, 18 March, 1971, when Great Britain revenged their defeat at Toulouse the previous month by winning 24-2. On this occasion, international new boy Steve Nash of Featherstone Rovers broke from a first-half scrum to pave the way for a try by St. Helens centre Billy Benyon, and his half-back partner Roger Millward (Hull K.R.) was also on the score sheet with two of his side's six tries. Few other Britons, however, enhanced their reputations.

The present offices and club shop were opened in October, 1972, whilst the Saints restaurant complex, which overlooks the terracing at the Dunriding Lane end was officially opened on 31 March, 1973 by the club president, Lord Pilkington, when Cathy Kirby was the evening's cabaret star. It was Pilkington Brothers who made it possible for Saints to up-grade the press facilities, and to install the nine executive boxes and the electronic scoreboard adjacent to the pavilion.

Knowsley Road's redevelopment is likely to start at the pavilion end (foreground) and the extension of the main stand (right) - Alex Service.

Improvements for the start of the 1989/90 season also included the provision of a police control room in the old scoreboard which had been opened by the Supporters' Club in September, 1954.

The ground's centenary celebrations got under way with the opening of a superb exhibition at the local museum in September, 1990, whilst on the field Saints were given the opening game of the Australians' tour. The legendary South African winger Tom Van Vollenhoven flew in especially for the match on 7 October and took part in a parade of past greats prior to the Australians' 34-4 victory. This memorable occasion was watched by a crowd of 15,216.

Looking at Knowsley Road's facilities it is difficult to imagine why the ground has not been allocated an international since 28 May, 1978, when England beat Wales by 60-13. That day Wales' ageing forwards suffered in the heatwave conditions, and the Welsh resistence lasted only ten minutes against England's high-speed attacks - with the game's top try-scorer, Stuart Wright of Widnes, helping himself to four of his side's 14 tries, and Saints full-back Geoff Pimblett kicking nine goals to extend his total at the top of the chart to 178. Whilst the ground's limit is now only 17,000, there is still a strong case for Knowsley Road, a designated Centenary World Cup venue, to be regularly used, ahead of Central Park, for future internationals involving teams such as Wales, France and Papua New Guinea.

Over the next five years, with grant aid and their share of the Super League money, Saints are hoping to develop Knowsley Road into a 20,000 all-seater stadium. The first phase is likely to be at the Dunriding Lane, pavilion, end, where a cantilever *"family stand"* will include enhanced social facilities, including a restaurant, an indoor bowl, a sports injury clinic, and a range of community meeting rooms.

Knowsley Road	
1939 England 9 France 12	10,000
1951 England 35 Wales 11	20,918
1953 England 24 Wales 5	19,357
1957 Great Britain 29 France 14	23,250
1960 Great Britain 17 France 17	13,165
1961 Great Britain 27 France 8	14,804
1968 Great Britain 34 France 10	6,080
1971 Great Britain 24 France 2	7,783
1978 England 60 Wales 13	9,759

WAKEFIELD

McEwans Belle Vue When Huddersfield moved from Fartown to the Alfred McAlpine Stadium for the start of the 1994/5 season, Wakefield Trinity's Belle Vue became the oldest ground in the Rugby League currently in use for first-team fixtures.

Founded in 1873 as part of the Holy Trinity Church Young Mens' Society, Trinity first played at Belle Vue on Easter Monday, 14 April, 1879, two days after winning the coveted Yorkshire Cup for the first time. The ground was then T-shaped with the second and third teams using a pitch at the Agbrigg Road end called *Heathfield*.

As founder members of the Northern Union, in 1896 Trinity formed a separate company, in order to raise capital for ground improvements. The first stand on the west side, behind which stood a new pavilion, originally had seating down to ground level. Around the rest of the field, which now incorporated a cycling and athletics track, spectators stood on wooden footboards. The re-built ground, which cost £2,134, was opened by the local M.P., Lord Milton, when Trinity lost 13-0 to Halifax on 24 September, 1898.

That day Belle Vue was full with a crowd of 10,000, but in 1901 there was room for 20,195 at the Trinity-Bradford Challenge Cup-tie. However, the narrow exits caused some crushing at the 1904 Challenge Cup semi-final when a similar number attended.

There was little chance of congestion at Belle Vue's one and only international, on 4 December, 1909, when there were less than 4,000 to see England beat Wales 19-13. The game started sensationally as a result of the Welsh full-back, Young, wearing an England jersey during the early stages of the match! This obviously confused his opposite number Tyson - who was standing in for Leigh's Clarkson who missed his train - as he allowed Young to put Wigan's Francis over for a try after only three minutes.

This farce continued until Young put on a Wakefield Trinity jersey, and immediately became the local's favourite. It was a genuine Trinity man, however, who gave England the lead, when half-back Newbould darted over from a scrum in the final quarter to put his side 9-8 ahead. Both sides were prepared to throw the ball about in difficult conditions, and the star of the match, Salford centre James Lomas, added England's fifth try before the gloom descended.

On 26 February, 1921 a new club record attendance of 30,676 was established at the first round Challenge Cup tie against Huddersfield; and in the club's jubilee year Belle Vue was the chosen venue for the 1923 Challenge Cup final, when 29,335 saw Leeds beat Hull 28-3.

The basic structure of the present East Stand, which currently seats about 1,500, was opened on 20 September, 1924, by Mr. R. Gale (Leigh), chairman of the Rugby League, prior to Trinity's 44-0 defeat of Widnes. At a cost of £3,200 the full length, partly-covered, terrace then provided standing room for about 8,500. A third of these were in the present uncovered sunken paddock, which was laid on the site of the cycle track. Subsequently, Belle Vue's ground record was increased to 32,095 at the 1930 Championship final when Huddersfield and Leeds drew 2-2. When bench seats were added under the cover in September, 1952 the ground's capacity was significantly reduced.

The 900-seater West Stand, which was demolished in 1986 following the Popplewell Report, was officially opened on 29 October, 1932 prior to Yorkshire's 30-3 defeat of Lancashire. This unique stand, which was only 30 yards in length, had a tiled roof, ornate roof fascia, and four rear chimneys. What remained of the cycle track was taken in by a

Belle Vue, early 1970s, with the now demolished West Stand and the Agbrigg Road end cover. - Aerofilms

sunken paddock. The dressing rooms, which were later converted into public refreshment rooms, remained under this stand until August, 1964, when the former St. Catherine's School was converted into a new clubhouse, and a tunnel was constructed in the East Stand. The old school was demolished in 1983 following the opening of the present clubhouse.

Later in 1932/3 season the ground record was extended to 36,359 - the highest at that in Yorkshire - at the Leeds-Huddersfield Challenge Cup semi-final. The present ground record of 37,906 was set on 21 March, 1936 when the same sides met at the pre-Wembley stage.

The Supporters' Club completed the present concrete slab terracing at the Kop end for the visit of the Australians in October, 1948, when a crowd of 20,040 watched a 26-19 Trinity win. The scoreboard, which once stood at the top of this banking was removed, along with the crush barriers, in the 1980s. Much needed cover was provided at the Agbrigg Road end with the erection of the South Stand, which was officially opened on 1 February, 1958 before Trinity's 17-12 league win over St. Helens. However, before Trinity's appearance at Wembley in 1979 this stand, which was subsequently sold to a local farmer for use as a Dutch Barn, was dismantled, and the banking levelled.

To see Belle Vue in its heyday you therefore need to turn to the cinema, Trinity's third round Challenge Cup-tie against Wigan on 23 April, 1962 having been used in the filming of *This Sporting Life*, in which Richard Harris starred as loose-forward Frank Machin. The all-ticket crowd of 28,254 created a new post-war ground record, subsequently beaten by the attendance of 28,736 at the Castleford-Widnes Challenge Cup semi-final replay on 22 April, 1964. Soon afterwards, on 4 October, 1967, Belle Vue's first £11,500 parallel floodlights were inaugurated, when a crowd of 19,376 saw Yorkshire beat Australia 15-14 in a ferocious match.

Ironically, with the levelling of the Agbrigg Road end in 1979, Belle Vue returned to something like its 1879 condition, although part of what was the site of *Heathfield* was built on with the opening in 1983 of the privately owned £250,000 social club (renamed the Coach House in 1991), under which Trinity have their dressing rooms, offices, board room and gymnasium. With Trinity facing bankruptcy, in 1986 a special members' meeting approved the sale of the ground, for £165,000, to Wakefield District Council. Later that year the West Stand was demolished on safety grounds, following

A view of Belle Vue's East Stand and social club at Trinity's game against Halifax in August, 1992 - Henry Skrzypecki.

which Belle Vue more than ever started to resemble its original 19th century state.

In the summer of 1991, however, Trinity became a limited company, and, with help of a £100,000 grant from the Sports Aid Foundation, new floodlights, switched on by the world-record points scorer, Neil Fox, M.B.E, before Trinity's 12-4 victory over Widnes on 19 February, 1992, created a new local landmark, the sleek 22-metre corner towers seeming somewhat out of place in a ground which is crying out for modern spectator amenities.

There were prospects of these when, after being renamed McEwans Belle Vue in September, 1993 as part of a three-year sponsorship, plans were immediately unveiled for a £500,000 4,000-capacity semi-cantilevered stand at the Agbrigg Road (southern) end of the ground. This was to have been funded by local authority and Sports Aid Foundation grants and completed for the start of the 1994/5 season.

Unfortunately, this has not happened, and at present it is sad to see this famous old ground in such a state of decay - particularly on the western side, where the sawn-off pylons of the old lights and the breeze-block supported executive boxes scar what was once the pleasantest area of the ground. It is difficult to know what the answer will be, for Belle Vue falls well below the Framing the Future report criteria for both cover and seating, and there appears to be no plans in the pipeline to raise the ground's capacity beyond its existing 8,300.

Belle Vue
1909 England 19 Wales 13   4,000

WARRINGTON

Wilderspool Stadium Warrington's move to Wilderspool in 1898, due to the building of Fletcher Street on a portion of their old field, was their fifth change of venue since their formation in 1879. Fortunately, after fears that Fletcher Russells had earmarked the adjacent land for development of their factory on Priory Street, Warrington were able to agree a ten-year lease on Wilderspool with their present sponsors, brewers Greenall Whitley, from whom they bought the freehold in 1914/5. The boundary fencing from Fletcher Street was re-erected and an enlarged stand built on the Priory Street side in time for the first game on 3 September, 1898, when Warrington drew 3-3 with Swinton and the home stand-off, R. Bate, scored the first points on the new ground with a try. A right-winger named Morgan Bevan was the Swinton try-scorer - an omen perhaps of the great try-scoring feats of his future Warrington namesakes, Brian and John.

The first 900-seater main stand with its pedimented gable, which survived until the fire in 1982, was opened on 2 September, 1911 by T. Locker, the club President, prior to the 16-10 victory over Leigh. Over 21,000 attended the Challenge Cup first round replay against Hull on 2 March 1921, during which season the club had a membership well in excess of available seats. It was not until the start of the 1925/6 campaign, however, that two bays were added to increase the seating capacity by about 600. Another short extension was also added later at the railway end.

In 1927 Wilderspool staged both the Lancashire Cup and Championship finals, the latter which was watched by a crowd of 24,432. At that time there was no terracing (only ash bankings) anywhere to be seen, and at the Fletcher Street end only a wooden hut which doubled as the dressing rooms and refreshment kiosk. A year later a familiar landmark appeared at that end, when the Supporters' Club presented the club with a scoreboard and clock, which was finally condemned in 1989. The present one was opened on 3 August, 1989 for the Student World Cup when England beat Ireland 65-12. It was only in the late 1950s that the present Fletcher Street shelters were built.

Although the former Warrington-Stockport freight line has always restricted one of the corners, by the 1930s the terracing at the railway end was considerably higher than it

Australian winger Pat McMahon, supported by centre Jack Horrigan (left), is pursued by the Warrington cover during the tour game in 1948 - Warrington Library

is today, thus enabling a new ground record of 31,565 to be set at the 1934 Championship final when Wigan beat Salford, 15-3. During the war Wilderspool was commandeered and the main stand used as a storeroom.

The 1948/9 season was marked not only by the 16-7 defeat of the Australians in front of 26,879 spectators, but the establishment of the present ground record of 34,304 at the league game against Wigan on 22 January. The Lancashire Cup final on 29 October, 1949, when Wigan beat Leigh, was made all-ticket, but although all 35,000 were sold only 33,701 turned up on the day and so the above record remained intact.

The first of Wilderspool's four internationals, when Wales staged a second-half revival to beat the eventual champions, Other Nationalities, was played on the evening of Wednesday 15 April, 1953. Three tries either side of half-time had given the latter a flattering 16-7 lead, but Wales stormed back, and in a thrilling finish Rochdale Hornets' centre Norman Harris got over for the equalizing try, which was converted by the Hunslet full-back Jack Evans, who thus gave the Welsh a deserved, 18-16, victory. Warrington's Australian forward and past captain Harry Bath kicked a couple of goals in this match.

The original Wilderspool floodlights were set on the main stand roof and the Priory Street cover, the latter which had been extended in September, 1958. They were officially switched on by Mr John D. Whitley of Greenalls on Tuesday, 28 September, 1965 for the friendly against Wigan. The fourth game under the lights, on 12 October, 1965 against Widnes, marked the opening of BBC2's Floodlit Trophy, which in those days was only televised in the south. The present £60,000 lights were first used for the game against Bradford Northern in October, 1992.

Wilderspool's appearance was dramatically altered, and its capacity likewise reduced, with the opening of the £300,000 Leisure Centre in November, 1972. As a result of the development the Priory Street stand was transferred to the railway end, and remains there today. There were a few rows of seats (taken out in August, 1991 to provide standing room) for vice-presidents and life members under the huge plate-glass windows, from which diners could watch the game in luxury.

But effectively Wilderspool had become a three-sided stadium holding no more than 21,000. However, these impressive social facilities, which are no longer owned by the club, soon guaranteed that Wilderspool was allocated its one and only

test match, during a period when interest in international rugby league in this country was at a particularly low ebb and a ground's capacity was not that important.

Because of the badly frozen and rutted pitch the third test against Australia on 1 December, 1973 should never have been played. However, because the Kangaroos could not delay their journey to France, the game went ahead, with Australia, seemingly oblivious to the dangers of playing on such a treacherous surface, convincingly beating the more wary home side, 15-5, in front of a crowd of 10,019.

The game started sensationally when Australia's Warrington-born half-back, Bobby Fulton, intercepted a pass at half-way to race over at the scoreboard corner. By half-time the British line had been crossed four times, including twice by the powerful Cronulla second-row forward, Ken Maddison, who seemed to revel in the arctic conditions. A finely worked try for Roger Millward shortly after the break raised hopes of a home revival, but within minutes this had been firmly quashed when a four-man move resulted in hooker Elwyn Walters going over for the Australians' fifth try. Robert Gate in his *The Struggle for the Ashes* concluded that, *"It was just as well that Eadie and Branighan could not land a goal from their seven opportunities or the home side would have been swamped"*. It is perhaps also worthy of mention that although Warrington won four trophies that season no member of this side was picked for this game.

Australian second-rower Ken Maddison crashes over for the first of his three tries in the 1973 test.

The Brian Bevan Stand and the Fletcher Street end at the game against Halifax in 1991 - Henry Skrzypecki.

There was better form shown by the two England sides which played at Wilderspool in the 1970s, although the standard of opposition was hardly on a par with Artie Beetson's men. Warrington and England coach, Alex Murphy, must have been highly delighted with the dazzling first-half performance of his side against Wales in the 1975 World Championship, when they raced to a 10 point lead after only 12 minutes play. Although having to retire after 64 minutes following a late head-high tackle, Salford stand-off Ken Gill had already done enough to earn the man-of-the-match award, although he was pushed all the way by his partner and captain Roger Millward (Hull K.R.). Wales recovered to trail by only 14-9 at the interval but with Castleford's Steve Norton also in brilliant form at loose-forward, the final score (22-16) was never in doubt.

In 1979 England's 12-6 victory over France, to retain the European Championship, was less important to the players than their own form as the match was played only days before the tour selections. Another stunning first 40 minutes, during which all their points were scored, guaranteed that the young England side was chosen almost en bloc. Bradford Northern full-back and man-of-the-match, Keith Mumby, booked his place, as did Leigh centre John Woods, who kicked three goals, and try scorers Tommy Martyn (Warrington) and Eric Hughes (Widnes).

It was from the front of the main stand that Warrington's world record try scorer, Brian Bevan had taken his farewell salute following Warrington's Easter Monday game against

Leigh in 1962. Unfortunately, almost twenty years to the day following this momentous occasion, this stand was burnt to the ground on the lunchtime of Thursday, 29 April, 1982. Flames quickly spread across its whole length and within twenty minutes the largely timber stand was completely destroyed and the floodlighting perished. Fortunately, the stand had been insured and together with an appeal fund the club were able to rebuild on the former site. The new 2,100-seater, which includes underneath the Touch Down Taverners social club, and new floodlights mounted on the roof, was opened on Sunday 6 February, 1983 prior to Warrington's 18-16 defeat of Hull.

On 21 July, 1991 this stand was named The Brian Bevan Stand in memory of the great Australian who died on 3 June of that year. Also the local council have erected in his honour a £20,000 statute, the unveiling ceremony being performed by Brian's widow, accompanied by actor and screenwriter Colin Welland, on 29 August, 1993. This can be seen in the centre of the Wilderspool Causeway traffic island on the approach to the ground. The plaque below the statue chronicles Brian Eyrl Bevan's remarkable contribution to the sport - played 688 games, scoring a world record 796 tries from 1945 until ending his career (with Blackpool Borough) in 1964. Amazingly, although he played 16 times for Other Nationalities (see Wigan for photograph), including the game at Wilderspool in 1953, scoring 29 tries in the process, the great man never once put on the Green and Gold jersey of his country.

The future of Wilderspool is in some doubt as Warrington, now a Super League club in their own right after the Rugby League's ill-conceived merger with Widnes was found to be a non-starter, are exploring, with the local council, the possibilities of developing a new 15-20,000 all-seater stadium. Nothing has yet been announced, although the pointers are that the Arpley Meadows, which is over the River Mersey near to their present home, will be the likeliest location for any such development. It may only be coincidence but that is also the direction in which the Brian Bevan statute is pointing.

Wilderspool Stadium	
1953 Wales 18 Other Nats. 16	8,449
1973 Great Britain 5 Australia 15	10,019
World Champ. 1975 England 22 Wales 16	5,034
1979 England 12 France 6	5,004

WIDNES

Naughton Park In 1932 Widnes had to rescue their present ground on Lowerhouse Lane from the bulldozers after it had been compulsorily purchased for future council housing. Its sale in 1994 to the local authority, who intend developing Naughton Park as a sports stadium and leasing it back to the club, might suggest that we live in more enlightened times.

Widnes, who started life in 1873 as the Farnworth and Appleton Cricket and Football Club before taking on the town's name in 1875, moved to their present ground for the start of the 1884/5 season when they met Liversedge in the first match. They had earlier had spells at what is now Ross Street, Simms Cross, Peelhouse Lane, and the Widnes Cricket Club field, the latter which was literally over the wall from the present ground. The club's once-familiar black and white hoops were introduced in 1895 when Widnes became founder members of the Northern Union.

A plan of the ground in 1899, when it was laid out for an athletics and cycling meeting, shows a stand on the exact site of the old shelter at the scoreboard end, which later became *"the boys pen"*, and a small stand on the present main stand side. During the 1902/3 season £98 was spent on new dressing rooms, which were then situated on the present popular side. The main stand was extended for the start of the 1911/12

A view of Naughton Park's popular side, circa 1950, from the pavilion end - Mike Flynn Collection.

90

season. Its wooden roof was not replaced until 1959, the five wooden rear staircases having been condemned in 1957.

Pre-First World War the rest of the ground was relatively undeveloped although there was also a wooden flat roofed stand with Y-shaped supports on the popular side which sported the advertisement *After the Match Visit the Empire Picturedrome and Century Cinema* on its roof fascia. This was replaced in two stages, in 1949 and 1956. Allowing for the fact that this stand still had two distinct parts, at the end of the 1990/1 season Naughton Park had no fewer than seven stands, prior to the demolition of the newest shelter, at the side of the pavilion, during that close season.

As mentioned earlier, following the First World War the ground was compulsorily purchased by the local council and earmarked for housing. The Chemics were granted a 5 year lease in 1926, but when this ran out it seemed likely that the ground would become part of the present Kingsway Council estate. Fortunately the Ministry of Housing and Local Government sanctioned the sale of the land to the club, and with the help of the Rugby League, who agreed to subscribe 10% of any money raised, the Supporters' Club completed the purchase in August, 1932 for £3,250.

Until 1971/2, the legal restriction, whereby the council had the right to buy back the ground at a similar price, inevitably influenced the club members' attitude towards major ground developments, although improvements were immediately made with surplus cash from the ground purchase fund.

The ground was subsequently officially named Naughton Park on 27 August, 1932, at the visit of St. Helens, in memory and appreciation of the late club secretary, Tom Naughton, who died in a motor accident in the year that his ground purchase scheme reached fruition. The adjacent Naughton Road, at the present scoreboard (electronic since 1990) corner, is also named after Mr Naughton.

The pavilion, which cost £1,479/9/0d, was officially opened by the Mayor preceding the game against St. Helens Recs

Australian half-back Tom Raudonikis dives over for a try in the tour match against Widnes in 1973 with Mick Adams (left) too late to stop him.

on Boxing Day, 1933. It then stood alone at the Lowerhouse Lane end, the present terraces largely obliterating the balcony.

When Widnes got to Wembley in 1934 there was a record crowd of 14,337 at the first round against Leeds on 3 February, and following the Second World War, with improvements to the terracing, the attendance record was increased as follows: on 31 January, 1948 v. Wigan 17,446; 26 March, 1948 (Good Friday) v. Warrington 20,286 ; and on 7 April, 1950 also against Warrington 22,729. The present record of 24,205 was set at the Challenge Cup first round replay on Thursday, 16 February, 1961 against St. Helens.

The ground's first parallel floodlights were opened by Lord Derby on 27 September, 1965 prior to the league game against St. Helens when the attendance was 17,319.

During the club's succesful period in the 1970s - Challenge Cup winners in 1975, 1979 and beaten finalists in 1976 and 1977, Division One champions in 1978 and Premiership winners in 1979 - Naughton Park staged three internationals.

In 1978, the Featherstone-born Welsh captain Bill Francis controlled the game from stand-off, scoring a try himself and setting up two others, after France had fought back to 9-7 at half-time thanks to a try and two goals by centre Marc Bourret. At the Friday night game in March, 1979, when England beat Wales 15-7 in atrocious conditions, snowbound roads over the Pennines prevented the arrival of Wakefield referee Fred Lindop, local official Ron Campell deputising. The following January Wales, who included eight new caps, struggled from the start against a lively French side, for whom classy loose-forward Joel Roosebrouck scored two tries in their 21-7 victory.

During 1984/5 a fire in the main stand had severely damaged the central press box area, and, following the Valley Parade tragedy at the end of that season, the insurers ordered Widnes to remove all the wooden seating. Consequently, for the start of the 1986/7 season, with loans from brewers Greenall Whitley, the Rugby League, and Halton Borough Council, £100,000 was spent on completely concreting the stand, erecting six front stairways to the paddock, and adding plastic tip-up seats, which totalled 1,043. Along with plans to install an artificial pitch (outlawed by the Rugby League) and an athletics track, a money-raising scheme for a new 3,000-seater stand had to

be abandoned in 1986 through lack of public interest and an underestimate of its true cost.

Whilst Doug Laughton and his committee were frustrated with the lack of progress in modernising Naughton Park they were far more adept at putting a champion side on the field. Having won the Premiership final at Old Trafford in 1988 and 1989 as champions, Widnes returned there on 4 October, 1989, when they defeated Canberra Raiders 30-18 in the Foster's World Club Challenge and earned £118,000 for their night's work. At the end of that season they also won their third successive Premiership.

In the final game of the Australian tour, on Sunday, 18 November, 1990, there was an all-ticket crowd of 14,666, which was slightly above the ground's present permitted limit. Although Widnes lost on that occasion, they can still claim to be the last English club side to beat Australia, when, on 25 October, 1978, an injury-time penalty from full-back Mick Burke gave them an historic first victory, 11-10, over the Kangaroos. By the time that Widnes again entertain the Australians Naughton Park's facilities should have changed beyond recognition from the present hotch potch of shelters.

The Naughton Park scoreboard in 1978 - Mike Flynn Collection.

Despite their earlier successes and a Wembley appearance in 1993, the club were recently faced with a financial crisis due to players' contracts. From 1991-1993 the Chemics' expenditure over income amounted to over £700,000 (excluding the sale of the bowling club and Martin Offiah to Wigan for a world-record £444,000), and at the end of

December, 1993 Widnes had little alternative but to change from being a members' club to a limited company.

Subsequently, at the first AGM shareholders gave the go-ahead for the sale of Naughton Park to Halton Borough Council for £300,000 with Widnes signing a 125-year lease. This has allowed for Naughton Park, now officially re-christened the Halton Community Stadium, to be redeveloped by Alfred McAlpine's at a cost of £5.2 million. To be carried out in three stages, the work will commence with the building of a three-storey amenity complex behind the proposed main south stand. As well as accommodating the new dressing rooms and multi-gym, this will also house the social club, a dance hall, a restaurant, and the souvenir shop, whilst there will be room under the stand for a range of community sports such as table tennis. There will eventually be covered cantilever seated stands on three sides and improved open terracing at the eastern (scoreboard) end, taking the ground's capacity to 15,000, including 12,000 seats. It is anticipated that the project will be completed by July, 1996 following the demolition of the pavilion and building of the new west stand.

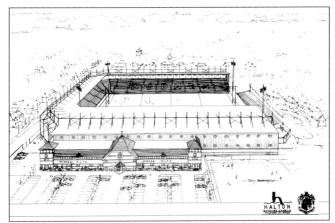

Artist Tony Babington's impression of the proposed Halton Stadium - Howard and Seddon Partnership.

Naughton Park	
1978 Wales 29 France 7	9,502
1979 England 15 Wales 7	5,099
1980 Wales 7 France 21	2,804

WIGAN

Central Park Having grown accustomed to watching one of the world's greatest club sides over the years, the Wigan public appear less interested in supporting representative games at Central Park. For example, although the ground has staged 39 internationals since 1904, there has been no higher attendance than the 27,500 who watched the England-Wales encounter in 1950, a figure which had been easily beaten when Wigan played the All Golds in 1907.

As the first Wigan club (formed in 1872) turned to soccer some time after February, 1878, The Riversiders clearly have their roots in Wigan Wasps who played their first competitive game at Upper Dicconson Street in 1879 and changed their name to Wigan in 1881. After being suspended for professionalism in November, 1894, Wigan were among the founders of the Northern Union, at which time they played at Prescott Street, which is now covered in light industry.

In 1901, Wigan moved in with Wigan United AFC at Springfield Park (the present home of Wigan Athletic), before taking a long-term lease the following year on Joe Hill's Field, which was named after the butcher who used it for grazing. The neighbouring area, extending beyond the present Kop, became known as the *"Bloody Mountains"*, being the site of the Battle of Wigan Lane in the 17th century Stuart-Cromwellian days.

Councillor J.H. Prescott, who supervised the volunteers who laid out the pitch and made the embankments from colliery waste, had apparently christened the field *"Central Park"* whilst watching pub teams play there on Sunday mornings. A Mr. Ablett built the original curved wooden stand (demolished in 1973) which ran the full length of the field on the River Douglas side. A press box was later installed in the roof.

At Central Park's opening on 6 September, 1902 winger Jimmy Barr scored the first points on the ground with a try against Batley, watched by an estimated crowd of 9,000. The dressing-rooms were then at the Princess of Wales, off Greenough Street, and at the drawn game against Hunslet, later that season, the referee had problems escaping from the ground due to a hostile mob. This incident resulted in the ground's suspension.

Even so, Central Park staged the Northern Union's first-ever international on Tuesday, 5 April, 1904 between Other

Nationalities and England. This was played 12-a-side but England started with only eleven men due to the late arrival of James Lomas. The game was further devalued as several selected players from Bradford and Broughton Rangers dropped out in order to play in the third round Challenge Cup tie at Park Avenue, where a ground record of 25,233 watched the second scoreless draw. There was slightly less interest in the historic game at Wigan, only 6,000 seeing Other Nationalities triumph 9-3.

But it was through such experiments that the Northern Union decided to introduce 13-a-side from the start of the 1906/7 season, England's first international under the new code being played at Central Park against the first-ever tourists, the New Zealand All Golds in 1908. On 9 November, 1907, when a brilliant hat-trick of tries by *"Gentleman"* Jimmy Leytham secured for Wigan a 12-8 victory a crowd of over 30,000 created a new record for Lancashire rugby. Only a third of this number turned up for the (non-test) international on 11 January, 1908, but the stayaways missed an intriguing match, which the home side were fortunate to win, 18-16. With the scores level in the second half Dally Messenger astonished the crowd by missing the easiest of penalties, and near the end the All Golds also threw away two simple try-scoring opportunities.

The brick pavilion and dressing-rooms was first used on 4 September, 1909 for the game against Hunslet. At that time, there was also a cover at the present Kop end, but because of timber shortages during the war this was sold in 1918 to the town's M.P. The first cover on the popular side was the so-called Dutch Barn, which was erected during the 1911/12 season.

Wigan became a limited liability company in 1921 and the first annual report confirmed that Central Park had been bought for £500. On a par with these important landmarks in the club's history was the signing, on 18 June, 1921, of Cardiff's 17-year old full-back Jim Sullivan. As Robert Gate informs us in the indispensible *Guinness Rugby League Fact Book*, at his retirement in 1946, Sullivan - a tourist in 1924, 1928 and 1932, and a future Hall of Fame member - was the world's record goal and points scorer who had played in more internationals (60) than any other man, before or since. On 8 August, 1979, his widow unveiled a plaque in his memory on the wall of number 1 Sullivan Way. This street overlooks Central Park, on which his ashes were scattered.

Wales' 13-2 defeat of England in the Central Park mud on Wednesday, 7 February, 1923, was popular with the 12,000 crowd as all the Welsh points were scored by Wigan players, with tries by Hurcombe (2), and Brown, and two goals from Sullivan. Although the result of this game was never in doubt once Jonty Parkin retired injured shortly after half-time, in the corresponding fixture in 1925 England were able to pull off an exciting 18-14 victory in the final minutes despite playing with twelve men for most of the game - England's five-man pack still managing to outplay the Welsh before Charlie Carr scored the winning try in the corner.

The Barrow winger also scored a brace of tries the following year when Great Britain beat New Zealand 28-20 in Central Park's first official test match. Despite being heavily penalised for technical offences Britain looked as if they could win as they pleased once Sullivan had kicked the first of his five goals, and only a late New Zealand rally in injury time made the score respectable.

In 1927 Central Park hosted the Challenge Cup final, when Oldham beat Swinton before a crowd of 33,448; and also in 1928 when Swinton, in their All Four Cups season, beat Warrington in front of 33,909. Earlier that season England had beaten Wales 20-12 in what was classed as a tour trial. It confirmed that Cumbrian loose-forward Harold Young, the oldest surviving Lion (1995), had booked his place on the tour, as did Jonty Parkin who was to captain the tourists for the second time.

An aerial view of Central Park during the 1930s, showing the "Dutch Barn" (opposite) and the pavilion (left) - Wigan Heritage Services.

Wigan became the first rugby league club to entertain royalty when the Prince of Wales (later King Edward VIII) visited Central Park on 23 November, 1932 to watch a demonstration of rugby league played by unemployed youths. Later that season he presented the Challenge Cup at Wembley.

A head stone in memory of former internationals Jimmy Leytham and Bert Jenkins was inserted by a well wisher into Central Park's new scoreboard, which was first used in 1947/8. During this season England beat Wales 10-8 in a disappointing match, in which two tries by pacy Oldham forward Les Thomas earned him a test place against New Zealand at Headingley. On the other hand, *"the extraordinary ineptitude"* of Ernest Ward and Frank Kitching ruled out both Bradford centres from the same match.

By June, 1949 the now familiar concrete perimeter wall had replaced the wooden railings, and 491 permanent ring side seats, which are now covered by advertising hoardings, were installed in time for England's 11-6 win over Wales on 1 March, 1950. Wigan winger Jack Hilton scored a hat-trick of tries but was still outshone by Halifax's Arthur Daniels, who scored just one. Immediately after the match the selectors met at Southport to name the tour party, and it was no surprise that both these players, together with Leeds Welsh stand-off, Dickie Williams, the man-of-the-match, were among those chosen.

With all Central Park's terraces finally concreted, finishing with the boys' pen at the pavilion end, a ground record of 44,529 was set at the traditional fixture against St. Helens on Good Friday, 1950.

Ted Cahill, the England full-back, tackles Tony Paskins as the Other Nationalities' centre passes to Brian Bevan during the international in 1953.

Although the roof of the Dutch Barn had been leaking since at least 1951, because of delays in obtaining building licences, it was not until 21 August, 1954 that its current replacement was opened at the game against Hunslet. This is now a family stand, seating 1,500, beneath which is the Jim Sullivan Bar. The present double pitched roof over the Kop was also completed in time for the visit of Warrington on 27 November, 1954.

During the early 1950s Central Park staged regular European Championship games, from which several players can perhaps be singled out for special mention. In 1951 the legendary Brian Bevan scored a hat-trick of tries, including a 75-yard interception, for Other Nationalities in their 35-10 victory over England. The following year England not only gained revenge, 31-18, largely due to a masterly display of ball distribution from Barrow stand-off Willie Horne, but also triumphed over Wales, 19-8. In the latter game, Horne had used his wits to carve out two of the tries, and when England again beat Other Nationalities 30-22 in 1953 to take the Championship it was his passing which had the stamp of genius about it. St. Helens centre Dougie Greenall also excelled in this department, giving Swinton's Peter Norburn the opportunity to score his four tries. In 1955 it was Leeds' Welsh wizard Lewis Jones, playing centre, who was largely responsible for Other Nationalities' trouncing of England, 33-16. Apart from his own try and six goals, his phenomenal change of pace allowed local hero Billy Boston to score a hat-trick of tries. On the other wing Bevan added two more, taking his try tally to nine in his four international appearances on the ground.

It was not until 1956 that Central Park was allocated its first Anglo-Australian test, when Great Britain had little difficulty in beating a disjointed Kangaroo side 21-10. The highlight of a bleak November afternoon occurred in the 49th minute, when Boston, from a play-the-ball inside the visitors' 25, weaved his way from the wing to the posts for his second try. Billy had a far more difficult time in 1957, when, despite Great Britain walloping France 44-15 he found himself outplayed by his opposite number, the crew-cut Raymond Contrastin.

A record attendance for an ordinary league fixture in this country, 47,477, was set on 27 March, 1959 for the 163rd meeting between Wigan and St. Helens. Although this attendance was originally announced as 47,747, Robert Gate has listed the preceding figure in his history, *Wigan versus Saints* due to it being entered as such at Rugby League headquarters.

What is not in dispute is the fact that Central Park was the venue, on 12 December, 1959, where Great Britain, 18-12 winners, last clinched a test series against Australia in this country. Six goals plus a try from his own up-and-under by world-record points scorer Neil Fox, and a last minute try to Oldham's right-winger Ike Southward, had staved off the threat posed by the brilliant Reg Gasnier. Who in the 26,089 crowd could have envisaged Great Britain's future traumas in attempting to repeat this feat on home soil?

After their humiliation in 1957, the French had quite an impressive record at Central Park during the 1960s, winning three and drawing one of their five games against home sides. They were less successful in the 1960 World Cup, when Central Park hosted two of their games, although they lost by only a single point to Australia and were unlucky that none of their drop kicks went over in the dying minutes. Their game against New Zealand, on the same afternoon that the decider was being played and televised from Odsal, was watched by less spectators than the average crowd for Wigan's "A" team. It was a grim spectacle, punctuated by mass brawls which resulted in the dismissal of Erramouspe, the French second-rower. In 1963, Neil Fox scored 21 points (9 goals and a try) in Britain's 42-4 win, which brought to an end a run of three successive defeats against the French. However, there were home defeats in 1966 and 1967, the latter being the last international under the old unlimited-tackle rules, whilst in 1969 Britain could only manage an 11-all draw.

Central Park's first £17,000 floodlights were officially switched on by the Earl of Derby on 26 September, 1967 for the drawn friendly game against Bradford Northern, which, because of their failure, took 98 minutes to complete. The present £36,000 lights were first used for the Roses match on 11 September, 1985.

Wigan also had teething problems with their £88,000 undersoil heating system, which failed to save the game against Hull on 29 December, 1985. The previously referred to scoreboard was converted into the director's board room in the 1980s, and was finally replaced with a £15,000 electronic one in 1985, paid for by H. J. Heinz & Co. Unfortunately, Wigan's problems with electricty continued when this was burnt out on 1 February, 1988 due to a short-circuit. With the opening of the new stand, the new electronic scoreboard now stands near the entrances on the popular side (continued).

The Sydney Football Stadium's spectacular "saddle-shaped" roof captured at the Anglo-Australian Centenary Test in 1988 - Varley Picture Agency.

Leeds United's Elland Road is now an established rugby league big match venue. The lower part of the new East Stand was first used at the Bradford Northern-Wigan Challenge Cup semi-final (pictured) on 27 March, 1993 - Mike Haddon.

The Stade de l'Amitie, Narbonne, the established home of the French Cup final and, for the last two years, the venue of the Championship final. On the left are the glass shields which protect the arena from the unusually high cross winds. - © Ville de Narbonne, PH. J. M. Colombier, Mairie de Narbonne.

There have been six venues in Christchurch used by the New Zealand Rugby League, with the Addington Showgrounds, pictured left, having hosted the large majority of tests in the city - Richard Cosgrove.

Following the success of playing the 1989 trans-Tasman test in Christchurch in the larger Queen Elizabeth II Stadium, Great Britain met New Zealand there in 1990. This picture shows the main stand on that day - Kirsty Beddard.

Knowsley Road, St. Helens, 1995, looking from the pavilion end towards the Edington End. The path of the former railway can be seen behind the main stand (right) - Alex Service.

The long-term future of Wembley, pictured at the World Cup final in 1992, will possibly hinge on the Sports Council's pending decision over the allocation of funds for the proposed new national stadium - Henry Skrzypecki

Central Park's Douglas Stand at Wigan's league game against Halifax in April, 1995. Wigan have announced proposals to redevelop this side of the ground after months of speculation as to the ground's future - Henry Skrzypecki.

After the season's wear and tear, Headingley's rugby pitch looks in remarkable condition compared to the cricket oval, pictured on the eve of the test against the West Indies in June, 1995. Under the first stage of the proposed redevelopment on the rugby side, Leeds Supporters' Club (bottom left) will be incorporated in a new South Stand (foreground) - Wood Visual Communications - AC 28724

The Stade Albert Domec's impressive main entrance archway (left) - Varley Picture Agency.

The Stade Albert Domec, Carcassonne, looking towards the main stand, during the Academy international in 1993, which was a curtain-raiser to Great Britain's 48-6 victory over France - Bob Evans.

St. Helen's, Swansea, has hosted 15 of Wales' post-war rugby league internationals. This superb view of the "Tanner Bank", pictured during one of the brawls in the exciting contest against Australia in 1975, would suggest that the official attendance fell well short of the true figure - Andrew Cudbertson.

Danny Leahy Oval, Goroka, in 1990, when Great Britain lost 20-18 to Papua New Guinea, and the scenes when police fired tear gas, which affected the players and caused the game to be halted in the 14th minute - Dave Hadfield.

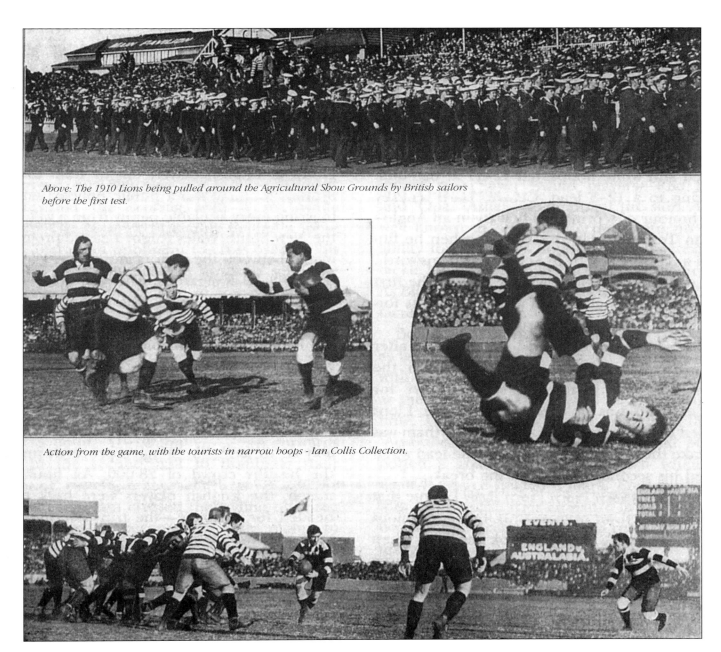

Above: The 1910 Lions being pulled around the Agricultural Show Grounds by British sailors before the first test.

Action from the game, with the tourists in narrow hoops - Ian Collis Collection.

tour of England. Messenger switched from his travelling companions and represented Australia under the captaincy of Arthur Hennessy, the founder and captain of the Souths club. New Zealand led 11-2 at half-time and won 11-10, although they had forward *"Massa"* Johnson sent off in the first half for punching Hennessy into unconsciousness. Unfortunately, Baskerville, who scored one of the All Blacks' (as they were called until they became the Kiwis in 1939) tries, soon contacted pneumonia and died in Brisbane eleven days after that historic game. The New Zealanders continued the tour, winning 24-12 in Brisbane and losing 14-9 when they returned to the RAS, the only test Australia ever won on the ground.

The first-ever test against England in Australia was played there on 18 June, 1910. It was preceded by a goal-kicking contest in which James Lomas defeated Messenger. The 42,000 fans, a world record for the game at that time, saw England prevail, 27-20, in a highly entertaining game. The Lions won there again, 23-5, on the 1914 tour. The last test on the ground, on 10 July, 1920, was won by England, 23-13, although their hosts had already regained the Ashes by taking the first two matches of the series.

Since those days, occasional matches have been played on the Showground, usually when other venues were unavailable. For example, Clive Churchill made his representative debut there before 50,253 fans on 7 June, 1947 for New South Wales Country Seconds versus Sydney Seconds. Also, several years ago, a club game was played during the annual Royal Easter Show, but not before the area had been carefully cleared of mementos left by the parading livestock! The RAS has been put to many other uses: during the great influenza epidemic of 1919 one of its newly built exhibition halls became a morgue; school examination papers and tax returns have both been assessed within its pavilions; and the ground was an Army depot in the Second World War. The main arena is currently the training quarters of the Sydney Swans *"Aussie Rules"* team. With the planned move of the Royal Easter Show to the Olympic Games site at Homebush, the NSW government has leased the RAS to Rupert Murdoch for use as a movie studio.

Royal Agricultural Society Showground	
1908 Australia 10 New Zealand 11	20,000
1908 Australia 14 New Zealand 9	13,000
1909 Australia 11 New Zealand 19	6,000
1910 Australia 20 Great Britain 27	42,000
1914 Australia 5 Great Britain 23	40,000
1920 Australia 13 Great Britain 23	32,000

Wentworth Park When Captain Arthur Philip sailed his First Fleet into Port Jackson in 1788 he established his settlement at Sydney Cove. If he had gone one inlet further up harbour, he may well have chosen Blackwattle Bay as his town site. The bay was wrongly named after the trees that covered the foreshores but which, as Collicoma Serratifolia are not really wattle trees. In 1789 Governor Philip granted the Church of England 400 acres bordering the bay as its glebe, to be used to support its clergy. In time, the suburb became known as The Glebe or just Glebe.

In 1870 the headwaters of Blackwattle Bay were reclaimed and city refuse dumped there until the area could be levelled and utilised. As part of the development, 32 acres of the reclaimed land was dedicated in 1885 as Wentworth Park, in honour of William Charles Wentworth, an explorer, parliamentarian and lawyer who, in earlier years had been shot at by escaped convicts as he rode through the bush there.

Playing fields were established and the park, less than a mile from Sydney's central railway station, became the home ground of the strong Glebe Rugby Union Club, which, in 1900 won rugby union's first inter-district premiership and five more before amalgamating with Balmain rugby union club in 1919.

As previously mentioned, when Australia's first rugby league premiership began in 1908 it met determined opposition, as a result of which the League were able to lease only three enclosed ovals where an admission fee could be charged - the previously referred to Royal Agricultural Showground at Moore Park, Birchgrove Oval on the Parramatta River and Wentworth Park.

The competition started on Easter Monday, 20 April, at Birchgrove Oval and Wentworth Park, as the Royal Easter Show was being held at the RAS. Two first grade games were played on each ground, lower grades being conducted elsewhere on unenclosed grounds. At Birchgrove, Souths beat Norths 11-7 and Balmain defeated Wests 24-0; whilst at Wentworth Park, Easts and Glebe triumphed over Newtown and Newcastle, 32-16 and 8-5, respectively.

In that first game at Wentworth Park Easts included current and future internationals in Dan Frawley, Albert Rosenfeld, Sid Pearce, Larry O'Malley and Lou Jones as well as future prominent officials Harry Flegg and Horrie Miller; whilst Newtown boasted Australian reps in Frank Cheadle, Tedda

Courtney and Bill Noble. Newtown's centre Jack Scott - one of Australia's fastest and leading bowlers of his era, who took over 200 first-class wickets and later became a test umpire - scored the first try from an intercept and added another try and two goals. Easts winger Jack Stuntz also scored three tries in a game in which three spectators jumped the fence to join in a less than friendly discussion between two players.

Among Glebe's stars, in a less spectacular second match, was Alec Burdon, whose uncompensated injuries had been factors in the League breakaway; and Tom McCabe, an English player whose knowledge of the laws of Northern Union football qualified him to be Australia's first rugby league coach.

Wentworth Park's moment of rugby league glory came early in the game's history when New Zealand were invited to tour Australia in 1909 to rescue the code's shaky finances, and the deciding test, of a series which Dally Messenger missed, was staged there on 3 July. The hosts led 15-3 at half-time following two tries by centre Charlie Woodhead and one by

Albert Conlon, supplemented by Herb Brackenreg's three goals, against a penalty try to New Zealand, and went on to win 25-5. Rival forwards Bill Cann (South Sydney) and H. Knight were sent from the field in the second half when they shaped up to each other without actually coming to blows. The All Blacks had earlier lost twice to NSW at the RAS, drawing 30,000 and 16,000, but could only attract 2,000 to Wentworth Park for their third game against the state team, when they won 20-8. The three tests had similar modest attendances, 6,000 in each case, perhaps because of Dally Messenger's absence.

Later that season, the second semi-final of the premiership was played at the Glebe ground, when Balmain defeated Easts, 15-8, before 3,000 spectators. They then forfeited the final against Souths because they did not agree with the game being a supporting fixture to a match between the 1908-9 Kangaroos, and those members of the 1908-9 Rugby Union Wallabies who had switched to the professional code after returning from Britain. Consequently, Souths were awarded the premiership by default.

Wentworth Park greyhound stadium, 1994, with the new grandstand on the left and the Sydney skyline, including the Centrepoint Tower, in the background - Noel Christensen.

In 1910 the first English tourists down-under played four internationals, and it was not until 1984 that it was determined that only the first two qualified as tests, the scheduled third test having been changed to Australasia (two New Zealanders appearing in the Colonial side) once the Lions won the first two.

An extra match, at Wentworth Park with 13,000 attending, was also played against Australasia, on Wednesday, 13 July, 1910, the day the tourists left for New Zealand. After being 15-0 in arrears Australasia, who again included two Kiwi representatives, and wore light blue, maroon and black jerseys, won 32-15. One sensational incident during this game was a collision between two wingers who were famous for hurdling would-be tacklers. Hunslet's Billy Batten attempted to leap over *"Opai"* Asher as the New Zealander had successfully done in the previous Saturday's drawn third *"test"*. Unfortunately, Batten's jump was not as effective and the pair collided, leaving Asher knocked out with a cut head. Although no longer recognised as a test, this game retains the status of *"international"*.

According to test referee Tom McMahon (the earlier of the two of the same name) one problem for visiting teams to Wentworth Park, if victorious, was the necessity to dodge stones thrown at their bus or, worse, their horse-drawn dray on the homeward journey through Glebe. When Glebe withdrew from the competition after the 1929 season Balmain adopted Wentworth Park as their home ground but drew only small crowds and therefore reverted to Birchgrove Oval in 1931.

Wentworth Park then ceased to be a premiership venue and was used for minor sporting events until greyhound racing commenced there in 1939. It is now controlled by the government appointed Wentworth Park Sporting Complex Trust, which built an unnamed grandstand, seating 4,500 under cover, which was opened by the Minister for Sport, the former test winger, Michael Cleary, in 1985. The Park's capacity is now claimed to be 30,000, including uncovered seating for 500, but this figure has never been tested. Despite its proximity to Sydney city centre, Wentworth Park has never been a big drawing ground for rugby league, and it seems unlikely that it will ever again be the venue for representative matches.

Wentworth Park		
1909 Australia 25 New Zealand 5		6,000
1910 Australasia 32 Great Britain 15 (non-test)		13,000

Sydney Cricket Ground In 1848 the British Army's Sydney garrison, the 11th North Devonshire Regiment, moved from near Sydney Harbour to the new Victoria Barracks, on the hills almost two miles south-east of the town. Subsequently, in 1851 they were granted 25 acres, just south of the barracks, as a shooting range, cricket ground and garden.

Known initially as the Garrison Ground, as it was developed and changed hands in the 1870s, the playing field was renamed the Civil and Military Ground, the (New South Wales) Association Ground, and finally, in 1894, under the control of a government appointed trust, the Sydney Cricket Ground (SCG). A second oval, Sydney Cricket Ground No. 2, was built next door and used for cricket and football training, and minor, usually social, matches.

The first recorded football match on the SCG was a rugby game in 1874; and its first cricket test in 1882 when Australia beat England. As well as rugby union and soccer internationals, other sports conducted there over the years include bowls, quoits, lawn tennis, baseball, and athletics, including the 1938 Empire Games. It is presently the home ground of Aussie Rules side, Sydney Swans. From 1896 until 1920 cyclists also raced on an asphalt track, on which in 1903 motor cyclists competed at night under acetylene gas lamps.

The first substantial grandstand, the Brewongle, which was named after the local tribe of Aborigines, was built in 1878 on the western side. It was replaced in 1980 by a $8.7 million triple-decker, with 24 private boxes, of the same name. The present members' and ladies' pavilions, at the northern end, were opened in 1886 and 1896, respectively. It was from the dressing rooms in the former pavilion that successive rugby league captains led out their teams, and in front of which Melba Studios have taken their famous wide-angle photographs of touring sides over the years.

Named after one of the New South Wales Cricket Association trustees, Philip Sheridan, the Sheridan Stand was built in 1909. This replaced the small Smokers' Stand, which was subsequently moved to the SCG No2 and in 1936 found its way to Belmore where it was renamed the Parry Pavilion. The Sheridan Stand was demolished in 1986 to make way for the Clive Churchill Stand, which is really an extension of the new Brewongle Stand.

The two-tier M. A. Noble Stand, which replaced the old Northern Stand dating from 1897, was built at the northern

Sydney Cricket Ground at the third test in 1958. On the immediate right is the M. A. Noble Stand with the old Bob Stand to the left on the famous Hill - Melba Studios.

end of the 130 x 165 metre oval in 1936. It was joined by its twin, the Don Bradman Stand, in 1973. The 1895 Bob Stand (a shilling entry fee), which was situated between The Hill and The Paddington Hill, was moved to the North Sydney Oval and replaced in 1984 by the Bill O'Reilly Stand (formerly called the Pat Hill's Stand after a long-serving trustee).

Small open stands, named after Dally Messenger and Doug Walters, have been added in recent years. Consequently, with the erection also of the giant electronic scoreboard in 1983, the once-famous grassed Hill is now covered by concrete and

seating. The present capacity of the all-seater SCG is in the region of 42,000, not much more than the eastern grass banks could once accommodate. The huge floodlight towers were erected in 1978 for Kerry Packer's World Series Cricket. Behind one of the open stands it is still possible to see the impressive 1904 scoreboard, which replaced groundsman Ned Gregory's wooden original further down The Hill.

The first rugby league match played on the SCG was New South Wales versus New Zealand on 22 June, 1911, the holiday celebrating the coronation of King George V. The

On his test debut, Great Britain stand-off Gus Risman receives a long pass from winger Stan Smith (9) during the third and deciding test at the Sydney Cricket Ground in 1932 - Les Hoole Collection.

SCG trustees would not normally let the professionals sully their sacred soil but the League's own ground, the Showground, was required by the government that day for a patriotic carnival. However, as the trust received a percentage of what were rugby league world record takings of £2,551 from a 46,000 crowd, they were persuaded to allow the NSWRL to lease the oval thereafter and club matches were held there regularly until 1987. Until 1974 the best club game, *"The Match of the Day"*, was held on the SCG every week-end.

The first of 57 tests held on the SCG was the second of the Lions 1914 tour on Monday, 29 June, when Australia, fielding seven changes from the side beaten at the Showground on the previous Saturday, defeated the injury-weakened Lions, 12-7, before 55,000 spectators. It was the third and deciding test, however - all three were played in Sydney as Queensland could not guarantee a profit - which was probably the most famous to be played on the ground.

Under strong protest against the tightness of their itinerary (in fact, the test had been due to be played in Melbourne), the tourists went into the contest on the following Saturday,

4 July, as directed by the Northern Union headquarters in England, whose cabled instructions included the Nelsonian rejoinder, *"England expects every man to do his duty"*. Under their outstanding captain, Harold Wagstaff, they certainly did so. For, although injuries reduced them to ten men for 20 minutes of the second half, they prevailed 14-6 and regained the Ashes, in what has since become known as *"The Rorke's Drift Test"* after a British Army unit's heroic battle in the 1879 Zulu Wars.

Another historic SCG test was the third of the 1950 series when, on a rain-soaked ground covered by forty tons of sand which made it just playable, Australia won the Ashes for the first time since 1920. Despite the downpours, 47,178 saw a gripping battle in which defences dominated until, with 15 minutes left, the not always reliable hands of lanky winger Ron Roberts held a pass and his long legs carried him clear of the British defence, and the clinging mud, to score in the right hand corner for Clive Churchill's heroes to win a famous victory, 5-2. As Alan Whiticker and Ian Collis point out in *Rugby League Test Matches in Australia*, it is perhaps appropriate that the Clive Churchill Stand now overlooks that particular corner.

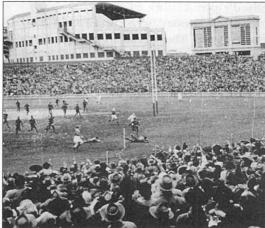

Above: Ron Roberts scores his famous try in the deciding test in 1950. The rear of the Show Grounds stand is prominent at the back of The Hill - Ian Collis Collection. Left: A graphic illustration of the conditions (only slightly improved on at the above game) during the first test at the Sydney Cricket Ground in 1950 - Associated Press.

In 1951 Australia were deposed as *"world champions"* by a French side whose style attracted over 400,000 spectators to see them on their first tour Down Under. The opening test was the first all-ticket international to be staged at the SCG, a crowd of 60,160 being enthralled by the French passing and the goal-kicking of Puig-Aubert (he landed 7 from 9 attempts) in their 26-15 victory. After Australia levelled the series at Brisbane, the tourists proved who were the masters with a breathtaking 35-14 win in the final test before a packed house of 67,000. Replacement stand-off Crespo scored three of his side's seven tries; and *"Pipette"*, whose record 210 tour points still stands, landed seven more goals, which brought him a record 18 in the series.

This was equalled the following year by Kiwi full-back Des White, who, after kicking a record 11 goals in the second test at Brisbane, kicked five in New Zealand's 19-9 success in the final test at the SCG. A crowd of 56,326, the largest ever to watch New Zealand, had been in the SCG for the first test.

One of the most sensational games at the ground was the Lions' second meeting with NSW on 10 June, 1954. On a rainy day, before 27,869 fans, Britain played forwards Geoff Gunney, Brian Briggs, and Jack Wilkinson in the three-quarters. What began as niggling disagreements developed into regular skirmishes until, in the 56th minute, a brawl erupted which no amount of whistle blowing could end. In despair, referee Aubrey Oxford gave a final blast for full-time and walked off the field, never to referee again. The Australian Rugby League issued warnings to both teams that there must be no recurrence in the third test a week later. There was not and 67,577 saw a hard but clean contest won by Australia, 20-16.

Skipper Johnny Raper (right) lifted the original World Cup trophy aloft in triumph after Australia beat France 20-2 in the 1968 final at the SCG. The St. George loose-forward was the last person to do so, as it was subsequently stolen from the Aussies' Bradford hotel during the tournament held in October and November, 1970. Although the World Cup miraculously reappeared twenty years later, Great Britain have had no such divine intervention in their forlorn attempts to recover the Ashes, which they last won earlier in 1970.

Following their opening 37-15 win at Brisbane, Australia were odds-on favourites to take the only 4-tackle series on Australian soil in the second test at the SCG. However, despite the dismissal of Leeds centre Syd Hynes on his test debut, Britain won comfortably 28-7, which included a record 20 points from stand-off Roger Millward. And it was Millward who also scored the decisive 75th minute try of the third test, after two minutes earlier Australian full-back McKean almost denied Britain victory with what would have been his eighth goal. Having scored five tries to one, however, Britain were deserved winners under captain Frank Myler.

The SCG's biggest crowd for a rugby league international (and a world record until it was beaten at the World Cup final at Wembley sixty years later) was 70,204 on 6 June, 1932, when England won the first of the series, 8-6. However, this was eclipsed at the New South Wales-Great Britain clash on 3 June, 1950, when a crowd of 70,419 saw the Lions score a 20-13 win. And, until the surprising attendance of 87,161 at the State of Origin clash at the Melbourne Cricket Ground in 1994, the SCG held the record for the game in Australia when an attendance of 78,056 was recorded at the St. George-South Sydney 1965 grand final and many more climbed the fences.

Since the opening of the Sydney Football Stadium the SCG has, more or less, ceased being a rugby league venue. The last test contested there was the second of the 1986 series against New Zealand when 34,302 saw Australia win 29-12; whilst the last of 53 grand finals and premiership finals, including replays, was on 27 September, 1987, when Manly beat Canberra 18-6 before 50,201 spectators. Although no Sydney club is now based at the famous old ground, which has changed for the worse in many people's eyes, the SCG is still used occasionally for nostalgia-generated club matches, such as the Balmain versus Souths games in 1993 and 1994.

In January, 1995, the NSW government announced plans for further development of the SCG. A new electronic scoreboard and a separate video screen, similar to those at the SFS, are to be built. A new building between the SCG and SFS will incorporate a lecture theatrette, VIP dining facilities and shops, and, on its upper floor, will feature an indoor cricket practice area with natural turf wickets under a translucent roof. Discussions are also to be held about the practicability of increasing the ground's capacity on what was The Hill and the replacement of the Dally Messenger Stand.

The modernised Sydney Cricket Ground at its last Grand Final day in 1987, viewed from the M.A. Noble Stand. The Bill O'Reilly Stand is to the left and the Clive Churchill Stand and the new Brewongle Stand on the right - Rugby League Week.

Sydney Cricket Ground

1914 Australia 12 Great Britain 7	55,000
1914 Australia 6 Great Britain 14	34,420
1920 Australia 21 Great Britain 8	40,000
1924 Australia 3 Great Britain 22	50,005
1924 Australia 3 Great Britain 5	33,842
1928 Australia 0 Great Britain 8	44,548
1928 Australia 21 Great Britain 14	37,380
1932 Australia 6 Great Britain 8	70,204
1932 Australia 13 Great Britain 18	50,053
1936 Australia 24 Great Britain 8	63,920
1936 Australia 7 Great Britain 12	53,546
1946 Australia 8 Great Britain 8	64,527
1946 Australia 7 Great Britain 20	35,294
1948 Australia 19 New Zealand 21	55,866
1950 Australia 4 Great Britain 6	47,275
1950 Australia 5 Great Britain 2	47,178
1951 Australia 15 France 26	60,160
1951 Australia 14 France 35	67,009
1952 Australia 25 New Zealand 13	56,326
1952 Australia 9 New Zealand 19	44,916
1954 Australia 37 Great Britain 12	65,884
1954 Australia 20 Great Britain 16	67,577
1955 Australia 20 France 8	67,748
1955 Australia 5 France 8	62,458
1956 Australia 12 New Zealand 9	46,766
1956 Australia 31 New Zealand 14	46,735
World Cup 1957 Great Britain 23 France 5	50,077
World Cup 1957 Australia 31 Great Britain 6	57,955
World Cup 1957 Australia 26 France 9	35,158
World Cup 1957 New Zealand 29 Great Britain 21	14,263
World Cup 1957 Australia 20 Rest 11	30,675
1958 Australia 25 Great Britain 8	68,777
1958 Australia 17 Great Britain 40	68,720
1959 Australia 9 New Zealand 8	38,613
1959 Australia 12 New Zealand 28	31,629
1960 Australia 8 France 8	49,868
1960 Australia 5 France 7	29,127
1962 Australia 12 Great Britain 31	70,174
1962 Australia 18 Great Britain 17	42,104
1963 Australia 7 New Zealand 3	48,330
1963 Australia 14 New Zealand 0	46,567
1963 Australia 54 South Africa 21	16,995
1964 Australia 20 France 6	20,370
1964 Australia 35 France 9	16,731
1966 Australia 13 Great Britain 17	57,962
1966 Australia 19 Great Britain 14	63,503
1967 Australia 22 New Zealand 13	33,416
1967 Australia 13 New Zealand 9	27,530
World Cup 1968 Australia 25 Great Britain 10	62,256
World Cup 1968 Great Britain 38 New Zealand 14	14,105
World Cup 1968 play-off Australia 20 France 2	54,290
1970 Australia 7 Great Britain 28	60,962
1970 Australia 17 Great Britain 21	61,258
1972 Australia 36 New Zealand 11	29,714
1974 Australia 11 Great Britain 16	48,006
1974 Australia 22 Great Britain 18	55,505
World Champ.1975 Australia 30 Wales 13	25,386
World Champ.1975 Australia 10 England 10	33,858
World Cup 1977 Australia 21 France 9	13,231
World Cup 1977 play-off Australia 13 Gt Britain 12	24,457
1978 Australia 24 New Zealand 2	16,577
1978 Australia 33 New Zealand 16	6,541
1979 Australia 24 Great Britain 16	26,387
1979 Australia 28 Great Britain 2	16,854
1981 Australia 43 France 3	16,277
1982 Australia 20 New Zealand 2	16,775
1984 Australia 25 Great Britain 8	30,190
1984 Australia 20 Great Britain 7	18,756
1986 Australia 29 New Zealand 12	34,302

Sydney Football Stadium For many years, although pleased with the historic traditions and atmosphere of the SCG, rugby league officials and supporters expressed a wish to have a ground designed for and dedicated to football and able to accommodate many more spectators. Various proposals were announced and plans published but none survived gestation. However, in 1951 the NSW Parliament passed an Act combining the trusts controlling the SCG and the adjoining Sydney Sports Ground (SSG), the latter which was opened in 1898, expressly for the purpose of rebuilding the SSG sometime in the future. In the early 1980s the NSW Minister for Sport, the former test winger Michael Cleary, persuaded his government to proceed with the project. Consequently, the Commonwealth government released adjacent Army land which, when added to that occupied by SCG No2 and SSG provided the 24.2 acres required. The last game on the Sports Ground was Easts' 21-14 victory over Norths on 29 June, 1986.

Demolition and excavation had begun in May, 1986 and the stadium, which cost $62 million to build, was opened with a concert on 24 January, 1988. Designed and built by Civic & Civic (architect Philip Cox, Richardson Taylor & Partners) the SFS features a unique continuous encircling roof, which rises and falls to create a spectacular *"saddle"* shape. The rectangular playing area, which is constructed 3 metres below natural ground level to reduce the scale of the building from outside, is 90 x 150 metres, and the external perimeter of the stadium is a perfect circle 220 metres in diameter. Lighting, set into the rim of the roof, provides four levels from 100 lux for training sessions to 1,200 lux for television coverage. The electronic scoreboard has an adjoining Mitsubishi Diamond Vision colour video screen on which the game is shown as it is being played plus replays of noteworthy incidents. Between the SFS and the SCG is a training or warm-up field, incorporating practice wickets.

The SFS' capacity, which was originally set at 40,000 to the disappointment of the NSWRL who had been hoping for double that figure, has since been increased to 42,500 with the building of 74 enclosed private boxes and two small cantilever decks at the northern end. The Members' Reserve on the western side and the 200 leased open corporate areas on the eastern side account for 10,000 seats. Members also have access to a gymnasium, heated swimming pool, tennis and squash courts, spa, sauna, restaurants, bars, and a 750 vehicle car park. South Sydney and Eastern Suburbs share the stadium as their home ground, with the trust, needing to provide entertainment for its members, guaranteeing the clubs a

Ellery Hanley gives a final word of advice to his colleagues before the Anglo-Australian centenary test in 1988 - Varley Picture Agency.

reasonable annual income from gate money. In the first premiership game there, on Friday night, 4 March, 1988, St. George defeated Eastern Suburbs 24-14 before 19,295 fans.

On 11 June of that year only 24,480 attended the first test against Great Britain, which was the first international (of any code) to be played on the ground, as well as the 100th between the old rivals. Public disappointment with the stadium's facilities, particularly the lack of cover in wet weather, together with $32 ticket prices, were contributing factors to the smallness of the crowd. Ellery Hanley's Lions led 6-0 at the interval but Australia finished the stronger, winning 17-6. Although Australia then clinched the series in Brisbane, nonetheless, there were still post-match scenes of rejoicing when Britain comfortably won the third test, 26-12, and thus stopped a fifth successive series whitewash. Among many highlights, from the British point of view, was the 80-metre try by Warrington loose-forward Mike Gregory, after a break by his namesake, Andy.

To celebrate the nation's Bi-Centenary Australia played The Rest of the World (comprising eight Kiwis, five Britons, a Frenchman and a Papuan) at the SFS on Wednesday night, 27 July, 1988 in front of only 15,301 spectators. The hosts won 22-10 but lost centre Mal Meninga, who broke his left arm for the fourth time in fifteen months.

All of Sydney's major rugby league representative games, including the State of Origin, are now played at the SFS, as are the final five play-offs, culminating in the grand final late in

The face of coach Mal Reilly hides the fact that, as the Sydney Football Stadium scoreboard shows, in 1988, Great Britain were heading for their first victory on Australian soil since 1974 - Malcom Scarth.

September, which are invariably sell-outs. Rugby union and soccer internationals are also held there, and it has also been the venue for baseball, opera and pop concerts. By the year 2000, however, the SFS's role will have greatly diminished with the opening of the previously mentioned new Olympic Stadium, which is currently being built at Homebush Bay.

Sydney Football Stadium	
1988 Australia 17 Great Britain 6	24,202
1988 Australia 12 Great Britain 26	15,994
1991 Australia 44 New Zealand 0	34,911
1992 Australia 22 Great Britain 6	40,141
1995 Australia 20 New Zealand 10	27,568

A model of Sydney's Olympic Stadium - S.O.C.O.G.

Parramatta Stadium This $15 million stadium can said to be the result of Parramatta supporters' over-exuberant celebrations when the western Sydney club won its initial first grade premiership in 1981. They not only burnt down the fence, but the old wooden, and only, grandstand at their home Cumberland Oval. This forced the building of the often dreamed of, but never previously realized, modern arena.

From the time that Parramatta were admitted to the competition in 1947, they trained and played their home games at Cumberland Oval, which was located just inside historic Parramatta Park, across the Parramatta River from the colony's Old Government House, 15 miles west of Sydney city centre. The oval (formerly known as Parramatta Oval from the club's inception in 1910) was shared with Parramatta Rugby Union Club and Cumberland Cricket Club.

The new Parramatta Stadium at its opening for the game against St. George on 16 March, 1986, when the Eels returned to the old Cumberland site for the first time since 1981 - Rugby League Week.

Parramatta Park was established by Governor Lachlan Macquarie (1810-1821) as the Governor's Parramatta Domain of 2,000 acres but was gradually reduced to its present 210 acres of historic buildings, gardens, playing fields and bushland, controlled by Parramatta City Council. The stadium is in a bend of the river on the eastern perimeter of the Park and just 100 metres from Parramatta Leagues Club.

With the ground un-usable after the 1981 post Grand Final festivities, Parramatta shared Belmore Sports Ground with Canterbury-Bankstown from 1982 until 1985, while their new headquarters were planned, approved and built. The state government gave control of the project to the Sydney Cricket Ground and Sports Ground Trust and it was decided that the new arena should be on the site of the old. It is built on a simple plan of two, almost identical, single deck cantilever grandstands both running the full length of each touchline with grassed hills behind each set of goal posts. There is individual seating for 17,000, half under cover and half on the open concourses. The ground's capacity is about 35,000. Each of the stands are named after famous Eels internationals. The stand on the western, dressing-rooms side, in which there are 24 private boxes, is named after Ken Thornett with the drinkers' lounge called the Ray Price Bar. Opposite is the Michael Cronin Stand which includes the Bob O'Reilly Bar.

Work was completed in time for the Queen to officially open and name it Parramatta Stadium on Wednesday, 12 March, 1986. The following Sunday the first games were played on its well-grassed surface, a luxury compared to the dust bowl condition of its predecessor. Before a crowd of 26,870, the Eels beat St. George 36-6 and suitably began a season in which they again won the premiership. The ground's record attendance for a club match is 27,243 when Parramatta and South Sydney drew 17-all on 17 August, 1986 and, following a violent game, were each fined $2,000.

The only test, so far, at Parramatta Stadium was a floodlit international against France on Wednesday, 6 July, 1994, which Australia won 58-0, which was then a record margin for Franco-Australian clashes. Before a surprisingly good crowd of 27,318 (the present ground record), captain Mal Meninga scored a try and five goals while Steve Renouf contributed a hat-trick of tries. Following this success, it is likely that more tests against less fashionable opponents will be held at the ground.

Parramatta Stadium	
1994 Australia 58 France 0	27,318

BRISBANE

Brisbane Exhibition Ground (*"The Ekka"*) Formed in 1875, the National Agricultural and Industrial Association of Queensland (QNA) took a long-term lease on 12 acres of the south-west corner of Bowen Park, where it held its first annual show on 22 August, 1876. The site close to Brisbane centre, was gradually expanded to become the present day Brisbane Exhibition Grounds, affectionately known as *"The Ekka"*. Although an organised rugby league competition was not started in Brisbane until 14 May, 1910 the ground had been used earlier for representative games and test matches.

The Albert Cricket Club had been allowed to use the ground from 1878, and in 1887 a new cricket pitch was laid in the enlarged show ring, where in 1893 rugby union games and cycle races were first held. From 1894 the Queensland Cricket Association leased the ground for intercolonial and international matches, thus improving the QNA's finances. However, because of the depression, at the end of 1897 the government was forced to rescue the QNA and take possession of *"The Ekka"*. Subsequently, in 1920 the QNA, which since 1922 has been commonly referred to as the Royal National Association (RNA), were granted a perpetual lease at a peppercorn rent.

To ensure that major fixtures were not lost to the rival Brisbane Cricket Ground, sports renting *"The Ekka"* for seasons of club matches had to guarantee that representative games would also be held there. Consequently, in 1907 Queensland's rugby union and Australian Rules teams played New South Wales, and in 1908 the Lacrosse Association met Canada, and the state cricket eleven played Fiji.

When Northern Union football came to Australia in 1907, the Queensland Rugby Union asked the QNA to refuse permission for the professionals to play on the same turf as themselves. However, when A. H. Baskerville's All Golds toured the nation in 1908 on their way home from England they were allowed to play several games at the Exhibition Ground. In the first, on 16 May, they beat a team selected from Queenslanders, whose inaugural competition had not yet started, 34-12. Having coached the locals during the previous week, on the day before this game the New Zealanders also played a practice match against them.

It was after watching this contest that Baskerville took ill and died of pneumonia three days later while his team were defeating Metropolis, 43-10, in a game which raised only £10 in gate money. The shocked players decided to continue the tour, and on the following Saturday at *"The Ekka"* played a 12-all draw against a Queensland side strengthened by the addition of Dally Messenger, who contributed a try, three goals and some strong defence.

On 30 May, 1908 *"The Ekka"* was the venue for the second test against the tourists, and the first to be played in the northern state. The Aussie team, captained by Arthur *"Ash"* Hennessy, included Messenger and men, in Jim Devereux (Hull) and Albert Rosenfeld (Huddersfield), who were later to shine with English clubs; whilst the great forward personality, Sid *"Sandy"* Pearce, appeared in the first of his 14 tests. After leading 15-2 at half-time and 22-4 well into the second half, the All Golds clinched the series with a 24-14 victory, Ernest Wrigley from Wairarapa (the first New Zealander to join a Northern Union club, Huddersfield) kicking six goals. The greatest thrill for the 4,000 present was a long run for a try by local forward Bill Hardcastle, one of four Bananalanders in the Australian team.

The first Lions tour to Australia in 1910 saw a 1908 Kangaroo, Jack Fihelly, referee the second test at the Exhibition Ground on 2 July, when many of the 18,000 spectators were accommodated in the new grandstand, which had been built in time for the previous year's Jubilee Exhibition. Possibly in an attempt to boost the code in the state and help attract what was Brisbane's largest league crowd to date, seven locals were selected and Bill Heidke of Bundaberg was appointed captain instead of Messenger. Australia led 11-10 at the interval, but Great Britain, despite the controversial dismissal of Broughton Rangers lock George Ruddick, were too strong in the second half, going ahead 22-11 before two late tries cut the final margin to 22-17. Wigan winger *"Gentleman"* Jim Leytham ran in four tries, still the record for Anglo-Australian tests.

In 1912 a further use was found for the arena, when American aviator, Arthur *"Wizard"* Stone, took off in his tiny Bleriot monoplane and returned later to complete the first aeroplane flight in Queensland.

Brisbane did not host a test in 1914 but *"The Ekka"* was allocated the first post-war clash in 1920, which Australia won 8-4 after being faced with a pre-match crisis. When two of the Australian team withdrew on the Thursday before the match, the selectors rushed to the Sydney club training venues to find emergency replacements in Alf *"Smacker"* Blair and Jack *"Junker"* Robinson, who were then faced with the problem of travelling 650 miles in 40 hours. Hurried arrangements were made for then to sail from Sydney Harbour at 11 o'clock that night to Newcastle, taking a car on board with them in order to drive the 480 miles to Tweed Heads, where they were to catch a train for the final 70 mile dash to the ground. All went well until they were slowed down by Tweed River floods, causing them to miss their train connection and what would have been their test debuts!

When Britain went north in 1924 they had already won the series in the two Sydney tests, but, captained by versatile Jimmy Craig, who was one of ten Queenslanders in the side, Australia defeated Jonty Parkin's men 21-11 after trailing 5-4 at the break. In brutal exchanges near the end, opposing forwards Jim Bennett and Frank Gallagher were sent off, and a disgruntled crowd of 39,000 booed the Lions off the field.

The first test in 1928, which was almost cancelled due to a disagreement over the referee, drew a record ground attendance of 39,300, with the legendary Dally Messenger leading out the teams and ceremoniously kicking-off. Captain Jim Sullivan sealed Britain's 15-12 win with his third goal from a penalty on the bell after the Aussies had fought back from a 13-7 half-time deficit to trail by only a point. Nine Australians, including the great second-rower George Treweek, made their test debuts as did five Britons, among whom were Jim Brough and Alf Ellaby.

"The Ekka" staged its first cricket test in December, 1928, when England outclassed Australia to win by 675 runs. Playing in his first test, Don Bradman scored 18 and 1, and was promptly dropped! The only other cricket test at the ground saw Australia beat the West Indies by an innings and 217 runs in 1930.

About this time the Queensland Rugby League (QRL) and the Queensland Cricket Association both decided to move their big games to the Brisbane Cricket Ground , one reason being that too many RNA members were attending their fixtures by gaining free entry through their respective membership cards. However, rugby union, soccer and speedway, the latter introduced there in 1926, continued to use *"The Ekka"*.

The Brisbane Exhibition Ground at the test against Great Britain in 1928 - Collection: John Oxley Library, Brisbane.

Rugby league returned to the Exhibition Grounds in 1946, primarily because it could accommodate a larger crowd than Brisbane Cricket Ground, which was still recovering from its war-time use. For the second test against Gus Risman's *Indomitables*, and despite there being little public transport because of a strike, fans queued from 4 a.m. for the doors to open at 7 a.m. - the record official attendance of 45,190 forcing the closure of the gates at 11.40 a.m., with even players, officials, and pressmen locked out for a time. Sydney league officials gained entry by pretending to be bag carriers to the players, but among those who were turned away and missed the match was Mr Vic Jensen, the President of the QRL!

Play was held up at the start whilst fans, thousands of whom had got in without paying by climbing over a railway embankment at one side of the ground, were cleared from the sidelines. So thick was the throng that some spectators climbed onto the four 300-foot radio towers and obstructed the view of those sat at the front of the grandstand. The Press Association concluded its report, *"A strike has some compensations. Had transport been available and double the crowd arrived the story may have ended in less happy fashion"*. As for the game, scrum-half Tommy McCue and lock Ike Owens dominated the dull match which Britain won 14-5, Halifax winger Arthur Bassett notching a hat-trick of tries on his test debut.

When in 1958 the old rivals returned to *"The Ekka"* for the last time the second test produced one of the sport's greatest against-the-odds victories. After his side had been easily beaten in the first test, Britain's coach, Jim Brough, surprised everyone by quartering his players at the pleasure seekers' paradise, the Gold Coast, to prepare for the second clash. Brough's move proved to be right, however, as his charges won 25-18, despite courageous captain, Alan Prescott, playing all but three minutes with a broken right arm, and five-eight Dave Bolton retiring with a broken collarbone in the 17th minute. Four other Lions also needed hospital treatment after the game, in which Vince Karalius, who moved from lock to cover for Bolton, Brian McTigue, and Dick Huddart began their brilliant test careers. Inspired by Prescott's refusal to leave the field, and the brilliant work of scrum-half Alex Murphy, who was playing in only his second test, Britain led 10-2 at the intermission and managed to reply to all Australia's second half challenges. The Lions went back to Sydney to confirm their superiority and their retention of the Ashes with a 40-17 triumph in the third test.

After 51 years New Zealand returned to the old ground in 1959 but lost 38-10, debutant and captain Keith Barnes

Alan Prescott holds his broken right arm off the ground as he tackles Australian full-back Gordon Clifford during the 1958 test at "The Ekka". - Brisbane Telegraph.

kicking 7 goals to supplement try hat-tricks by Reg Gasnier and Ian Moir. The last international at *"The Ekka"*, before the QRL's Lang Park became the code's Brisbane headquarters, was Australia's 56-6 demolition of France in 1960, when captain Barnes contributed 10 goals. Among the try scorers were Bob Bugden and Ken Irvine with three each, and two-try Lionel Morgan, a lay preacher, who thus became the first Aborigine or Islander to represent Australia in a test.

A palm-fringed arena in a natural amphitheatre, the Brisbane Exhibition Ground is now used generally for only minor sporting events and commercial displays but it becomes the centre of Brisbane's interest every August when the eagerly awaited Annual Exhibition is held.

Brisbane Exhibition Ground	
1908 Australia 12 New Zealand 24	6,000
1909 Australia 10 New Zealand 5	6,000
1910 Australia 17 Great Britain 22	18,000
1920 Australia 8 Great Britain 4	28,000
1924 Australia 21 Great Britain 11	39,000
1928 Australia 12 Great Britain 15	39,300
1946 Australia 5 Great Britain 14	45,190
World Cup 1957 France 14 New Zealand 10	22,142
1958 Australia 18 Great Britain 25	32,965
1959 Australia 38 New Zealand 10	30,994
1960 Australia 56 France 6	32,644

The Ron McAuliffe Stand, which originally had standing terracing on the lower tier - Tony Jesson.

The first international at Lang Park was the second test on the Lions 1962 tour when 34,766 saw Britain, captained by Eric Ashton, lead all the way to win 17-10 and thus retain the Ashes. Lang Park has not been Britain's happiest hunting-ground, however, this win being their only success in eight test and World Cup visits, whilst on 16 June, 1979 the 35-0 thrashing in the second test was the biggest margin between the sides on Australian soil. In that game, which was the first floodlit test in Australia, Mick Cronin equalled the test world record with 10 goals.

In 1978 Australia had beaten New Zealand, 38-7, by a then record margin (bettered in 1995) in Trans-Tasman tests. The Kiwis, however, have a slightly better test record than Britain on the ground, having won on three of their thirteen visits, including the first, in 1963, which ended in dramatic fashion, following a sweeping movement which saw Kiwi winger Ken McCracken score the winning try with only three minutes remaining.

Earlier in this game rival forwards Peter Gallagher and Maunga Emery had been sent off for fighting. Their conduct, however, was exemplary compared to the behaviour, in 1985, of props Kevin Tamati and Greg Dowling, who continued their fisticuffs on the sidelines on their way to the sin-bin. In a reversal of the 1963 ending, John Ribot's touchline conversion of his own last minute try not only gave Australia a 26-20 victory but produced scenes of Pandemonium when fans invaded the pitch.

Lang Park at a State of Origin night game, looking towards the Burke Stand - Varley Picture Agency.

One of the dourest of modern tests was the second on Britain's 1966 tour, when in front of 45,057, still the ground record, the Australian captain Keith Barnes kicked three penalty goals, from seven attempts, to Arthur Keegan's two from five, and Australia won 6-4. It was the first tryless test since England won 4-0 at Belle Vue in 1933. Barricades were erected along the sidelines in attempt to control the crowd which overflowed onto the field, but one spectator did manage to swing a punch at Keegan as Barnes lined up a kick at goal. In a violent game referee Col Pearce sent Hunslet forward Bill Ramsey from the field on a kicking charge although others must have gone perilously close to the same fate. Britain had a great chance to score the winning try 12 minutes before the final bell but winger Billy Burgess dropped a pass with the line at his mercy. It was a costly miss for Australia went on to retain the Ashes by winning the third test at Sydney.

In contrast to this turgid stuff, the floodlit test in 1984 produced, if not the best game, certainly one of the finest scores in the history of Anglo-Australian tests. This classic try resulted from a move, started deep inside the visitors' half, in which the youngest ever Lion at that time, Hull's 18-year old centre Garry Schofield, handled three times in linking with Andy Goodway and Des Drummond before diving over in the corner. It was a score which deserved to win any match, but unfortunately it was not to be as Australia ran out comfortable winners, 18-6.

In 1993, after continuous disputes, the Brisbane Broncos who had been Lang Park tenants since they were admitted to the NSW premiership in 1988 moved to ANZ Stadium and the QRL decided to redevelop the ground. The Burke Stand was replaced by the double-decker Suncorp Stand, which is 140 metres long and seats 13,000, including 1,000 in corporate boxes. Because approval was obtained to build the tiered seating at a 34 degree gradient, instead of the standard 30 degrees, spectators are three metres closer to the playing area and all able to see the near touchline. The ground's capacity has been increased to a safety level of 40,000, which was the estimated attendance when New South Wales beat Queensland, 27-12, on 20 June, 1994. The Broncos best crowd at Lang Park was 33,245 on 20 August, 1989, when they beat Parramatta 16-8.

On 8 July, 1980, Queensland and New South Wales met in the first of the now nation-stopping State-of-Origin clashes. From the moment the Maroons' captain Arthur Beetson punched his club mate, friend, and Blues' star, Michael

Cronin, a legend began, a symbol of which is Lang Park's 8-foot high bronze statue of Wally Lewis, the *"Emperor of Lang Park"*, which depicts Wally holding the State of Origin Shield above his head. Costing $10,000 and paid for by over 600 of his fans, this was unveiled on 20 May, 1992, the night Queensland beat New South Wales 5-4. NSW players have come to be wary of the *"cauldron"* atmosphere that Lang Park and the Brisbane night crowds can engender, and it is unlikely that more modern facilities and a change of name will lessen it.

Suncorp Stadium	
1962 Australia 10 Great Britain 17	34,760
1963 Australia 13 New Zealand 16	30,748
1963 Australia 34 South Africa 6	10,210
1964 Australia 27 France 2	20,076
1966 Australia 6 Great Britain 4	45,057
1967 Australia 35 New Zealand 22	30,122
World Cup 1968 Australia 31 New Zealand 12	23,608
World Cup 1968 Australia 37 France 4	32,662
1970 Australia 37 Great Britain 15	42,807
1972 Australia 31 New Zealand 7	20,847
1974 Australia 12 Great Britain 6	30,280
World Champ. 1975 Australia 36 New Zealand 8	10,342
World Champ. 1975 Wales 12 England 7	6,000
World Champ. 1975 Australia 26 France 6	7,612
World Cup 1977 Australia 19 Great Britain 5	27,000
1978 Australia 38 New Zealand 7	14,000
1979 Australia 35 Great Britain 0	23,051
1981 Australia 17 France 2	14,000
1982 Australia 11 New Zealand 8	11,400
1983 Australia 12 New Zealand 19	15,000
1984 Australia 18 Great Britain 6	26,534
1985 Australia 26 New Zealand 20	23,000
1986 Australia 32 New Zealand 12	22,811
1987 Australia 6 New Zealand 13	16,500
1988 Australia 34 Great Britain 14	27,103
1991 Australia 40 New Zealand 12	29,139
1992 Australia 16 Great Britain 10	31,500
1993 Australia 16 New Zealand 4	31,000
1995 Australia 26 New Zealand 8	25,309
1995 Australia 46 New Zealand 10	20,803

WAGGA WAGGA, NEW SOUTH WALES

Eric Weissel Oval 300 miles south-west of Sydney on the Murrumbidgee River, Wagga Wagga, which in Aborigine language means *"place of many crows"*, is commonly abbreviated to just Wagga. The first Europeans to see the fertile riverlands were those with Captain Sturt in 1829, and as white settlement spread west from Sydney and over the Great Dividing Range, the township of a few hundred grew until it is now the largest inland city in New South Wales (population 55,000), and the administrative centre of the Riverina district.

Because Wagga is closer to Melbourne than Sydney, the Riverina Rugby League has had to battle the *"Aussie Rules"* code ever since prospectors from Sydney and northern England took the 13-a-side game with them to the West Wyalong goldfields in 1911. During that year, Arthur Hennessy, a founder of South Sydney Club and Australia's first test captain in 1908, coached the Goldfields team which visited Sydney and took back the basis for the game's development.

Visiting overseas teams did not venture to the Riverina until the 1924 Lions, hoping for an easier start to their schedule than on previous tours, defeated Southern NSW, 31-4, at Cootamundra in their second game. The first touring team to play at Wagga were the 1932 Lions, who drew 8,000 to the Wagga Showground in their final match, when they defeated Group Nine, which is part of the NSW Country Rugby League Riverina Division. For the next 22 years, the Division's tour matches were shared between Leeton, Junee, Cootamundra, Albury and Young. In 1954 Britain returned to the Showground and, before 13,000 spectators, finished strongly to win 36-26 after trailing Riverina by ten points eight minutes from the final whistle. Thereafter, all divisional teams meeting tourists at Wagga - France being the next overseas guests, who attracted 11,000 fans to the Showground in 1960 when they won 25-14 - were designated Riverina.

In 1962, however, when Eric Ashton scored three tries and five goals in a classical display of centre play to lead Britain to a 34-7 victory, the scene had changed to the Robertson Oval, Wagga. This ground in Bolton Park was also the venue in 1970 when, in a stormy game, Britain only just scraped home, 12-11. That day, the 11,000 crowd cheered a strong effort by the home side who were coached by former test captain Arthur Summons who later became secretary-manager of the Wagga Leagues Club.

Situated on Wagga's north-west fringe, what is now a palatial three storey, licensed, sports and entertainment centre, was established in 1956 after the club President, *"Butcher"* Dixon, saw the site's potential and an energetic committee purchased a one room tennis clubhouse and the adjoining 2.5 acres of swampland. This was then reclaimed and developed as playing fields for the local club games.

On the death of local resident and former Australian five-eighth Eric Weissel in 1972, the Leagues Club decided to honour his sporting achievements and fine character by naming its oval after him. As a teenager, he had played against the Lions at Cootamundra in 1924 and went on to appear in eight tests against them. He was top scorer on the 1929-30 Kangaroo tour and was one of the heroes in the 1932 *"Battle of Brisbane"* test, kicking two goals as well as sprinting and hobbling 60 yards on an injured ankle to set up the game-clinching try. He refused all offers to transfer to Sydney clubs, preferring instead to represent his birthplace, Cootamundra, and other Riverina towns, Temora,

Eric Weissel

Barmedman, Narrandera and Wagga Magpies until he retired in 1939. Weissel also enjoyed another claim to sporting fame, having caught and bowled Don Bradman in 1926 in a country inter-district carnival. He also top scored for Riverina, only one run short of Bradman's total of 43.

The Eric Weissel Oval was completed in 1972, the year that its floodlights were turned on by the then Australian captain, Ron Coote. The Schnelle-Harmon Grandstand, named in honour of two founder directors of the Leagues Club, seats 800 under cover, and was officially opened by the Prime Minister, Gough Whitlam, in time for Great Britain's visit in 1974, when the Lions won 36-10 on a heavy ground. Despite being held to a 15-7 half-time lead, Britain scored eight tries, including a hat-trick to Bradford Northern winger Dave Redfearn. The ground's international baptism drew an audience of 8,498, confirming its suitability for major contests.

After losing to the Kiwis in 1978 and 1982, and Britain in 1979 and 1984, Riverina, who included Les Boyd in the second-row, achieved their first victory over a touring party in 1986, New Zealand succumbing 16-14 before 5,000 happy locals.

A more important historic moment, however, came on 20 July, 1988, when the Eric Weissel Oval staged the first test ever to be played outside of Sydney and Brisbane, and a record attendance of 11,685 saw Australia notch 14 tries in a merciless 70-8 romp over an heavily outweighed Papua New Guinea. Michael O'Connor's 30 points and the Australian score and winning margin were all test world records at that time. In his first test, scrum-half Alan Langer won the Man-of-the Match award and another debutant, veteran forward Gavin Miller, displayed all his attacking skills.

Eric Weissel Oval's claimed capacity of 14,000 has never been tested but its playing surface surely has, with 176 games of rugby league having been played on it in 1974 alone! The oval, which has also been used for cricket, hockey, concerts, rodeos and stunt shows, is now fully established as the premier rugby league ground in the Riverina, and future plans include the installation of an electronic scoreboard and additional seating.

Eric Weissel Oval
1988 Australia 70 Papua New Guinea 8   11,685

Skipper Wally Lewis kicks majestically during the test against Papua New Guinea in 1988 - Daily Advertiser, Wagga Wagga.

PARKES, NEW SOUTH WALES

Pioneer Oval Parkes, which is twinned with Coventry (UK), is a town of 10,000 inhabitants on the Great Western Highway, 227 miles west of Sydney. The settlement, which started as a *"canvas town"*, known as Currajong, when gold was discovered there in 1862, was renamed in 1873 after a visit to the miners' diggings by the Prime Minister of New South Wales, Sir Henry Parkes. Now a regional administrative and tourist centre for mid-western New South Wales and an important road and rail freight interchange, Parkes' main tourist attraction is the Australian Radio Telescope Observatory with its 64 metre diameter antenna dish.

Spicer Oval, located in Spicer Park, was the first headquarters of rugby league in Parkes. Controlled by the Shire Council, in the early part of the century the oval, with its modern grandstand and fine playing surface, competed for the allocation of the Western Division's matches against touring teams with rival centres, Bathurst and Orange, which shared the games against the 1910, 1914 and 1920 Lions.

Jonty Parkin's 1928 Lions were the first visitors to play at Parkes, defeating Western NSW, 22-9, at Spicer Oval. At the time, the attendance of 9,000 was the largest at any provincial game against a touring team. In 1930 a New Zealand team, which did not play a test, had a harder tussle, only beating Western Division 20-16, but Jim Brough's 1936 side, who attracted 7,000, overwhelmed the Western countrymen 33-16.

After World War II, Parkes Rugby League moved to Pioneer Oval, which is also in Spicer Park. A natural amphitheatre, it was considered more suitable for future development and it has since become the venue for all the town's major fixtures. The first overseas visitors to play there were the 1955 Frenchmen, captained by the irrepressible Jean Dop, who just prevailed, 11-8, in front of a crowd of 8,303. During this game, giant prop Kevin Hansen could not pacify opponent André Carrere so he simply upended him and sat on him until the volatile visitor regained his composure! That day, Ian Walsh, who later captained Australia, was hooker for the Western Division.

Pioneer Oval's main amenities block, the C. J. Dwyer Pavilion, was opened on 22 May, 1963, when New Zealand easily accounted for Western Division, 36-11 - Kiwi full-back Gary Phillips kicking nine goals. Only 3,400 watched this game, but

Pioneer Oval during the quarter-final of the Toohey's Challenge on 18 February, 1994 when Illawarra beat Canberra 18-12 - Parkes Shire Council.

131

on a bitterly cold night in 1966 8,306 saw Britain beat the Westerners 38-11, winger Berwyn Jones notching three tries.

In 1985 the NSW Department of Sports and Recreation and the Parkes Sports Council introduced a development programme to transform the oval. An underground automatic watering system was installed in 1986, and a year later new perimeter fencing shaped the playing field to rugby requirements. As a result of these improvements, in 1989 10,000 saw Brisbane meet Canberra in the mid-week, nationally televised, Panasonic Cup. Later that season the BARLA tourists also played Western Schools at the ground.

From 1990 new entrances and outer security fencing have been erected; and a new roof and individual seats have been added to the official stand, where corporate sponsors boxes and a permanent camera platform have also been installed. The grassed embankments have also been extended. There are also three terraces on to which, as in many country ovals, patrons can drive their vehicles and, from them, watch the entertainment in warm comfort on the cold winter afternoons and nights of the football season. The more hardy (or foolhardy) make a grandstand of their truck trays and stand huddled together, cheering their team while defying the biting westerly winds.

The 1990 season started with a pre-season Tooheys Challenge Shield double-header (Souths-Balmain, Canberra-Illawarra) at Pioneer Oval, which attracted nearly 12,000 fans, but the Australia-France World Cup-rated night test on 27 June, 1990 remains the ground's most prestigious event to date.

The pitch had been flooded in April but was in excellent condition when referee Graham Ainui of Papua New Guinea got the test under way. Probably feeling the cold more than anyone, he controlled a one-side contest attended by 12,384 shivering fanatics who braved the below-zero temperature. It was so cold that the players had buckets of hot water placed by the sidelines into which they could plunge their hands to help keep some feeling in their fingers.

Injuries had changed the selected Australian team - for example, Mal Meninga became captain when Wally Lewis broke his arm in a club game - but they were still strong favourites against a French side who had beaten Britain at Headingley a few months earlier. Rightly so, for Australia's giant forwards overpowered the courageous but out-classed French pack and the hosts ran out winners, 34-2. Australia

scored eight tries, including those to test debutants, lock forward and Man-of-the-Match Brad Mackay (3) and centre Mark McGaw (2), but five kickers could register only one goal between them.

Britain's itinerary was altered in 1992 and, instead of Western Division, they met Combined NSW Country at Pioneer Oval, where, despite backs Deryck Fox and Joe Lydon ending the contest as temporary forwards, the tourists won an ill-tempered game, 24-6, in front of 8,014 spectators. Winger Paul Eastwood's try and six goals, allied to his timely cover defence, won him a place in the victorious second test team.

Pioneer Park has also hosted two Australian Schools fixtures: in 1993 when the home team beat BARLA 24-12 after trailing 4-12 at the break; and in 1994 when the much bigger Junior Kiwis were defeated 56-30.

There seems no doubt that Pioneer Oval, centrally located on the NSW Western Plains, with its, as yet untested, capacity of 20,000, will continue to be a popular venue for other major rugby league matches in the region.

Pioneer Oval	
1990 Australia 34 France 2	12,384

TOWNSVILLE

Sports Reserve 850 miles north of Brisbane, Townsville (population 130,000) is Australia's largest tropical city. First settled in 1864 as a port for the export of minerals and pastoral produce from the northern regions of Queensland, Townsville is now also a thriving tourist centre and gateway to the Great Barrier Reef.

In 1900 the town council separated a section of Queens Park Botanical Gardens by building Burke Street through it. The excised 13.5 acres, in the suburb of Northward and a quarter of a mile from the Coral Sea, was dedicated to recreation as the Townsville Sports Reserve (TSR), and a Trust of five prominent citizens, including the Mayor, was appointed to administer it. Three playing fields were then developed and used for rugby and cricket; and a single-storey pavilion built, its wide sun-stopping verandah enabling the ladies to promenade with their complexions safely protected.

Learning of rugby league inroads down south and also being dissatisfied with the rugby union administration, leading players formed the Townsville Rugby League in 1914, inaugurating a competition with just three clubs, Souths, Norths and Natives. The first President was J. C. *"Dardy"* Lynam who, when the North Queensland Rugby League was established in 1919, became its founding President. In 1915 a combined Townsville team travelled down to Brisbane and nine of its players gained selection for Queensland, including Jack Egan who had previously played for the state against Harold Wagstaff's 1914 Lions.

Touring teams did not venture further north than Rockhampton, where they played Central Queensland, until 1928, when Jonty Parkin's side attracted 11,000 to the TSR to see them defeat Northern Queensland, 30-16. Britain's six tries were shared and the great Jim Sullivan kicked six goals. Although Sullivan was captain in 1932, forwards Martin Hodgson and Joe Thompson, who also scored a try, each landed two goals in the 20-2 victory. In the depths of those

Depression years, the crowd was 7,000 but rose to 8,000 when the 1936 tourists won 39-3.

All later Great Britain-Northern Queensland games, except in 1974 and 1988, have been played at the Reserve, where there have been some extremely large scores, attributable both to the relative playing strengths and the tropical conditions. Eric Batten got four of the fifteen tries in the 55-16 win in 1946; whilst in 1950, Ernest Ward led Britain to a 39-18 drubbing of a side containing five Australian internationals. Although, in 1954, scrum-half Gerry Helme retired in the first minute and, in the reshuffle, forward Nat Silcock moved to the wing, Britain still prevailed, 39-13. Billy Boston was apparently hit on the head with an umbrella when the powerful winger ventured too close to the crowd encroaching on the sideline, but this did not stop him from scoring four tries, along with Oldham's Terry O'Grady. In 1958 it was the turn of Lions captain and prop Alan Prescott

The undeveloped Townsville Sports Reserve is to the right of this photograph taken circa 1920 - Collection: James Cook University of North Queensland.

A view of Townsville Sports Reserve's main stand during Great Britain's game against North Queensland in 1984 - Bob Evans.

to turn out as a winger, and despite having played 240 miles away the day before, Britain still won 78-17 - Warrington full-back Eric Fraser being successful with 15 of his 18 kicks and second-rower Dick Huddart (Whitehaven) scoring four of the 16 tries. The attendance that day was 6,312, and this rose to 8,278 in 1962 when Britain won 47-14.

The second country to grace the Reserve, France had a comfortable 50-17 win in 1951, before which game Puig-Aubert gave an exhibition of his amazing kicking skills by guiding the ball between uprights from the corner-post hole! On the Chanticleers' fourth visit to the ground, in 1964, Northern Queensland were able to celebrate their first success over a visiting country, when, on an overcast day, a crowd of 6,623 saw future test and World Cup winger Lionel Williamson notch three tries in their 35-21 triumph. And there was even greater glory for the home team in 1966 when Britain were defeated 17-15 to the delight of 6,000 locals, and five Northern Queenslanders were immediately selected for the state squad to tour New South Wales.

New Zealand, having previously won at the Reserve in 1952, 1956 and 1963, redressed the balance of the travellers by beating Northern Queensland, 22-18, in 1967 - since which date Britain have visited Townsville on another five occasions, including World Cup warm-up games in 1968 and 1977.

After Great Britain opened their 1992 tour with a 14-10 victory against Queensland Residents, Townsville's biggest league event came later that season, on 15 July, when

Australia met Papua New Guinea, whom they had beaten in five previous tests with the closest result being 40-6 in Port Moresby in 1991. However, a long and demanding representative and club programme had reduced the commitment of the Australian players and, after Laurie Daley scored after only three minutes play, they appeared over-confident and lethargic in the enervating humid conditions. The crowd of 12,470, while appreciating the superior strength and skills of the home team, also sensed their casual attitude, and so cheered the determined and courageous efforts of the underdogs.

Australia led only 8-0 at the break and, although they far out-measured the Kumuls in weight, height, experience and technique, they scored only eight tries and four goals to Papua New Guinea's three tries and a goal. Winger Graham Mackay's two try effort earned him the Man-of-the-Match award but the crowd's favourite was, undoubtedly, Kumul half Aquila Emil who, late in the game, scored a brilliant individual try, regathering his chip-kick over the defence and bewildering Daley in the run to the line. At full-time his team mates hoisted him up on their shoulders before they took a loudly-cheered lap of honour. Full-back Philip Boge had also startled the spectators with his strong defence on the much bigger Australians, saving at least two certain tries.

The grandstand, built in 1976 when a local soccer team made an unsuccessful venture into the State League, replaced an earlier timber structure. It has recently had its iron roof replaced, no doubt corroded due to the salt air from the nearby ocean, and 900 individual seats installed. The ground also has some tubular steel portable stands with plank seats, known locally as *"Curly Bells"*. The athletics track now hosts the Australian Masters Games (for veteran athletes) and the Oceania Games, which is contested by the Pacific Islands.

Although Townsville has shown that it can successfully stage major games, the restructuring of any future tours (Super League permitting), in order to concentrate on playing premiership teams, will make it difficult for remote centres to be allocated fixtures. It is also likely that Townsville games will be played at Willows Park, now renamed Stockland Stadium, the newly developed headquarters of the North Queensland Cowboys, who were admitted to Australian Rugby League premiership in 1995.

Sports Reserve
1992 Australia 36 Papua New Guinea 14   12,470

MELBOURNE

Olympic Park's Western Sportsground Renamed Olympic Park in 1956 for the Olympic Games, the former Friendly Societies Gardens and Amateur Sports Ground (FSG) was built in Yarra Park in 1900, after radical changes had been made to the parkland following the widening and straightening of the Yarra River.

In 1924 Melbourne Motordrome Ltd., owned by the controversial entrepreneur John Wren, leased the FSG for five years on condition that they improved the then run-down oval. Wren spent £40,000 developing the complex into a suitable venue for professional athletics, boxing and speedway, the last-named starting in December, 1924. In 1935 he successfully staged the second (Aussie Rules) football match played in Victoria under lights, Richmond meeting South Melbourne, and in 1936 he tried to have Richmond make his arena their headquarters. He claimed that because their home ground, Richmond Oval, only a few hundred yards from the motordome, was part of a dedicated common it was illegal for the club to charge admission there; and he arranged for several hundred people to cite this technicality and force their way into Richmond's matches without paying. However, once legislation was rushed through parliament to legalize the levying of admission fees Wren's interest waned.

After the Second World War the Victorian Athletics Association took control of the ground and retained it as their headquarters until Melbourne was granted the 1956 Olympic Games, when the state government renamed it Olympic Park and created a statutory trust to control the complex. Facilities were rebuilt with both the Eastern and Western Sportsgrounds being used during the Games for soccer and hockey and the latter as an athletics warm-up track - the track and field events being held at the nearby Melbourne Cricket Ground. After the Games the specially built cycling velodrome was demolished and the new swimming pool transformed into the Melbourne Sports and Entertainment Centre, which is now used mainly for basketball and pop concerts.

Since 1956 the two arenas have been further developed: their location, just over a mile from Melbourne's central business district, helping to make them popular sporting centres. The Eastern Sportsground, with a capacity of 17,500, is the city's greyhound venue and is also used for American Football, hockey, lacrosse, and school sports.

The Western Sportsground, the real subject of our story, has the only soccer pitch in Victoria accepted by FIFA for international games. It also has an eight lane 400 metres synthetic athletics track and is the home of the state's

Olympic Park, 1990. Aside the Yarra River, the Western Sportsground is sandwiched between Olympic Park's Eastern Sportsground (in the foreground) and the Melbourne Sports and Entertainment Centre. The floodlight towers of the Melbourne Cricket Ground are prominent in the top right corner - P. Gregory, The Herald and Weekly Times.

amateur athletics. A claimed capacity, possibly optimistically overstated, of 30,000 includes 10,699 seats, 6,937 of which are under cover, and covered standing accommodation for 5,000. There are four light towers providing 1,200 lux power, as well as a computer controlled electronic scoreboard. As well as the usual function rooms the stadium also houses a sports medicine centre.

Since its early days in Australia, the Rugby League has made ineffective attempts to interest Melbournians in its game. In the founding year of 1907, in cooperation with the earlier mentioned John Wren, the NSW Rugby League tried to arrange a match by the All Golds but the New Zealanders tight travel schedule would not allow it. In 1914, the three tests were originally scheduled for 27, 29 June (in Sydney) and 4 July (in Brisbane). Britain's manager J. Clifford protested about this tight scheduling and the NSW management committee agreed to switch the third test to Melbourne on 5 August, after the Lions' return from New Zealand.

However, without even consulting the tourists, the New South Wales Rugby League general committee decided against the switch to Melbourne and the game, to become famous as *The Rorke's Drift Test*, went ahead in Sydney on the original date, 4 July. What was then intended to be a showpiece game against New South Wales at Melbourne Cricket Ground on 5 August was therefore affected by the acrimony which had preceded it, and, unfortunately, the players considered that they had scores to settle from the hard-fought tests. NSW lock Frank Burge said *we belted the daylights out of each other* and Lions captain Harold Wagstaff described it as *the dirtiest match ever played*. Britain won a vicious battle, 21-15, before an encouraging crowd of 12,000 who thought the altercations were a normal part of rugby. There were also drunken skirmishes that night and the unsavoury events set back the rugby league cause in Victoria by many years.

Following the dynamic Harry Sunderland becoming the President of the southern state's Rugby League and initiating a competition in 1923, Britain opened their tour against Victoria at Fitzroy Aussie Rules home ground, the Brunswick Street Oval, on 24 May, 1924. Victoria, supported by 15,000 spectators and captained by 1921-2 test five-eighth Harry Caples, wore the red, white and blue, and the Lions played in white with a red bar. Despite being penalised 41-0, the visitors scored 11 tries to win 45-13. When Sunderland returned to Queensland the Victorian enterprise faded into insignificance.

The brilliant 1951 Frenchmen attracted only 4,460 in rainy weather when they defeated an Australian Selection, which included two Victorians, 34-17, at Melbourne Showground. In this victory Puig-Aubert took his points tally for the tour beyond 200; his final total of 236 being a record for any tourist. In 1955 Jean Dop starred when France repeated the experiment, beating Victoria 44-2 on 21 May, before only 2,311 at Richmond Oval.

On 18 March, 1978 Manly defeated Western Suburbs 12-5 in a Festival of Football at Junction Oval, St. Kilda. It was a spiteful clash, luckily in front of only 1,000 Victorians, which generated a longlasting feud between the Manly *Silvertails* and Wests *Fibros*.

In recent years, however, rugby league has been able to generate remarkable interest in the heartland of Aussie Rules. After plans to use the Melbourne Cricket Ground or other Aussie Rules venues were rejected, $100,000 was spent on improving seating and lighting at Olympic Park's Western Sportsground for the State of Origin clash on 30 May, 1990 (see picture below), when a sellout 26,800 saw NSW win 12-6 in a game remembered by Queenslanders for referee Greg McCallum's decision to penalise Alan Langer for stealing the ball, which they claim turned the match.

Encouraged by this attendance, the Australian Rugby League then decided to play its first ever opening test outside of NSW and Queensland at Olympic Park, when strong

© *Action Photographics*

favourites Australia were beaten 24-8 by New Zealand on the Western Sportsground on 3 July, 1991. An apparently capacity crowd, variously reported as being between 26,900 and 28,000, which included many Melbourne resident Kiwi expatriates, saw Australia lead 6-2 at half-time after hooker Steve Walters celebrated his first test by surging over from dummy-half for Mal Meninga to convert. Early in the second session Wally Lewis, making his final representative appearance after earlier dominating the State of Origin series, was ruled to have been unable to touch down; and this reprieve, by English referee John Holdsworth, seemed to revitalise the Kiwis, who, throwing the ball around in a dramatic change of tactics, ran in four second half tries. Robust winger Richard Blackmore was prominent in the build-up to the first and scored the second himself, whilst the others by Clayton Friend and Tawera Nikau came from enthusiastically followed kicks. The giant Australians had no excuses, in a game in which they were outplayed by Kiwi guile, but they regathered their forces to win the second and third tests by margins of 44-0 and 40-12.

Olympic Park	
1991 Australia 8 New Zealand 24	28,000

Optus Oval (formerly Princes Park)

The former Princes Park is the home of Carlton Australian Football Club, the most successful team in the history of what the eastern states rugby fans refer to as Aussie Rules football, or less respectfully, *"aerial ping-pong"*. The ground has recently been renamed Optus Oval, after a sponsor.

Carlton were formed in 1862, three years after the Victorian game had its rules codified by members of the Melbourne Cricket Club, and first played on a sloping, pebble strewn and unenclosed area on the brow of a hill in Royal Park, Carlton. In 1871 club uniforms were introduced and Carlton elected for a navy blue jersey which earned them their current nickname, *'The Blues'*. The game's haphazard scheduling of matches was replaced by the formation of the Victorian Football Association (VFA), of which Carlton was a foundation member and the first premiership winners. In 1897 they were one of eight clubs which, seeking a higher standard of competition, broke away to create a new controlling body, the Victorian Football League (VFL), which is now called the Australian Football League (AFL). Although they did not win their first VFL premiership flag until 1906, *'The Blues'*, with 15 titles, have won more than any other club.

In 1879 Carlton were given permission to share with Carlton Cricket Club a section of Princes Park, a reserve next to Melbourne Cemetery, providing they did not build any fences or upset passing funeral processions. This arrangement proved unsatisfactory and, in 1894, the clubs obtained from the Victorian Board of Land and Works a grant of 10 acres of an old rubbish tip on the northern edge of Princes Park. Enthusiastic working-bees of players and supporters had the ground ready for the official opening on the Queen's Birthday Holiday, 22 June, 1897, in the VFL's inaugural season.

The oval was gradually developed as the club continued to succeed and attract the support of wealthy businessmen. When the John Elliott Stand, named after the club President and Carlton United Brewery's chairman, was built in 1987, three-quarters of the arena, which can accommodate 41,000 spectators, was surrounded by covered stands. As with all Aussie Rules grounds, the playing area is much bigger than those required for rugby, being 180 yards by 153 yards.

Following the packing of Olympic Park in 1991 against New Zealand, it was agreed that when Britain toured in 1992 a venue with a greater capacity was required, and therefore the Carlton club, eager to bolster their finances and prove themselves suitable hosts for further events, were allocated the second test.

Having lost the first test in Sydney, 22-6, the injury-ravaged Lions showed improved form in beating Newcastle but lost Ellery Hanley for the rest of the tour in that game. Nevertheless, roused by the media's dismissal of their chances, the tourists were fiercely determined to prove their competitiveness. What Syneysiders regard as typical Melbourne weather produced a wet and slippery surface but did not deter the 31,005 fans who squelched their way to Princes Park on 26 June, 1992, when captain Mal Meninga equalled the record of Reg Gasnier by appearing in his 36th test.

Fielding an all Wigan pack, the first time one club had provided the six, Britain's ferocious attacks upset the home team who, failing to adjust to the greasy conditions, made uncharacteristic handling errors and conceded two early penalty goals to winger Paul Eastwood. The Lions' first try came in the 17th minute, when young lock Phil Clarke took a Daryl Powell pass, and, in his 25 yard run, dummied through shell-shocked defenders to score for Eastwood to

Optus Oval (then called Princes Park), July, 1993. The pitch for the test in 1992 ran from left to right at the top end of the oval - Carlton Football Club.

add the extras. Paul Newlove was next to cross after benefitting from Shaun Edwards' neat chip kick. After captain Garry Schofield, playing in his 35th test, scored by the posts after regathering his own kick as full-back Andrew Ettingshausen slipped attempting to claim the ball, Britain led 22-0 at half-time, and all Australia was stunned.

After Schofield dropped a goal to edge the lead to 23-0, the locals began their fight-back, reducing the margin to 23-10 with 20 minutes left. However, the Lions pack regained ascendancy, and full-back Graham Steadman speared down the blindside touchline to cross wide out. Martin Offiah completed the rout by scoring when Schofield again regathered his own kick and passed to the flying winger. Eastwood missed his only goal attempt but the final tally was 33-10, a margin which equalled Britain's biggest in Anglo-Australian test, 40-17 in the third in 1958. However, having recovered from the mauling at Princes Park, Australia retained the Ashes, winning 16-10 in the Brisbane decider.

In 1994 Balmain, with a possible view to relocating to Melbourne, arranged to play three of its home games at Princes Park, but after badly losing the first two before small crowds, the future Sydney Tigers abandoned the experiment.

On 8 June, 1994, the second of the season's State of Origin matches was played at the Melbourne Cricket Ground, Australia's biggest sports arena, and drew a national rugby league record attendance of 87,161 to see NSW beat Queensland 14-0. This indicated that the code had out-grown Princes Park as a venue for major games, and again encouraged administrators to consider establishing a Melbourne club. All proposals since, to reduce the number of premiership clubs and form a Super League, have included a Melbourne club in the competition plans.

Optus Oval
1992 Australia 10 Great Britain 33   31,005

FRANCE – *Robert Fassolette*

Although it was 1933 before the first game of rugby league was played in France, plans had been made to introduce the sport to that country in the 1920s. It was partly due to this possible expansion to the Continent that the Australians argued that the term *"Northern Union"* was too parochial, leading to the game's title being changed at the 1922 AGM.

PARIS The Australian team manager, George Ball, visited Paris during the English leg of the 1921 tour and negotiated for the proposed game against England to be played during January, 1922 at the Stade Pershing; and one was also fixed, again in Paris, for the 23 January, 1927, between England and New Zealand. However, neither event took place. The later match was apparently cancelled because the New Zealanders were depleted by injuries, although, perhaps significantly, the decision came on the very day that five of the Kiwis forwards went on strike. The proposed game in 1921 was aborted by the French Rugby Union's threat to boycott the ground.

Such obstructionist tactics by rugby unionites have continued to this day, but it was their own internal problems which resulted in the introduction of rugby league to France. The Club Championship, which aroused great community interest, particularly in the south-west of the country, was known to be the root cause of the introduction of veiled professionalism, and, allegedly, much rough play. This lead to France's banishment by the Home Unions from international competition from the 1930/1 season. Although the twelve clubs, who had resigned from the French Rugby Federation (F.F.R.) in 1930 to form their own body (the Union Francaise de Rugby Amateur), returned to the fold in 1932, the climate was still ripe for the French public and its players to be made aware of Rugby à Treize.

There was little progress however until the arrival of the 1933 Kangaroos to England. John Leake, the Welsh Commissioner in Newport, had apparently contacted the editor/proprietor of the *L'Echo des Sports*, Victor Breyer, and it was largely through Breyer's assistance that the first game of rugby league in France was arranged. On his recommendation, a four-man deputation, including the Rugby League secretary, John Wilson, inspected both La Piste Municipale du Bois de Vincennes (now officially renamed Velodrome Jacques Anquetil but known as La Cipale) and the **Stade Pershing** in October, and decided that the last-named ground should be the venue for an exhibition between England and Australia on 31 December.

Also located in the Bois de Vincennes, about five miles from the heart of Paris, Stade Pershing is named after John Joseph *"Black Jack"* Pershing, the commander-in-chief of the American expeditionary force in Europe during the First World War. The US Army built the 25,000-capacity stadium as a gift, and it was officially opened for the Inter-Allied Games held between the victors after the war. The stadium had staged Olympic soccer matches in 1924, and had previously been used for French Cup finals.

Much of the pre-match propoganda in 1933 was orchestrated by Harry Sunderland, the Australian tour manager, who flew to Paris with John Wilson in November to finalise the arrangements. Although he is said to have been aware of rugby league since 1931, it was apparently through reading an article of Sunderland's in the popular sports paper *Toulouse Olympique* that Jean Galia, the French international forward and amateur boxing champion, went to see the new game for himself.

Australia on the attack during their 63-13 victory over England at a snow covered Stade Pershing on 31 December, 1933.

In the Paris area, of course, it was Victor Breyer who was responsible for publicising the game, which sowed the seeds for the eventual development of the game in France. The Rugby League officials stayed behind to watch the France-Germany rugby union international on New Year's Day at Colombes, where there was neither the skill nor the excitement shown at Stade Pershing.

Having beaten Wales 51-19 at Wembley the previous day, the Australians were not only in top form but far happier on the frozen and snow covered pitch than the badly organised Englishmen. By the manner in which they ran in 15 tries in their 63-13 victory the Australians captured the hearts of those Parisians present, to such an extent that not only did some of the 8,000 crowd show their appreciation by throwing their red seat cushions over the heads of the tourists, but at the end they carried Vic Hey and Dave Brown, the latter who had scored 27 points with 9 goals and three tries, shoulder high in triumph. The spectacle inspired Jean Galia to organise a six match tour of England in March, 1934, during which his pioneers lost 32-16 to a Rugby League XIII at Headingley. Following his death at the age of 44 in 1949 Jean Galia's widow presented the Jean Galia Memorial Trophy for the game's European Championship.

This historic match was the only occasion on which a rugby league international or representative game was played at Stade Pershing. But the ground has one other claim to fame in that it was also the home of the first ever official rugby league club in France, Sports Olympique de Paris, an amateur section of this multi-sports organisation which was formed on 24 January, 1934 in the immediate aftermath of *"the revolution in rugby"*.

They played at Pershing as the ground had been banned by the French Rugby Union due to its *"professional use"*. This ruling also affected the Paris University (R.U.) Club, but, conquered by the new game, some students from this club finally managed to establish the Quarter Students Club, whose chairman was Louis Jacquinot, a future Minister for the Navy. Even though they obviously found it more enjoyable to play the *"new game"*, it was socially profitable to maintain their union links and they therefore played league under assumed names for fear of being banished from rugby union. Until the start of the Second World War, this club also used Pershing, where all the stands have long since been demolished and today the site is used only for recreational sport.

With hindsight, and given the links between rugby league and cycling - before the war Victor Breyer was a member of the International Cycling Federation, and, after the war, the league's dynamic chairman, Paul Barriere, was its vice-chairman - La Cipale would perhaps have been a far better choice for the 1933 exhibition game. This is because the velodrome, having staged the finish to the Tour de France from 1968 until 1974, has always had a high media profile, which would certainly have helped to maintain in people's minds the historical link with the birth of rugby league. La Cipale is nowadays the only ground where rugby league has a firm foothold inside Paris, despite the continuous aggressive attempts by rugby union to secure such a coveted venue.

It was in order to maintain rugby league's presence in Paris that the French Rugby League chose La Cipale to stage their 50th anniversary celebrations on 14 April, 1984, when national television covered the event. The commentator remarked on the fact that *"the grass was as scarce as the spectators"*, but the dust-bowl conditions were no problem for an Oceania side, captained by Wally Lewis, who beat an hastily-selected European combination, 54-4, for whom Des Drummond scored their only try. The choice of La Cipale was symbolic, being only a couple of miles away from the historic Pershing at the other end of the wood of Vincennes, and only five miles from the site of the former **Stade Buffalo**, which was situated south of Paris in the suburban town of Montrouge.

Buffalo was chosen by the newly-formed (on 6 April, 1934) Ligue Francaise de Rugby a Treize for France's first international, on Sunday, 15 April, 1934, against an England side containing three Welshmen. A 24,000-capacity velodrome, complete with a restaurant and superb medical facilities, Stade Buffalo, which was demolished in the early 1950s to make way for a residential complex designed by the famous architect Fernand Pouillon, was to become the pre-war home of rugby league in France. The stadium's managing director, Louis Delblat, a former administrator of the *L'Echo des Sports*, was elected treasurer to the French Rugby League at their first executive meeting, which was held in the Restaurant Prunier in the rue Duphot the day after England's 32-21 victory.

Basking in the 82 degree heat, the 20,000 crowd at Buffalo fully appreciated the action, which produced eleven spectacular tries, including five to the home side. The best was scored by Salford stand-off Jenkins, who side-stepped his

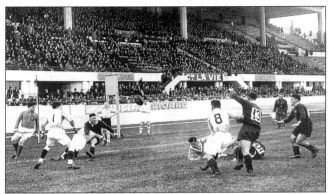

France on the defensive during their 35-6 defeat by Australia at Stade Buffalo in 1938

way past six men from half way to help kill off a French rally. As in so many matches, however, it was the goalkicking of Jim Sullivan which in the end proved decisive. At the post-match dinner, held in the banqueting hall of the Restaurant Marguery, Victor Breyer echoed the sentiments of many when he said, *"You have come and you have conquered; the game has arrived to stay in France."*

Following this game a 10-club professional league (Albi, Sport Olympique de Beziers, Bordeaux, XIII Catalan, Cote Basque XIII, Lyons, Celtic de Paris, Pau, Roanne, and Villeneuve being the ten founder members) opened its season on Sunday, 30 September, 1934, when only three games, Roanne-Villeneuve, Lyon-Beziers, and Bordeaux-Cote Basque were played. The game at Roanne was under threat from a rugby union ground ban, and it was only because of the friendship between the French Rugby League President, Francois Cadoret, a socialist M.P., and Roanne's Mayor, Albert Serol, who was also a prominent socialist M.P. who later became Employment and Justice Minister, that the game went ahead. All three home sides won, with Roanne's defeat of Jean Galia's Villeneuve, who had just returned from a six match tour of England, being the shock of the day.

At that time the French Rugby League only had guaranteed access to six grounds throughout the whole of France. These were Parc de Suzon (Bordeaux), Stade Bourbaki (Pau), Parc des Sports (Roanne), Stade Georges Lyvet (Lyon-Villeurbanne), the only stadium of the six currently hosting first-grade rugby league, Stade du Pont de Marot (Villeneuve

sur Lot), and Stade Emile Lagreze (Albi), a stadium which has quite a unique history.

In those days, under rugby union pressure, the Albi city council banned rugby league from their municipal facilities, which compelled the league club to build their own ground. Unfortunately, when it came to pay for the wooden grandstand Albi could not raise the money. However, a deal was subsequently struck by which the joiner waived his charges in return for having the ground named after him, and thus the Stade Emile Lagreze, which still exists, was born!

In the second week of that inaugural season the Perpignan town council also refused access to their municipal grounds (rugby union pressure again) for a planned game, which was subsequently transferred, 200 miles away, to Villeneuve. Because of these ground problems only two of the ten clubs managed to fulfil their maximum 18 fixtures, and on many occasions home and away fixtures were played on the same ground. No play-off was organized, however, and Villeneuve were declared champions on points aggregate.

In those formative years Leeds, who took over a Yorkshire side, Bramley, Hunslet, Salford *("Les Diables Rouges")*, Castleford, and Widnes all toured France; several players were also released by their clubs to act as player-coaches with French sides; and English referees were asked to take charge of the French Cup final, for which Lord Derby had donated a trophy, and the early internationals. All this support, of course, was necessary, but it was more because of their abundant enthusiasm for the new game that the French officials - against vehement rugby union opposition - managed to get Rugby à Treize established. Thankfully, their task was simplified by the ability of the converted players to immediately compete at international level.

In fact, after defeating Wales at Bordeaux in January, 1935 France also came close to beating England two months later at Buffalo. Having led 10-2 at half-time, they regained the lead through a magnificent try by their genius of a stand-off, Max Rousié. However, in the 72nd minute, Rousié's opposite number, Todd, levelled the scores, 15-all, with the third try of the afternoon for Hunslet men - second-rower Smith having scored two in the visitors' second-half rally.

Before the international in 1936, in which England, the 25-7 winners, gave their Gallic hosts a *"lesson in rugby"*, there was a one minute silence by the record crowd of 25,000 in memory of King George V. This was an impressive attendance considering that the championship had already been won by Wales, whose successful defence of the title included a 9-3 victory at Buffalo on 6 December, 1936. The nearest the French actually came to beating England at Buffalo came in March, 1938 (having earlier that season lost 35-6 to the Australians) when Warrington's giant second-rower Jack Arkwright caused a sensation by dropping a goal, which proved to be the decisive score, the game ending 17-15.

Prior to the outbreak of the Second World War the Stade Buffalo had therefore staged six internationals, each resulting in defeat for the French, and three other representative games (28 April, 1935 French XIII 12 Rugby League XIII 32; 26 April, 1936 France 8 Dominions XIII 5; and Monday, 31 October, 1937 France 0 Empire X111 15 for the Paris Exhibition Cup). It was also the home of the Paris XIII and Paris Celtic clubs.

However, because of the bitterness by rugby union - which up to 1948 successfully contested the right for rugby league to be admitted to the national committee of sports, thus depriving the game of most of the official municipal stadiums - there were still problems experienced because of Buffalo's use by the Stade Francais rugby union club.

This stemmed from an agreement signed in 1924, which gave the Stade Francais sole tenancy between October and April in return for a yearly guarantee and a share of their takings. By 1938 the rugby union gates were so poor that the French Rugby Union were subsidising the rent and the Buffalo board would have gladly ended the arrangement. This was particularly so following the Stade Francais' court action in February of that year, which gave them the right to occupy the ground on the day of the proposed game between Paris XIII and Villeneuve, a fixture which would have attracted over 10,000 spectators.

Stade Buffalo Velodrome	
1934 France 21 England 32	20,000
1935 France 15 England 15	18,000
1936 France 7 England 25	25,000
1936 France 3 Wales 9	17,000
1938 France 15 England 17	18,000
1938 France 6 Australia 35	11,500

By 1939, with the Rugby Union having lost 313 of its 784 clubs, and the fledgling Rugby a Treize having already 220

clubs under its wing, there appeared to be only one eventual winner. This latter figure, however, could well have been much higher but for the obstructionist tactics of the rugby union authorities who set about banning as many grounds as possible. For example, even the well-established Paris based club was unable to obtain a permanent ground during the 1937/8 season and had to play their homes games at...Bordeaux! Catastrophe then struck the game with the outbreak of war, when fervent rugby union members of the pro-Nazi Vichy regime banned the game and confiscated all its assets valued at 1.2 million francs.

The French Rugby League had therefore to re-build from scratch in 1945. Their offices in Bordeaux had been ransacked, but officials were surprised to find that when they returned after the war there were still some documents that had not been destroyed. A photograph, presented by Hunslet during their tour in 1938, was among items which survived and was now given pride of place. For the 1945/6 season there were 18 clubs in the premier league, including new ones at Libourne, Lézignan and Avignon.

A breakthrough was made on 6 January, 1946 when the **Parc des Princes,** on the Bois de Boulogne (opened as a velodrome in 1897 and the venue of rugby union internationals from 1906-1920) opened its doors to rugby league for the first time. On that day, Eric Batten celebrated by scoring a hat-trick of tries in the English Rugby League XIII's 19-6 victory over their French equivalents. This game, watched by a crowd of 10,000, helped to establish the newly-formed Racing Club de Paris, who lost 36-19 to a Rugby League XIII on 28 April, 1946.

Before a British side again played at Parc des Princes, New Zealand had played in two tests on the ground; in 1947 when they won 11-7, and in 1951 when a crowd of 23,459 saw France gain their revenge with an 8-3 victory after breaking down the Kiwis' stubborn defence late in the second half with tries by centre Jacques Merquey, the most penetrative back on the field, and winger Constrastin. A 34th minute try by Hough had earlier shocked the home side and it was not until the 57th minute that the legendary Puig-Aubert, *"Pipette"*, replied with a 50 metre penalty.

In 1952 a broken-nose injury to Great Britain captain Ernest Ward proved the turning point, with the home side seizing the initiative during Ward's absence to score 11 points, including two tries from scrum-half Crespo, which gave them

French scrum-half Verge cuts through the centre during the game against Australia in 1964 at Parc des Princes - Hulton Deutsch.

a 22-12 victory. Later that year the Australians beat France 16-12 in an exciting match in which each side took the lead three times, and France trailed by only one point until Hazzard scored the Kangaroos fourth try in the 75th minute. Although France had lost both their opening games in the 1953 championship there was still a crowd of 25,000 at the Parc des Princes to see England score a 15-13 victory after playing brilliantly in the first half - St. Helens' centre Dougie Greenall scoring two tries in the first quarter.

Having unsuccessfully proposed a World Cup in 1934 (see Bordeaux), twenty years later the French Rugby League hosted the inaugural competition, which was staged at six venues, including the Parc des Princes where both the opening game, in which France beat New Zealand 22-13, and the final play-off, on Saturday 13 November, 1954, between France and Great Britain, took place. There had been so many withdrawals from their original squad that Great Britain were considered no-hopers in this competition. But, before a crowd of 33,000 and a live television audience in England, they pulled off a memorable victory, 16-12, and the players chaired their captain, Dave Valentine, and Gerry Helme, the scorer of the decisive try, off the field at the end.

ST. OUEN After their defeat in 1955 it would be 13 years before Britain next played at Parc des Princes. However, during that period both Australia and New Zealand were visitors to the stadium, and in 1961 Paris was also a test match location when France drew 5-5 with New Zealand in the

northern district of St. Ouen, at what, as the current home of the famous Red Star soccer club, is now named **Le Stade de Paris.** In the 1960s the stadium had room for only about 7,000 but nowadays, located immediately off the Peripherique ring road, its capacity has risen to 21,000 with cover on three sides.

Le Stade de Paris	
1961 France 5 New Zealand 5	3,307

In 1968 Leeds full-back Bev Risman marked his Great Britain debut at the Parc des Princes by scoring two tries and five goals in his side's unexpected 22-13 victory, bearing in mind France's triumphs over Australia in the recent tests. Another debutant that day was Widnes second-rower Ray French, who was among the best of the British forwards. In 1969, following their inclusion in the forthcoming World Cup in Australia, Wales made their first appearance at the stadium, losing to France 17-13 after conceding a gift try to stand-off Jean Capdouze in the 5th minute, and suffering the loss of his opposite number David Watkins with a cheekbone injury.

The Parc des Princes, which had been totally rebuilt in 1932, was again redeveloped, from 1967-1972, at a cost of £8 million. Before rugby union internationals recommenced at the new 48,700-seater stadium, Australia beat New Zealand, 9-5, there in the 1972 World Cup. The future of the stadium, which is the home of Paris St. Germain soccer club and now run by Canal Plus, the leading sports and movie channel, is now in some doubt. It is not large enough to guarantee that all rugby union internationals are staged there, and its status will be further threatened with the building of the 85,000 all-seater national stadium at St. Denis, which is only a couple of miles from Le Stade de Paris, for the 1998 World Cup soccer

Parc des Princes, 1995 - Robert Fassolette.

finals. The French Super League side plan to play some games at the Parc des Princes. Time will only tell whether rugby league in France will ever regain its pre-war status, and perhaps one day be able to fill this ground or the new Grand Stade.

Parc des Princes	
1947 France 7 New Zealand 11	15,000
1951 France 8 New Zealand 3	23,459
1952 France 22 Great Britain 12	16,466
1952 France 12 Australia 16	20,000
1953 France 13 England 15	25,000
World Cup 1954 France 22 New Zealand 13	13,240
World Cup 1954 final France 12 Great Britain 16	30,368
1955 France 17 Great Britain 5	18,000
1955 France 24 New Zealand 3	14,752
1956 France 8 Australia 15	10,789
1959 France 19 Australia 20	9,864
1964 France 8 Australia 16	5,979
1968 France 13 Great Britain 22	5,500
1969 France 17 Wales 13	6,189
World Cup 1972 Australia 9 New Zealand 5	6,000

BORDEAUX The birth of a rugby league club in Bordeaux was directly attributable to the Leeds/Yorkshire side playing at the **Parc de Suzon,** which was owned by the President of the S.A. Bordelais (rugby union) club, Mr Loze. The suspension of the ground by the French (R.U.) Federation resulted in Mr Loze going over to rugby league, with whom he became a national committee member, and Bordeaux XIII becoming the champions of France in 1937. The first staging of an international outside of Paris, on New Year's Day, 1935, resulted in France's first-ever victory: the 18-11 defeat of Wales, who have lost on each of their five visits to Bordeaux, taking place at Suzon. Wales were handicapped with the early loss of Oldham prop Rees and finished with only ten men, but France's historic victory was well deserved with Jean Galia superbly leading his forwards, who ran and passed like backs.

Parc de Suzon	
1935 France 18 Wales 11	15,000

Before the game a conference was held between French and English League representatives to discuss the proposal by France for a World Cup to be staged there during May. The Rugby League later decided against such a competition, partly because they were heavily committed to sending tour sides to France at that time.

Subsequent internationals in Bordeaux were held at the **Stade Velodrome Municipal.** This stadium and the other sports facilities on the eight hectares of the Park Lescure had been built after the First World War on the initiative of architect Alfred Duprat and a number of Bordeaux *"sportsmen"* who created their own society and financed the construction. In 1930 the town council voted 3.8 million francs for the purchase of the old stadium and 1.5. million francs towards its repair, but these estimates were rapidly exceeded when a major reconstruction of the sports complex, a collaboration between architects Raoul Jourde and Jacques d'Welles and Italian engineer Dabbeni, was undertaken from 1933 until 1938.

The original stadium was transformed with the completion of a 20 million francs concrete velodrome, which was opened on 12 June, 1938 for the Brazil-Czechoslavakia World Cup soccer game. At its opening, the continuous cantilever roofs of the Stade Velodrome Municipal covered every seat and gave the stadium a futuristic appearance. Joining the higher and lower roofs at each corner are twin-decked press observations rooms, which were said at the time to resemble *"the bows of a hydroplane"*. The dressing rooms are set within a trapezoidal courtyard adjacent to the stadium, and the players enter the field from a tunnel behind the goals.

In the new stadium, on 16 April, 1939, a crowd of 25,000 saw France take the European Championship for the first time in

The original cycle track at Bordeaux's Stade Municipal has now been removed to accommodate extra seating.

their history by defeating Wales 16-10; whilst in March, 1946, in the first full post-war international in the country, the scoreline was 19-7. Wales had dominated both these games in the early stages but had been unable to match the French for pace. The Welsh remained a major attraction, however, and a year later thousands were locked out when more than 26,000 saw France stage a remarkable second-half rally which took the scores from 7-13 to 29-21. Each side scored five tries but Puig-Aubert, as so often, proved the match-winner with seven goals.

For the game at Bordeaux in November, 1948 the Rugby League rejected the innovation of flying to France on the Friday due to the risk of delays through fog. But the long overland journey appears not to have affected the English side, who were paying their second visit to the ground, and they scored ten points in the last two minutes to snatch an astonishing 12-5 victory. A 75th minute penalty by full-back Barreteau appeared to have sealed the game until the Belle Vue Rangers' left-winger Stan McCormick brought the crowd to their feet with a brilliant side-stepping run to score under the posts. Ernest Ward, whose try had been the only score in the mud-bath in 1946, converted to regain England the lead; and then, with only 30 seconds remaining, his co-centre, Warrington's Pimblett, scored his sixth international try of the season. Both Wigan's Jack Hilton and Bradford Northern's Ken Traill each scored tries on their internationals debuts at Bordeaux in 1949, the latter at a crucial stage in the game when England trailed 7-5 before running out winners 13-7.

Another outstanding all-round performance by Puig-Aubert, who kicked five goals, was the major factor in France's 16-3 defeat of Other Nationalities in 1950. Whilst in 1952 it was again *"Pipette's"* brilliant kicking (seven goals, including two drop goals) which helped France to a 20-12 victory over the unfortunate Welsh. Brian Bevan had been Other Nationalities' only scorer in 1950, and it was his two characteristic tries which were the highlight of Other Nationalities' 15-10 win in 1953.

Only twice have Great Britain graced the Bordeaux pitch; in the 1954 World Cup, when they beat New Zealand 26-6; and in 1960 when they scored four tries in the second half in beating France 21-10, despite being heavily penalised by the French referee and seeing little of the ball during that period.

Stade Municipal	
1939 France 16 Wales 10	25,000
1946 France 19 Wales 7	–
1946 France 0 England 3	24,100
1947 France 29 Wales 21	26,000
1948 France 25 New Zealand 7	22,000
1949 France 5 England 12	26,000
1949 France 0 Australia 10	17,365
1949 France 5 England 13	20,598
1950 France 16 Other Nats. 3	28,000
1952 France 20 Wales 12	15,678
1951 France 17 New Zealand 7	11,110
1953 France 5 Australia 0	23,419
1953 France 10 Other Nats. 15	12,190
World Cup 1954 Great Britain 26 New Zealand 6	14,000
1956 France 6 Australia 10	11,379
1959 France 2 Australia 17	8,848
1960 France 10 Great Britain 21	5,127
1961 France 6 New Zealand 6	2,375
1963 France 8 Australia 5	4,261
World Champ. 1975 France 2 England 48	1,581

England second-rower Bill Hudson is tackled during their 3-0 win over France at Bordeaux in 1946 - Les Hoole Collection.

Wreaking their revenge for being nilled themselves in 1949, France beat Australia 5-0 in the second test in 1953 through a second minute try by Carrère and a wonder goal from touch by full-back Rives. The crowd of 23,419, however, voiced their dissatisfaction at the quality of this particular game. A decade later and the next generation had voted with their feet, for only 4,261 paid to see France beat the Kangaroos in their fifth and last meeting with them in Bordeaux.

For the last international staged in Bordeaux, a city which had been one of the post-war strongholds of the game, the figure dropped to only 1,581 paying spectators. This was at the 1975 World Championship, when Salford's flying winger, Keith Fielding, scored a record four tries in England's 48-2 annihilation of the home side. Unfortunately, in contrast to earlier times, with such a sparse crowd there was little or no atmosphere in the vast stadium. Apart, that is, from the traditional band, which not only celebrated each score but even burst into tune during the actual play!

Under the eye of architect Guy Depuis, in 1986 the stadium was tastefully refurbished so that now it holds over 50,000, the cycle track having been removed and regraded for the installation of extra seating.

MARSEILLE Although no rugby league club was formed in Marseille until after the Second World War, the French Rugby League had used the **Stade Velodrome** for the second test against Australia in 1938, when the Kangaroos had won 16-11 in front of 24,000 spectators.

This was designed by architect Henri Ploquin, and officially opened on 13 June, 1937 with an athletics and cycling meeting followed by a soccer match between Turin and the traditional and current main user, Olympique de Marseille. The almost identical Jean Bouin and Ganay Stands originally seated 28,500 with standing room for a further 15,800 at the open ends. The Olympic-style scoreboard at the rear of one of these terraces still survives, although since 1970 the pink cycle track has been built on to provide extra seating, and executive boxes have been installed on two levels at the rear of the main Jean Bouin Stand. Having once held nearly 55,000 its present all-seater capacity is nearer 45,000.

Since the war the ground has hosted 15 rugby league internationals involving France, of which they have lost only four. It was at Marseille in 1948 that a crowd of 32,000 saw England win the European Championship for the second successive year, after building an unassailable interval lead with the help of the elements. However, in 1951, in front of a crowd of 31,810, they were routed by the French 42-13, conceding ten tries in the largest defeat since the championship was inaugurated.

Wales have been unsuccessful on each of their four appearances at Marseille, in 1947, 1949, 1951, and 1953, although on the latter occasion it was only a last-minute try

French forward Georges Ailleres on the charge against New Zealand at Marseille in 1965.

by winger Constrastin, his second of the match, which sealed the game 23-22. In 1951 all three back-row forwards scored tries, including a hat-trick by loose-forward Perez, in France's 28-13 success. That day Puig Aubert kicked eight goals and was in his usual immaculate form. However, in 1952 it was his mistakes when under pressure that led to some of Other Nationalities' five second half tries, and defeat for his side.

Great Britain's last visit to the Stade Velodrome, in 1981, was a painful one, when, having thrashed France 39-0 at the Boulevard two weeks earlier, they were soundly beaten themselves in the return, 19-2. The French victory owed much to two superb first half tries by Tonneins right winger and international debutant, Patrick Solal. Although stretchered off in the second half with concussion, his display was so impressive that he was immediately signed after the game by Hull, thus making him the first French player to emigrate to an English first division club.

On Saturday, 23 November, 1985, the live televised test against New Zealand, for what was the Kiwis' fifth visit to the stadium, attracted a mere 492 paying spectators in an estimated crowd of only 1,500. All of which was a far cry from earlier games on the ground, and the welcome which greeted the all-conquering French tourists on their triumphant return from Australia in 1951, when an estimated 60,000 lined the streets of Marseille to see the American-style parade, with each player standing in a Peugeot 203. Three years later and the Stade Velodrome was used for the inaugural World Cup fixture between Australia and New Zealand, which the Kangaroos won 34-15. Of the three so far unmentioned venues where that historic tournament took place, two, at Nantes and Toulouse, had never hosted full internationals, whilst only one test had previously been played at Lyons.

Stade Velodrome

1938 France 11 Australia 16	24,000
1947 France 14 Wales 5	24,500
1948 France 10 England 25	32,000
1949 France 11 Wales 0	30,000
1949 France 10 Australia 29	15,796
1950 France 8 Other Nats 3	22,580
1951 France 28 Wales 13	18,000
1951 France 42 England 13	31,810
1952 France 10 Other Nats 29	17,611
1953 France 23 Wales 22	25,000
World Cup 1954 Australia 34 New Zealand 15	20,000
1965 France 14 New Zealand 3	30,431
1967 France 7 Australia 7	5,193
World Cup 1972 France 20 New Zealand 9	20,748
World Champ. 1975 France 12 New Zealand 12	26,879
1981 France 19 Great Britain 2	6,500
1985 France 0 New Zealand 22	1,492

NANTES It was at the **Stade Malakoff** (now called **Stade Marcel-Saupin**), on Thursday, 11 April, 1954, that France qualified for the final of that first competition, beating Australia 15-5 in a keenly-fought game before what was then a record attendance for any sporting event in Nantes of 12,000 (9,837 paying) France led 10-5 at half-time, but their heroic defence was hard pressed by the dominant Australian forwards, who looked likely to salvage at least a draw. Then, in the 75th minute, after making a blind-side break from a scrum on the right, Puig-Aubert immediately cross-kicked, and left-winger Cantoni took advantage of a favourable bounce to score under the posts, and thus guarantee the Tricolours' place in the final.

Named after the road on which it now stands, the Stade Malakoff was built near to the site of the former Stade du Champ de Mars, the home of the Stade Nantais University (R.U.) Club since 1912, which was demolished in 1938. Malakoff had an initial capacity of about 9,000 and was constructed principally for rugby, but since the war, during which the stadium was damaged by bombing, and up to

France attack against Australia at Nantes in 1954 through, from right to left, Cantoni, Puig-Aubert and Constrastin.

1984, it was principally the home of soccer club, F. C. Nantes. It was renamed Stade Marcel-Saupin in 1964, prior to Nantes winning six French Championships from 1965-1983, and its capacity being progressively raised to about 27,000.

Rugby maintained its traditional access to the stadium until about 1960. For example, apart from the World Cup game in 1954, Stade Malakoff also hosted the France "B" - Wales (24-11) game on 19 May, 1955, and Australia's game against a regional selection on a foul night in December, 1959, when the attendance was only 900. Four rugby union "B" internationals have also been played there.

Bordered on the south by the River Loire, the stadium had no room for expansion, and in order to host games in the 1984 European soccer championships, a new stadium, La Beaujoire, had to be built. This 45,000 capacity stadium is one of the country's most important international rugby union venues, whilst the Stade Marcel-Saupin is now used for Nantes F.C. second team games and other sports but not rugby league.

Some ten years ago there were six rugby league clubs in the Nantes area, but today there is only Nantes XIII, a club which is in the third division of the French Rugby League as part of the Paris district. They play at a neat little stadium, Stade Michel Lecointre.

Stade Malakoff

World Cup 1954 France 15 Australia 5	12,000

LYONS Rugby League officials in charge of the Dominions side which played a French XIII on Sunday, 21 March, 1937 at the **Stade de Gerland**, near the River Rhone, were amazed to find that the pitch was waterlogged to a depth of between six and nine inches up to the 25-yard lines and at least two inches overall. However, as there was an attendance of 17,000 already inside the ground watching a curtain-raiser between two local sides, it was found impractical to cancel the main event, which the Dominions went on to win, 6-3. Such were the conditions that the visiting captain, Warrington's Bill Shankland, suggested, unsuccessfully, that the 25-yard lines should be used for the goal-lines.

Designed by architect Tony Garnier, this colossal stadium on l'avenue Jean-Jaures was intended as the centre-piece of the Lyons Exhibition in 1914. However, the war, during which German prisoners worked on the stadium's construction, interfered with its progress. Ironically, it was German reparations which eventually paid for its completion in May, 1926. Of the rectangular-shaped rugby stadiums, the Stade de Gerland ranked as the largest in the world; the pitch being surrounded by a 500 (sic) metre athletic track, which in turn was enclosed by a 666.66 metre cycle track (to allow exactly 2km for 3 laps) with banked corners, whilst along each straight (in front of the main stand) there was room for a 200 metre sprint track. The arena was also used for gymnastic and other mass displays. The main architectural features of the stadium were the four monumental concrete arches at each entrance. Despite its initial size, the stadium's

capacity was no more than 30,000, most of whom were seated on open concrete terraces.

The first test match on the ground was a fierce affair in 1953, when, thanks to five goals from Puig-Aubert, including one 50-yard effort just before the end, France beat Australia 13-5. Following one second-half incident play was stopped whilst the Australian managers and an interpreter came on the field to discuss matters with the French referee, who appeared to have sent Keith Holman off for swearing. When play resumed, however, Holman was still on the field.

On 3 January, 1954, when snow fell throughout the match, France beat a Combined Nations side 19-15 at the Stade Gerland to commemorate the 20th anniversary of the French Rugby League. As well as hooker T. McKinney, who was born in Northern Ireland, and representatives from England, Australia, Wales, and Scotland, the Combined side also included the Italian Vigna, who scored a try, and three Americans.

The latter were from the All Stars side which was then touring France. This team of gridirons players were included by the French in the original World Cup draw later that year, but were withdrawn after objections from the English Rugby League. In that tournament Great Britain beat Australia 28-13 in front of 10,250 spectators at Gerland.

The last international to be played in Lyon was the World Cup final in 1972 when Great Britain took the trophy, having headed the qualifying table, despite only drawing 10-all with Australia after extra time. It was perhaps not the most satisfactory way to end such a prestigious tournament but it was nonetheless well deserved. Australia led 10-5 mid-way through the second half, and their massive pack and 15 stone centre Mark Harris threatened to overrun the British defence. However, the Kangaroos lacked ideas near the line, and Britain were the better side in the last quarter and throughout injury time. Tireless Dewsbury hooker, Mick Stephenson, had scored his third try of the series, and captain Clive Sullivan produced one of the most memorable tries in international rugby, with a breathtaking run from his own half, to level the scores. Unfortunately, on a wet day, there was a crowd of only 4,000 to witness this major event.

By that time Gerland had been substantially altered from its original design, with the cycle track having been removed in 1966 to accommodate seated terraces, and the athletics track

The pre-match ceremony of the Australia-Great Britain World Cup game at Lyons in 1954.

Stade de Gerland circa 1970.

reduced to standard Olympic dimensions. The major step was taken in 1982 when it was decided to remove this track and remodel the stadium in order to host the 1984 European soccer championships. Tony Garnier's external architecture, including the columns, were retained but new stand roofs, supported by 125 metre long horizontal girders, were erected.

The Stade de Gerland presently has an all-seater capacity of 42,326 and the ground's main user is the national league first division soccer club, Olympique Lyonnais, who moved there in 1950. Rugby Union also organise big games at Gerland, and that sport still holds the ground record with an attendance of 36,161 paying spectators for the Grand Final between Beziers and Brive in 1972.

Stade de Gerland	
1953 France 13 Australia 5	17,454
World Cup 1954 Australia 13 Great Britain 28	10,250
1956 France 23 England 9	–
1956 France 22 New Zealand 31	7,051
1957 France 21 Australia 25	5,743
World Cup 1972 final Australia 10 Great Britain 10	4,231
(After extra time - Great Britain won on better points aggregate).	

TOULOUSE Rugby League started in Toulouse in 1936 under the guidance of Jean Baylet, the director of the regional newspaper *La Depeche du Midi*. Toulouse Olympique's first coach was Jean Galia who by that time had retired from playing. The ground situation in Toulouse was

different from other areas of France in that the city council arranged for a new stadium, the **Stade des Minimes**, to be dedicated to rugby league. However, as construction work was not completed for the start of the season, the first six games were played away from home. According to former players this worked to their advantage in so far as the home supporters were spared the early thrashings which the inexperienced team suffered. By 1939 Toulouse were good enough to reach the Cup final, which was held in the city at the Stade Chapou, losing 7-3 to XIII Catalan.

The Stade des Minimes was used by France as their training ground prior to the first full international to be staged in Toulouse. This was the 13-all draw between France and Great Britain in the 1954 World Cup, played on Sunday, 7 November, at the **Stade Municipal** (known locally as Le Stadium). The attendance that day of 37,471 is a record for a rugby league game in France. The stadium is the traditional home of the Championship final but nothing approaching this figure has ever been recorded for any domestic event.

Situated in a large Parc des Sports, and nowadays cut off from the central hall by a flyover, the new stadium was not completed until 1950, although work on its construction had started before the war, in 1937.

Great Britain played two matches there in 1957. In March they turned a 17-2 deficit into a 19-17 lead with a Lewis Jones interception try in the 71st minute, but were apparently *"robbed"* when the home referee awarded France their 29th penalty and their brilliant stand-off

French second-rower Guy Delaye makes a break during the 13-all draw with Great Britain in the 1954 World Cup at Toulouse watched by a record crowd.

Benausse levelled the scores. In November, former international scrum-half turned referee, Jep Maso, was equally hard on Britain, but his handling of the game brought only praise. In this game, which Britain won 25-14, Oldham full-back Bernard Ganley marked his international debut with a try and five goals, and Wigan's £9,500 world-record signing Mick Sullivan scored two memorable tries. However, the highlight of the match was provided by Oldham loose-forward Derek *"Rocky"* Turner who scored a 70-yard solo try to enlighten a scrappy first-half.

It was Turner's tackle in 1960 on scrum-half Fages which resulted in his dismissal and precipitated a 66th minute brawl. However, Turner, who was then with Wakefield Trinity, was instructed by his captain, Jeff Stevenson, not to leave the field as the referee had appeared to change his mind after signalling that a French forward should also walk. The five-minute stalemate was only broken when Rugby League secretary, Bill Fallowfield, escorted Turner from the field. This incident marred a fine game in which France wiped out an 11-point deficit to win 20-18 - the match-winning try coming only four minutes after the brawl when eight men handled for outstanding prop Quaglio to score.

A Welsh XIII easily lost to France, 23-3, at Toulouse in 1963, and in full internationals, in 1975 (World Championship) and 1977, Wales again failed despite winning an abundance of possession on both occasions.

The Stade Municipal, Toulouse - Services techniques de la mairie de Toulouse.

Because of flooding of the Le Stadium by the Garonne river, the test against New Zealand in 1965, which resulted in a 28-5 win for France, was played at the Stade des Minimes.

Stade des Minimes	
1965 France 28 New Zealand 5	7,000

There was a surprise for Great Britain in 1969 when they were beaten 13-9 at Toulouse, mostly thanks to the old guard of George Ailleres, who led his powerful pack by example, and Claude Mantoulan who scored France's second try and set up their third after intercepting. However, one of the greatest upsets in international rugby league history was reserved for Australia, who, after their rampage through England and Wales, were beaten 11-10 at Toulouse in 1978, substitute Jean Marc Bourret scoring the winning drop goal in the 67th minute.

Stade Municipal	
World Cup 1954 France 13 Great Britain 13	37,471
1956 France 24 New Zealand 7	10,184
1957 France 19 Great Britain 19	16,000
1957 France 14 Great Britain 25	15,762
1959 France 25 Wales 8	25,000
1960 France 20 Great Britain 18	15,308
1963 France 9 Australia 21	6,932
1967 France 7 Australia 7	5,193
1968 France 16 Australia 13	5,000
1969 France 13 Great Britain 9	7,536
1970 France 14 England 9	6,587
1971 France 3 New Zealand 3	5,000
1971 France 16 Great Britain 8	14,960
1972 France 9 Great Britain 10	11,508
World Cup 1972 France 9 Australia 31	10,332
1973 France 3 Australia 44	5,000
World Champ. 1975 France 14 Wales 7	7,563
1977 France 13 Wales 2	5,827
1978 France 11 England 13	6,000
1978 France 11 Australia 10	7,060
1980 France 3 New Zealand 11	1,956

Unfortunately, the game in France was unable to capitalise on this famous victory due partly to the extraordinary scenes of player violence at the 1981 Championship final in the same stadium, which not only resulted in XIII Catalan being suspended, but actually made the headline news on BBC television! The pictures were also broadcast in many other countries as French TV sold the pictures as an illustration of violence in sport. Certainly, those few minutes of madness did untold harm to the game's credibility in France.

As part of a 15 million franc redevelopment, for the start of the 1983/4 season seating was added to what had been the banked cycle track, thus increasing the stadium's capacity to just over 38,000, with most seats being undercover. In his *Football Grounds of Europe* Simon Inglis has likened Le Stadium, the home of Toulouse FC, to *"a miniature Wembley"*, and, with twin towers at its entrance and an almost identical roof, it is easy to see why.

GRENOBLE The Alpine city of Grenoble, which hosted the 1968 Winter Olympics, had its first taste of rugby league during January, 1935 when a Rugby League XIII beat the South East Selection (Lyons/Roanne) 24-8. It was not until 2 March, 1958, however, that a 13-a-side international was played there. That day, at the **Stade Municipal**, Great Britain triumphed, despite being seven points down after only twelve minutes play and referee Jep Maso awarding them only two of 28 penalties. Full-back Lacaze's three penalties (from eleven attempts) kept France in the game, but in the last 15 minutes Great Britain scored three tries, two of which were converted, to run out easy winners. The capacity attendance (estimated at 17,000, 14,700 of whom paid) and the receipts of 6.674 million francs were both records for this velodrome.

On a spring-like day in 1959, a paying audience of 8,527 (estimated attendance 10,000) saw France chalk up their first victory over Great Britain since the fixture was granted full test match status. Having scored 50 points at Headingley three weeks earlier, Great Britain were punished for their over confidence, France scoring two tries in the first four minutes and leading 19-0 at the break. On his international debut, Neil Fox scored two tries to rally his side, but a second try by stand-off Benausse on the hour made the game safe for France.

Stade Municipal		
1958 France 9 Great Britain 23		17,000
1959 France 24 Great Britain 15		10,000
World Cup 1972 France 4 Great Britain 13		5,321
1974 France 5 Great Britain 24		4,100

In terms of internationals, the ground was next used for one of the qualifying games in the 1972 World Cup, when the Hull Kingston Rovers' second-row, Phil Lowe, scored two solo 30-yard tries and created a third for Clive Sullivan

A section of the record crowd at Grenoble in 1958 - Dauphiné Libéré.

The Alps make a dramatic backdrop as Great Britain centre Neil Fox is tackled during the test at Grenoble in 1959 - Dauphiné Libéré.

with the last move of the match to help beat France 13-4. The last time an international was staged at Grenoble was in 1974 when international rugby league debutant Keith Fielding scored three sparkling tries in Great Britain's 24-5 victory. According to Alfred Drewery, writing in *The Yorkshire Post*, *"The last of Fielding's tries was as breathtaking in one way as was in another the sight of the setting sun tipping the snow-covered peaks which surround this picturesque ground."*

ROANNE A founder member of the French League in 1934, Roanne (50 miles north-west of Lyons, population 40,000)

had no large facilities to compare with the two other major cities of the Rhone-Alpes region. Therefore, although the Australians played Roanne on 1 December, 1937 during their first tour of France, as we have seen, representative games were staged at either Lyons or Grenoble. Indeed, what was to be the Kangaroos' last match of their 1960 tour, the third test on Sunday, the 17th January, was scheduled to be played at Lyons. However, the Stade Gerland was frost and snow-covered and with no alternative ground available, and the Australians due to fly home before the following week-end, it seemed that the test, for the first time in rugby league history, would have to be cancelled.

A view of Parc des Sports' original grandstand during Roanne's game against the 1980 Kiwis - Bernard Vizier (Roanne R.L.).

However, at his own expense, the chairman of that year's champion club, R. C. Roanne, quickly arranged with the local authorities for the test to be played on Wednesday, 20 January, at the **Parc des Sports** - the only problem being that the old wooden ground had no floodlights. To guarantee a reasonable crowd, Monsieur Devernois, who was also President of the French Rugby League, therefore approached his colleagues and fellow club directors in the town's hosiery trade, to persuade them to free their workers for the afternoon. With them readily agreeing to this, and the town being almost entirely dedicated to hosiery, the crowd for the test reached a satisfactory 3,437 - the record for the ground being a capacity 7,066 paying spectators who watched the *"Hosiers"* meet the Carcassonne *"Canaries"* on 2 February, 1947. The scores were level at 8-all up to the 47th minute but due to injuries France finished with only ten men and Australia ran out winners 16-8.

Since then a new sports complex named Malleval has been built at the other end of town and is shared by the local rugby league, rugby union and soccer clubs, whilst the Parc des Sports is only used for training purposes by the same clubs. Only weeks before Malleval's new floodlights were opened, the 1980 New Zealand tourists beat a determined Roanne side, 16-11, under the ground's adequate training lights. On this occasion, Kiwi coach Ces Mountford was reunited with his Roanne adversaries from 1948, Crespo, Abadie, and his opposite number, Taillantou, whom he had faced when wearing Wigan's colours in a two-legged competition between the French and British champions.

A view of Stade Gilbert Brutus' main stand at the France – Great Britain game in 1992 – Christian Ratcliffe.

victory over the Australians, 20-5. It was here also that in 1961 New Zealand were convincing 23-2 winners against France in the first international to be staged in Perpignan.

Stade Jean-Laffon
1961 France 2 New Zealand 23	9,020

XIII Catalan repeated their feat of 1948 against Reg Gasnier's 1964 Kangaroos, beating them 15-11, but by this time the club had moved to the new **Stade Gilbert Brutus**. Known simply as *"Brutus"*, the stadium, which includes an athletics track, is named after a famous Catalan rugby union player who died under Nazi Gestapo torture in 1944. Including seating for about 6,000, Brutus' capacity is in the region of 12,000, with the smaller of the two grandstands, which houses the dressing rooms and press facilities, being fully cantilevered. This is faced by the popular-side propped cantilevered stand, Tribune Dr. Henri Bonzoms, which is named after a former President of the club who was partly responsible for the re-birth of the game after the war. The one open terrace, at the opposite end to the scoreboard, is popular with British fans.

During the 1960s Great Britain managed only one win in five visits. Two of these were in 1962, the year that Brutus was opened. Because France held a commanding, 21-5, half-time lead in March they happily conceded penalties in the second half; whilst in a rough game in December they had the match won by three-quarter time. Hunslet centre Geoff Shelton scored two tries on his international debut in 1964, when snow, which was the first to fall in Perpignan during March

Parc des Sports
1960 France 8 Australia 16	3,437

From the 1960s internationals have increasingly been played in the code's heartland, in the extreme south of the country near to the Spanish border, and along the Mediterranean coast.

PERPIGNAN Since their formation at the Cafe de la Poste on 24 August, 1934, a meeting which was attended by fellow Catalan and rugby league founder, Jean Galia, XIII Catalan, who were winners of the first Grand Final in 1936, have been among the most successful and best supported clubs in the French game's turbulent history. As part of their 50th anniversary celebrations they invited Salford over to play them as a tribute to *Les Diables Rouges'* momentous visit in 1934.

From their formation, XIII Catalan played at **Stade Jean-Laffon**, where at Christmas 1948 they scored a famous

The Tribune Dr. Henri Bonzoms is prominent as Great Britain applaud their supporters on the open terracing following France's 30-12 defeat at Perpignan in 1992 - Joe Ratcliffe.

for 30 years, turned the pitch into a quagmire and left France floundering in the mud.

Ironically, in December of that year, it was a shirt-sleeved crowd who urged France to victory. Berwyn Jones' speed in scoring a 40-yard try brought unbelieving gasps from the partisan crowd, but it was the French right-winger Bruzy who had the last laugh with two tries in his side's 18-8 success. On that occasion Alex Murphy put in one of the worst performances of his otherwise brilliant international career, thrice conceding penalties for kicking the ball directly out of play from kick-offs - an error which he, along with fellow Hall of Famer, Neil Fox, repeated at Perpignan in 1966, thus costing Britain the game.

Wales' first win on French soil for 34 years came in January, 1970, when a last-minute try by Clive Sullivan, his second of the match, gave them a 15-11 victory. Unfortunately, the occasion was marred by a spectator's attack on the referee, Mr. R. L. Thomas, at the conclusion of the game, which resulted in the Oldham official being hospitalised and the ground being suspended from staging further internationals that year.

It was this Catalonian trait, the so-called *"temperament of fire"*, which caused the player violence which resulted in the previously referred to abandonment of the 1981 Championship final at Toulouse, and the subsequent suspension of XIII Catalan. They immediately bounced back,

however, to win an unprecedented four successive Grand Finals, culminating in their victory over Le Pontet in 1985.

A few months earlier at Brutus, France had pulled off a brilliant 26-16 victory over Britain, debutant winger, Didier Couston, scoring a hat-trick of tries, including one 80 yard interception.

This success was stunning in so far as they had conceded 50 points only a fortnight earlier at Headingley. There have been no such surprises on the ground since, although France's performance at Perpignan in 1990, when missed goals cost them dearly, was the precursor of their historic win at Headingley three weeks later. In 1991, however, Britain posted their highest score and highest winning margin, 45-10, on French soil.

Stade Gilbert Brutus	
1962 France 23 Great Britain 13	12,500
1962 France 17 Great Britain 12	12,500
1964 France 5 Great Britain 11	4,326
1964 France 18 Great Britain 8	7,150
1965 France 6 New Zealand 2	9,000
1966 France 18 Great Britain 13	6,000
1970 France 11 Wales 15	12,000
1971 France 11 New Zealand 27	3,581
World Cup 1972 Australia 21 Great Britain 27	6,324
1973 France 9 Australia 21	7,630
1975 France 9 England 11	7,950
World Champ. 1975 France 2 Australia 41	10,440
1980 France 6 New Zealand 5	6,000
1985 France 24 Great Britain 16	5,000
1985 France 0 New Zealand 22	3,045
1986 France 2 Australia 44	2,532
1990 France 4 Great Britain 8	6,000
1990 France 10 Australia 34	2,000
1991 France 10 Great Britain 45	3,965
1992 France 12 Great Britain 30	5,688

CARCASSONNE A.S. Carcassonne rugby union club transferred to rugby league in May, 1938 following a disagreement with the French Rugby Union over the transfer of two players. A.S.C.'s ground, the **Stade Albert Domec (formerly le stade de la Pepiniere)**, which sits within the shadow of Carcassonne's medieval walled-city, is named after a local rugby union centre three-quarter who was capped against Wales in 1929. A charcoal merchant by profession, Domec was nicknamed *"Bamboo"* because of his slender physique. Such was his popularity that the municipality had no hesitation in renaming in his honour following his premature death in 1948.

A rain-swept Domec at the France-Wales game in 1995. For a brighter view of the stadium see the colour section - Margaret Ratcliffe.

1978 they scored a famous victory against the Kangaroos, 13-10, with a try from Naudo and five goals from Moya. The Aussies had a long wait to gain their revenge on the ground but when it came it was in the form of a then world-record test margin of 52 points to nil, Dale Shearer scoring four of their ten tries.

England's only game at Carcassonne was a full-blooded affair in 1977, when captain Roger Millward was knocked out by a punch, and world-class centre Jean-Marc Bourret scored two tries and five goals in France's 28-15 championship-clinching victory. Bourret also scored a hat-trick of touchdowns in the 15-2 victory over Papua New Guinea in 1979 on a quagmire of a pitch.

Similar conditions also greeted Jonathan Davies' Welsh side earlier this year when they won the European Championship for the first time since 1938. France led at half-time but in the end had no answer to the power of the Welsh pack, strengthened as it was by the Wigan front-row and their new found ancestral blood.

Stade Albert Domec	
1967 France 13 Great Britain 16	10,650
1967 France 10 Australia 3	4,193
1971 France 11 New Zealand 27	5,200
1977 France 28 England 15	12,000
1978 France 13 Australia 10	6,000
1979 France 15 Papua New Guinea 2	–
1983 France 5 Great Britain 20	3,862
1986 France 0 Australia 52	1,574
1987 France 10 Great Britain 20	1,968
1987 France 21 Papua New Guinea 4	2,204
1989 France 14 New Zealand 16	4,208
1989 France 0 New Zealand 34	4,200
1993 France 6 Great Britain 48	5,500
1993 France 11 New Zealand 36	3,500
1995 France 10 Wales 22	6,000

Having bought the ground in 1919 for 95,000 francs, A.S. Carcassonne sold it a year later to the town council who built the two present stands, one which seats about 3,000 and the other opposite which provides shelter for a similar number. At that time they also laid the banked cycle track. Apart from the addition of lattice tower corner floodlights, there have been no fundamental changes to the ground's original design, although Domec's present capacity of less than 10,000 is way below the record figure of 23,500, set on 22 May, 1949 for the Championship Final between A.S. Carcassonne and Marseille.

Because France had not yet adopted the 4-tackle rule, the first international to be played at Carcassonne, in 1967, was under the old rules, of which France took full advantage to retain possession for long periods. Full-back Lacaze's third drop goal looked to have sealed the match until Clive Sullivan produced a spectacular 77th minute try to give Britain a dramatic victory. The man of the match, however, was Alan Hardisty who scored two masterly touchdowns in his first game as Britain's captain. As with New Zealand, Britain have never lost at Domec, although the Aussies have found it a far more harrowing place.

Later in 1967 France beat Australia 10-3, with all their points coming from the boot of stand-off Jean Capdouze; whilst in

PAU Although Pau XIII were founder members of the league in 1934, when they played at Stade Bourbaki, they were very much isolated inside a rugby union stronghold and permanently under attack. The only international played at Pau was during the 1972 World Cup, when Leeds stand-off John Holmes scored an international record 26 points (10 goals and 2 tries) in Great Britain's 53-19 defeat of New Zealand. The local press, who had earlier emphasised the league authorities' *"extreme difficulties"* in securing

Phil Lowe in full flight against New Zealand at Pau in 1972.

both ends having substantial semi-circular standing terraces, which were flattened in 1987 to allow for the construction of an eight-lane Olympic standard athletic track.

In 1977, when Albi reached the Grand Final against Carcassonne, because of extremely bad weather conditions this prestigious match was transferred by the French Rugby League from Toulouse to Albi. Both sets of directors were in agreement over this unprecedented move which resulted in a town record crowd, estimated at over 20,000 (18,325 paying), watching R.C. Albi win their fifth and, so far, last title, 19-10.

Shortly afterwards, Le Stadium was then the scene of another historic event when, on Sunday 14 October, 1979, Papua New Guinea played their first ever test in Europe. A highlight of the game was the 80 yard try by left-winger Volu Kapani in the 55th minute which put Papua New Guinea into a 9-8 lead, and it was only in the last ten minutes that an over-confident French side came out on top, 16-9.

Le Stadium
1979 France 16 Papua New Guinea 9   2,415

NARBONNE Since being officially opened on 29 August, 1976, the **Parc des Sports d'Egassiairal**, which is now called the **Stade de l'Amitie**, has been the regular venue for the national knock-out Cup finals. In 1994, however, whilst this event was transferred to Carcassonne, Narbonne staged its first Championship final when XIII Catalan took their tenth title by defeating village side Pia, 6-4.

On the 20 May this year Pia went one better by winning the Max Rousie Shield for the first time in their history by beating favourites St. Esteve, 12-10. This game, watched by a crowd of 13,200 paying spectators and a national television news audience, gave rugby league its highest profile for many years. And with over 250 teams also taking part in mini league on the three adjoining training pitches, the day was very reminiscent of the stadium's opening ceremony in 1976, which was followed by a children's athletic meeting on the tartan track, and a local sports festival.

The stadium initially seated 20,000 in its two cantilevered stands, but its capacity has since been raised to about 25,000 with further development at one end. At the opposite end, what must be the largest double-glazing contract in the world now protects the pitch and the

le **Stade du Hameau** for this game, were also impressed with the outstanding two-try performance of Hull Kingston Rovers' second-row, Phil Lowe. Despite live television, some 7,500 spectators (5,467 paying) attended the game, which was also filmed by Spanish television.

Since then the stadium has been refurbished with the opening, in October, 1983 of a new 4,600-seater fully-cantilevered grandstand, opposite which is a temporary stand seating 3,200. Unfortunately, there is no longer a rugby league club in the town to avail itself of these new facilities.

Le Stade du Hameau
World Cup 1972 Great Britain 53 New Zealand 19 7,500

ALBI Another founder member club, R.C. Albi, have also been honoured only once with a full international. Their ground, **Le Stadium,** which has a 1,800-seater cantilevered grandstand and a small (unseated) stand opposite for 1,200, was opened in 1964. Despite these modest figures, the stadium used to accommodate thousands more, thanks to

problem. Progress was steady during the first few years. In 1922 the terraces, then thirty inches high, were cut down by half to increase capacity, a big stone wall was erected at the Stanley Street end, and caretaker Rangi Hayward could put aside his previous hand and horse-pulled mowers and use a motorised model. Electric lighting was installed and a match even held under that lighting in 1923. But it was to be 1975 before floodlights were erected, and they were upgraded twelve years later.

Hot showers had been provided by the time Jonty Parkin's 1924 Lions arrived, and the New Zealand team celebrated by achieving its first win over Britain on home soil. *"Gig"* Wetherill scored the first test try on the park, and replacement Frank Delgrosso the first goal when he converted New Zealand's third try. Player comfort was further improved in 1929 with the purchase of a heating plant from the tepid baths.

The original 1921 grandstand, which held 640 patrons, was doubled in size in 1922, but within a decade could not handle the crowds. Auckland R. L. chairman G. Grey Campbell was the motivating force behind its replacement, and in 1934 a record club attendance of 17,000 applauded as Governor-General Lord Bledisloe declared open the 2,000-

The opening of Carlaw Park in 1921.

seat wooden edifice which is still in use. Generations of rugby league writers have gingerly climbed the rear stairway and roof-top walkway into the press box which seems to hover above the grandstand touchline, offering an unparalleled view of the action.

Records attribute the 1928 British tourists as attracting the biggest (estimated) rugby league crowd to Carlaw Park, with 28,000 watching the Kiwis' 17-13 win in the first test. The current capacity is 17,000, with 2,000 seated in the Railway Stand, 7,500 on the concrete terraces, and standing room for another 7,500. The terraces were concreted and covered in 1954, after the Auckland R. L. borrowed £18,790 from the New Zealand R. L. Professional boxing, international soccer, supercross motorcycling, and American evangelist Billy Graham have featured at Carlaw Park, which also had a golf driving range from 1965 to 1968. A second playing field at the Stanley Street end, running at right angles to the main ground, was used for club football until 1993.

Carlaw Park was purchased by the Auckland R. L. from the Auckland Hospital Board for $200,000 in October, 1974, financed by a loan of $180,000 from the hospital authorities. That was a bargain, with the land being valued as worth millions of dollars in the 1990s. The railway embankment behind the Railway Stand was bought from Railcorp for $35,000 in January, 1994, while the road access from Stanley Street to Carlaw Park cost $239,500 in 1993.

The muddy state of Carlaw Park frequently frustrated visiting and home teams alike, though one Australian journalist was the victim of a prank when he reported that surface water appeared whenever it was high-tide in the nearby harbour! But the condemnation by one French manager that Carlaw Park was *"mud, mud, mud"* has not been echoed for some time. Between 1985 and 1993 the surface was greatly improved by sand slitting and laying of a sand carpet, and the installation of a sprinkler system with electronic timing.

No other ground in the rugby league world has so dominated a country's international programme. Carlaw Park has been the venue of 59 of New Zealand's 95 home tests, and eight of its eleven World Cup fixtures. Between 1920 and 1992 the Kiwis played 67 of their 95 test or World Cup games at *"headquarters"*. With Auckland provincial teams often being the equal of New Zealand test sides, Carlaw Park was indeed a graveyard for overseas teams. Of the many memorable matches staged there, the only test of

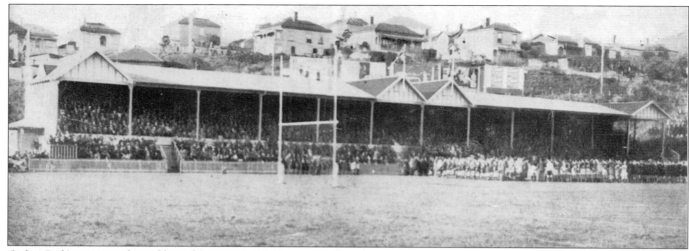

Carlaw Park's main stand, possibly on the occasion of the farewell to the 1939 Kiwis before their war-curtailed tour of Great Britain.

the 1951 French tour stands supreme for sheer drama. Kiwi scrum-half Jimmy Haig had his cheekbone fractured in the 10th minute but, despite being a man short, the Kiwis wrested a 14-7 lead. Midway through the second half French hooker Martin refused to go when ordered off for throwing mud at referee Jim Griffin, but French manager Antoine Blain and New Zealand R. L. president Jack Redwood escorted Martin to the sideline. The twelve remaining Frenchmen surged back and edged ahead at 15-14. Worse for New Zealand, stand-off George Menzies suffered a broken jaw and followed Haig to hospital. Only seconds remained as the Kiwi backs launched a last, desperate raid, and winger Bevan Hough was obstructed. The penalty, just in from touch on the 25-yard line, was goaled by full-back Des White to complete a 16-15 scoreline after the full-time hooter had sounded.

In modern times the 1985 trans-Tasman series would take some beating. Having lost the first match narrowly at Brisbane's Lang Park, the Kiwis were beaten in the last 30 seconds at Carlaw Park as Wally Lewis and Garry Jack sent John Ribot away for a converted try and a 10-6 victory. But one week later coach Graham Lowe, captain Mark Graham, and a magnificent Kiwi combination whitewashed Australia 18-0 to take sweet revenge. The previous season Fred Ah Kuoi had led the Kiwis to an unprecedented 3-0 cleansweep over Great Britain, with two of the tests at Carlaw Park.

Unfortunately, today Carlaw Park's future is very much in doubt. The New Zealand R. L. justified its seemingly permanent move to Mount Smart Stadium in 1993 by

Watched by Phil Jackson, the New Zealand winger Cyril Eastlake is tackled by Billy Boston during the second test in 1954 - Central Press/Science & Society Picture Library.

pointing out Carlaw Park could not have catered for the 22,000-plus crowd which attended the first Australian test. When Auckland Warriors, after a long and often vigorous debate, settled on Mount Smart for their 1995 Winfield Cup entry, the chances of big developments at Carlaw Park were virtually extinguished. Consequently, with the land valued at $8 million and the park's running costs up to $300,000 a year, in November, 1994 the Auckland Rugby League voted by 11-9, sixteen clubs failing to send representatives to the meeting, to sell the famous old ground. As the issue has strongly divided the clubs, however, at the time of writing Carlaw Park had still not been put on market and no announcement had been made as to its future.

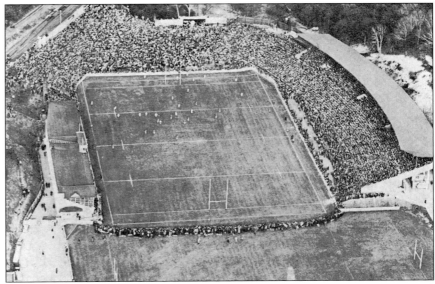

Above – A view of Carlaw Park during one of the 1958 tests against Great Britain

Left – Carlaw Park, February, 1995, looking towards the old main stand on the railway side. It will be noted that the second field is now used for car parking - The New Zealand Herald.

Carlaw Park

1924 New Zealand 16 Great Britain 8	22,000
1928 New Zealand 17 Great Britain 13	28,000
1932 New Zealand 9 Great Britain 24	25,000
1932 New Zealand 18 Great Britain 20	6,500
1935 New Zealand 22 Australia 14	20,000
1935 New Zealand 8 Australia 29	9,000
1935 New Zealand 8 Australia 31	20,000
1936 New Zealand 8 Great Britain 10	25,000
1936 New Zealand 11 Great Britain 23	17,000
1937 New Zealand 8 Australia 12	12,000
1937 New Zealand 16 Australia 15	20,000
1946 New Zealand 13 Great Britain 8	10,000
1949 New Zealand 10 Australia 13	12,361
1950 New Zealand 20 Great Britain 13	20,000
1951 New Zealand 16 France 15	19,229
1953 New Zealand 16 Australia 18	16,033
1954 New Zealand 7 Great Britain 27	22,097
1954 New Zealand 6 Great Britain 12	6,186
1955 New Zealand 9 France 19	20,500
1955 New Zealand 11 France 6	12,000
1958 New Zealand 15 Great Britain 10	25,000
1958 New Zealand 15 Great Britain 32	25,000
1960 New Zealand 9 France 2	17,914
1960 New Zealand 9 France 3	14,007
1961 New Zealand 12 Australia 10	11,485
1961 New Zealand 8 Australia 10	12,424
1962 New Zealand 19 Great Britain 0	14,976
1962 New Zealand 27 Great Britain 8	16,411
1963 New Zealand 3 South Africa 4 (Unofficial)	–
1964 New Zealand 24 France 16	10,148
1964 New Zealand 10 France 2	7,279
1965 New Zealand 8 Australia 13	13,295
1965 New Zealand 7 Australia 5	11,383
1966 New Zealand 8 Great Britain 25	14,494
1966 New Zealand 14 Great Britain 22	10,657
World Cup 1968 England 2 France 7	15,760
World Cup 1968 New Zealand 10 France 15	18,000
1969 New Zealand 10 Australia 20	13,459
1969 New Zealand 18 Australia 14	9,848
1970 New Zealand 15 Great Britain 19	15,948
1970 New Zealand 16 Great Britain 33	13,137
1971 New Zealand 24 Australia 3	13,917
1974 New Zealand 13 Great Britain 8	10,466
1974 New Zealand 0 Great Britain 20	11,574
World Champ.1975 New Zealand 17 England 17	12,000
World Champ.1975 New Zealand 13 Wales 8	9,368
World Champ.1975 New Zealand 8 Australia 24	20,000
World Cup 1977 Great Britain 23 France 4	10,000
World Cup 1977 New Zealand 12 Australia 27	18,500
World Cup 1977 New Zealand 28 France 20	8,000
1979 New Zealand 8 Great Britain 16	9,000
1979 New Zealand 18 Great Britain 11	7,000
1980 New Zealand 6 Australia 27	12,321
1980 New Zealand 6 Australia 15	9,706
1981 New Zealand 26 France 3	12,200
1981 New Zealand 25 France 2	8,100
1983 New Zealand 4 Australia 16	18,000
1983 New Zealand 60 Papua New Guinea 20	7,000
1984 New Zealand 12 Great Britain 0	10,238
1984 New Zealand 32 Great Britain 16	7,967
1985 New Zealand 6 Australia 10	19,132
1985 New Zealand 18 Australia 0	15,327
1986 New Zealand 8 Australia 22	14,566
1988 New Zealand 66 Papua New Guinea 14	8,392
1991 New Zealand 60 France 6	7,000
1992 New Zealand 66 Papua New Guinea 10	3,000
1992 New Zealand 16 Great Britain 19	10,223

Eden Park The staging of the 1988 World Cup final at Eden Park, home of Auckland rugby union and cricket, was not quite a unique occasion. Rugby League was played there in 1912, before rugby union became the winter tenant, while seven years later Auckland beat Hawkes Bay in a provincial match at Eden Park.

The land upon which New Zealand's premier sports stadium now sits was rough, swampy farmland, pitted with tussock and scarred by low stone walls as late as 1899. Some friendly cricket games were held before district inter-club cricket was introduced in 1903 and the Eden club made a successful bid for the area. An official opening was held on 9 November, 1903. The Auckland Cricket Association assumed responsibility for Eden Park in 1911-12, and after lengthy negotiations the Auckland Rugby Union signed a 21-year lease on 1 August, 1914.

Eden Park became Auckland's rugby union test venue when South Africa toured in 1921, and cricket tests since 1929-30 have produced wildly fluctuating results. It was the scene of New Zealand's first victory over the 1955-6 West Indians, but only twelve months earlier England had bowled the home team out for a world record low of 26. In 1950 the Empire Games opening ceremony and track and field events were held at Eden Park.

Kiwi winger Bevan Hough won a silver medal in the long jump at those games. Verdun Scott, a utility back on the ill-fated 1939 Kiwi visit to Britain, regularly distinguished himself on Eden Park as an Auckland and New Zealand opening batsman after the war which curtailed his rugby league tour.

World Cup fever swept New Zealand leading up to 9 October, 1988 and temporary seating was erected to increase Eden Park's capacity to 47,343, easily the biggest attendance at a rugby league match in New Zealand. But for Kiwi fans the game did not live up to expectations.

Australia, led by Wally Lewis until he retired with a broken arm, scored the first 25 points and cruised to a 25-12 victory.

When the New Zealand R. L. sought to re-hire Eden Park for test football, the rugby union-dominated trust board, which controls the grounds, declined, saying that the World Cup final had been a one-off occurrence outside the normal winter season.

World Cup final 1988 New Zealand 12 Australia 25   47,363

Eden Park, February, 1995 - The New Zealand Herald.

Ericsson Stadium (formerly **Mount Smart Stadium**)

Stern opposition was mounted against Mount Smart Stadium by many traditional rugby league fans who preferred the intimacy of Carlaw Park, where the big *"hits"* could not only be seen, but heard, and almost felt! After 15,000 of them had tasted test football, Mount Smart-style, in the 1989 World Cup-rated loss to Australia, less than 8,000 returned to see the 1990 Lions clinch their series with a 16-14 second test success.

The traditionalists argued they were too far away from the action because of the athletics track between the football field and the seating areas. It was also claimed Mount Smart was remote, not served by public transport, and had no facilities nearby. In 1993, however, almost 23,000 spectators thrilled to the first-ever trans-Tasman draw in 80 matches and 85 years as Australia escaped with a fortuitous 14-14 result.

When the Auckland Warriors preferred Mount Smart over Carlaw Park (comparing their options to the Brisbane Broncos decision to adopt ANZ Stadium at the expense of Lang Park), the 1990 Commonwealth Games stadium had its rugby league destiny decided.

Located in the Penrose industrial district of Auckland on a land area of 22 hectares, Mount Smart, which has been renamed the Ericsson Stadium following a sponsorship, lies within the crater of an extinct volcano and was for many years a quarry. Development for athletics began in the early 1960s when the sport had a high profile in New Zealand because of the feats of Olympic champions Peter Snell and Murray Halberg. A Crown reserve, Mount Smart was vested in the Auckland Regional Authority in 1979 to develop as a multi-purpose sport and recreation centre. A second football field is also encircled by another synthetic athletics track, with terraces and grass banks capable of holding 10,000 spectators. The Supertop, a mammoth tent behind the main grandstand, can also accommodate 12,500 people for indoor events. Before the Commonwealth Games, the main stadium hosted the home games of New Zealand's march to the 1982 World Cup soccer finals in Spain and some representative rugby union and American football exhibitions have also been featured.

A major NZ$8 million face-lift, which included improvements to the already adequate floodlighting, before the Warriors' Winfield Cup debut was underwritten by the Auckland Regional Council. Paramount in the plans was the need to bring spectators nearer the action by erecting additional seating across the existing running track. Of the stadium's 22,000 seats, 9,000 are under cover in the main two-tier Western Stand where there are now 40 corporate boxes, 19 corporate booths, and the Immortals Club, the latter which is situated in the former media centre under the grandstand

An artist's impression of the Ericsson Stadium after improvements to the stands for Auckland Warriors's entry to the Australian premiership.

roof. A new open stand, seating 7,000, was built opposite, and one also erected at the southern end accommodating a further 5,000 spectators. Together with two grassed embankments the Ericsson Stadium can now hold approximately 32,000 for Warriors' games, a figure which was sold out weeks in advance of their historic opening game against Brisbane Broncos on 10 March, 1995. In their first five home fixtures the Warriors averaged more than 28,300, having budgeted on average attendances of only 11,000.

Ericsson Stadium	
1989 New Zealand 14 Australia 22	15,000
1990 New Zealand 14 Great Britain 16	7,843
1993 New Zealand 14 Australia 14	22,994
1995 New Zealand 22 France 6	15,000

CHRISTCHURCH

Sydenham Park Originally set up under the Public Reserves Act of 1881 as a recreation ground, Sydenham Park is a typically inner-city Christchurch suburban park, a green patch bounded on two sides by busy streets, with a bowling green, tennis club and pensioners' cottages adjacent. There is a pavilion in one corner, shared by local cricket and hockey clubs, built in 1973.

The park is little changed from 1919 when New Zealand beat Australia 26-10 at rugby league, other than the current pavilion replacing a wooden structure which then served as changing rooms. Spectators stood around the perimeter of the playing area to witness the home side's only success in a four-match series.

Referee Arthur Brunsden infuriated the Australians with his interpretations of the rules. Australian reports described his rulings as *"eccentric"*; but a Christchurch newspaper praised him as *"a first-class referee, sticking closely to the New Zealand rules, which resulted in frequent penalties against the visitors, whose play is, in certain small features, a little different."*

Sydenham Park was the venue for many inter-provincial matches until the Show Grounds became permanent headquarters, and was used for club football until relinquished by rugby league when some Christchurch City Council grounds were reallocated some years ago.

Sydenham Park	
1919 New Zealand 26 Australia 10	7,200

Lancaster Park Only two rugby league matches have been held on Lancaster Park's main oval, the home of cricket and rugby union in Christchurch. Great Britain beat New Zealand 19-3 in the second test of the 1920 series, and accounted for the Canterbury provincial side 29-14 two days later. In 1921 the Addington and Sydenham clubs met on the south ground as part of a benefit day for a deceased representative player in both rugby codes.

Otherwise, Lancaster Park has been the subject of frequent requests by the rugby league authorities to play there, and just as many rebuffs by the rugby union-dominated Victory Park Board which administers it. Ironically, Lancaster Park had been opened free of debt in 1920 by Dr H. T. J. Thacker, who was not only Mayor of Christchurch but also President of the Canterbury R. L. The most bitter battle occurred when Britain toured in 1946, and was to play South Island in Christchurch. Controversy ranged for months, even into the New Zealand House of Parliament, and was further inflamed by rugby union authorities scheduling a match between Canterbury and New Zealand Army for the same day. Eventually the rugby union conceded to the extent that it waived its right to the Show Grounds for the day and agreed to an earlier kick-off so that many fans could get there by tram from Lancaster Park.

Lancaster Park 1959 on the occasion of the rugby union international between New Zealand and the British Lions - V. C. Browne & Son.

Lancaster Park was originally opened in 1881. Albert Shaw's England XI met XVIII of Canterbury in the first representative cricket match, and it was New Zealand's first test venue in 1929-30. Peter Snell set world 800 metres and 880 yard running records on its grass track in 1962. In the past cycling and harness racing, Davis Cup tennis, national athletics, and Australasian swimming championships, hockey and soccer internationals, war-time baseball, marching, and even exhibition hurling, were held there. Big crowds attended royal visits, a Billy Graham crusade, a Pope John Paul II blessing, and a Tina Turner concert. But the attendance record of 62,000 was set at a Dire Straits concert. Its capacity has been reduced to about 35,000 by ground developments.

The construction of a new grandstand, comprised mostly of corporate suites, in 1994 was the first stage of planned developments which include floodlighting. Old prejudices have been diluted sufficiently for park authorities to seek major rugby league fixtures in their quest to promote Lancaster Park as an international sports and entertainment venue.

Lancaster Park	
1920 New Zealand 3 Great Britain 19	10,000

English Park Although the Canterbury R. L. had its own ground, Monica Park, it hosted the deciding test of the 1928 Great Britain tour at the then Canterbury Football Association-

English Park, 1950 - V. C. Browne & Son.

owned (since 1923) English Park in the near-city suburb of St. Albans. The match was a box-office bonanza, so much so that the police ordered the gates closed with 21,000 spectators crammed inside and thousands of others locked out. The players responded in fitting fashion. Tries by British backs Les Fairclough and Tommy Askin either side of half-time eventually saw the tourists through to a nail-biting 6-5 decision.

English Park is the traditional home of soccer in Christchurch, though the playing field is encircled by a cycling track. It is now the property of the Christchurch City Council, which purchased it when the Football Association was experiencing difficulties in 1943. A wooden grandstand looks out to an open stand, a low sweeping embankment, and a modern amenities building. The park was considered as a possible cycling venue for the 1974 Commonwealth Games but the cost of upgrading it was considered too great. The first floodlit rugby league club match in the city, between Linwood and Marist, was played there on 30 September, 1970.

English Park	
1928 New Zealand 5 Great Britain 6	21,000

Monica Park (later called **Athletic Park**) International rugby league's nomadic existence in Christchurch continued when Great Britain beat New Zealand 25-14 at the Canterbury R. L.'s own Monica Park in 1932. Although English Park was again offered by the Football Association there was concern a cinder track had been constructed near its playing field. Monica Park, in suburban Woolston, was also said to have a superior tram service, better crowd control, and more wind shelter.

Named after the wife of Canterbury R. L. president Dr H. T. J. Thacker, the ground was opened on 18 April, 1925 by Sir Joseph Ward (then between terms as New Zealand's Prime Minister). It featured a grandstand capable of seating 1,000 people above four dressing rooms, hot showers, a tea room, and a ladies room. The enclosure accommodated another 2,000 spectators and was to be raised. Five months later Canterbury scored its first win over Auckland by 6-5 in muddy conditions, a result not to be repeated anywhere for 37 years. But while there were some great days at Monica Park, they were more than offset by years of antagonism over its administration and financing. By 1928 three of the 33 acres had been sold for housing. As a gimmick *"motorcycle football"* was once introduced as half-time entertainment!

Jim Sullivan leads out his side for the test at Monica Park in 1932.

Monica Park was reopened as Athletic Park on 19 July, 1947, with the staging of a Queen Carnival as the first step towards raising the £10,000 needed to purchase the land and renovate the buildings. Australia beat South Island 38-8 there in 1949 (after an application for the Show Grounds had been turned down). By 1955 the Athletic Park mortgage had been reduced by only £1,000 and the grandstand needed a major overhaul. In January, 1957 Kerridge Odeon advised Athletic Park was not suitable as a drive-in theatre and two months later Canterbury clubs voted the land be sold. Some went for housing, the rest was retained for sport as nearby Linwood High School's playing fields.

Monica Park	
1932 New Zealand 14 Great Britain 25	5,000

Addington Show Grounds Although the Canterbury Agricultural and Pastoral Association's Show Grounds complex in the inner suburb of Addington has rugby league links tracing back to the very first fixture in Christchurch, it was fifth in the city to host a test match.

On 7 September, 1912 a Canterbury team lost by a last minute penalty goal to Wellington, 5-4, in the city's introduction to rugby league, and the Show Grounds was also the venue for the first club matches the next April.

The A and P Association had moved to Addington in 1887, having purchased 35 acres from the Reverend Joseph Twigger at £200 per acre and being gifted another five acres after his death. A well, reputed to be the deepest in New Zealand at 319 feet 10 inches was sunk, and a wooden grandstand (capacity 1,600) was completed in 1896. Harness racing was held there until 1899.

By 1917 rugby union was the regular winter tenant, though other sports were played occasionally. It was at the Show Grounds that the 1936 and 1946 Great Britain rugby league sides beat South Island opponents. The Show Grounds achieved test status on 29 July, 1950, when the Kiwis scored a 16-10 success over the British in front of 10,000 spectators.

Both rugby codes applied for winter occupancy from 1951, with the A and P officials favouring rugby league's bid for an

The Show Grounds at the 1963 A & P Show before the present stands were built. In the top left corner on the western side is the grandstand of the Addington Raceway (trotting) - V. C. Browne & Son.

initial five-year lease. In all, nine tests and two World Cup fixtures have been held there, second only in New Zealand to Auckland's Carlaw Park.

Development of the ground accelerated in the mid-1960s. The main grandstand which seats 2,400 and contains the players' facilities, was opened in 1967, when embankments were raised at both ends and at the western flank of the two end-on-end football fields. An old Secretary's Stand and small wooden stand on the eastern side were demolished. The Canterbury R. L. contributed an interest-free loan of $60,000 towards the $200,000 costs.

The original wooden grandstand on the western side became victim to the notorious *"Addington Arsonist"* in 1975 and was replaced by a 1,600-seat structure. Because

A view of the Show Grounds from the main stand showing the Number 2 Stand and the southern embankment - Richard Cosgrove.

the destroyed stand was insured for less than replacement cost, the Canterbury R. L. paid 16 years advance rent, totalling $85,000, to roof the new stand.

What was once a second inter-club playing field behind the main stand had become a camping ground. Floodlights to the value of $20,000 were installed on the main field in 1974, and the No2 field was lit at a cost of $100,000 in 1989. Rock concerts, supercross motorcycling meetings, American football, exhibitions, and, of course, various animal shows, parades, and competitions have been staged at the Show Grounds.

New Zealand made winning rugby league debuts there against Great Britain (1950), Australia (1953), and France (1964), but the Lions struck back with three test wins and a World Cup victory in the 1970s. Dane Sorensen kicked six goals in his 1975 Kiwi World Cup debut when France was beaten 27-0 on a day when hypothermia was a distinct threat. Gary Freeman signalled his arrival on the international scene with two tries as a substitute in the 12-10 win over Great Britain which advanced New Zealand into the 1988 World Cup final.

The biggest officially recorded rugby league crowd up to that time, 9,536, packed in to see Canterbury beat Auckland in the 1993 first division championship final. By then the future of the Show Grounds was clouded with A and P authorities wishing to develop a rural site in the near future. The 38 acres, with motor camp, football facilities, buildings, houses, yards, and pavilions had a Government valuation of $5.8 million. But rugby league is likely to stay at Addington, with the Christchurch City Council indicating it will purchase the football fields and lease them back to the code. The Canterbury Rugby League has set itself a fund-raising target of $500,000 as negotiations continue.

A Show Grounds rugby league attendance record, officially recorded at 12,811, was set on the night of 18 January, 1995 when Canterbury were beaten 26-12 by Auckland Warriors in the latter's first trial match.

Among the guests were officials of many other sports. But it is unlikely any of them signalled the start of their own competitions in the manner of Peter McLeod, the chairman of the Warriors, who bungy-jumped from a helicopter at the Show Grounds as part of the pre-match entertainment!

Addington Show Grounds	
1950 New Zealand 16 Great Britain 10	10,000
1953 New Zealand 25 Australia 5	5,509
1964 New Zealand 18 France 8	4,935
1970 New Zealand 9 Great Britain 23	8,600
1974 New Zealand 8 Great Britain 17	6,316
World Champ. 1975 New Zealand 27 France 0	2,500
World Cup 1977 New Zealand 12 Great Britain 30	7,000
1979 New Zealand 7 Great Britain 22	8,500
1984 New Zealand 28 Great Britain 12	3,824
1988 New Zealand 12 Great Britain 10	8,525
1991 New Zealand 32 France 10	2,000

Queen Elizabeth II Park When the New Zealand R.L. decided to play the 1989 trans-Tasman Tests in large multi-purpose stadiums, Queen Elizabeth II Park, in Christchurch's eastern suburbs, was hired after Lancaster Park was again unavailable. An athletics stadium with an international swimming pool backing onto it, the QEII complex was built for the 1974 Commonwealth Games. Temporary turf was placed over some of the artificial athletics surfaces to bring the playing area up to international requirements.

The move was justified when 17,000 attended, many more than the Show Grounds could have accommodated. However, Australia won easily and the stadium lacked atmosphere. After the Commonwealth Games most of the western side had been dismantled (the capacity dropping from 34,000 to 20,000) and crowd noise from the

A view of Queen Elizabeth II Park from the main stand during the test against Australia in 1989 - The New Zealand Rugby League Annual.

171

grandstands dissipated over the few rows of seating left and out to barren countryside.

A weakened British side did not draw well in 1990, and after New Zealand lost the first two tests, few more than 3,000 attended the third at QEII Park. Those who stayed away missed an entertaining 21-18 Kiwi victory. An adjacent playing-field, an athletics warm-up area at the 1974 Games, has regularly been used for club rugby league.

Queen Elizabeth II Park	
1989 New Zealand 6 Australia 26	17,000
1990 New Zealand 21 Great Britain 18	3,133

DUNEDIN

Tahuna Park Cut away from a sandhill in the popular Dunedin seaside suburb of St. Kilda, Tahuna Park was formed in time for the third annual parade of the Otago Agricultural and Pastoral Association in October, 1884. The A and P links remain, with the main ground doubling as judging ring for horses and cattle, and stables situated alongside the second and third playing fields. Tahuna Park gives little hint it has hosted rugby union (1905) and rugby league (1924) internationals. When the All Blacks beat Australia 14-3 the more comfortable of the 3,000 spectators were seated in a

A view of Tahuna Park during the 1993 Under-15 Grand Final showing part of the original old grandstand. - Carey Clements.

grandstand erected in 1902 and which still stands. Army camps, athletics events, and brass band contests preceded the third rugby league test of Great Britain's 1924 tour.

Controversy raged for some time before the match as other prospective venues, such as Forbury Park and Culling Park, were declined by the powerful Otago Rugby Union, which had the backing of the Dunedin City Council. Tahuna Park was made available a few days before the test, the fledgling Otago R. L. paying the Otago R. U. £75 and the A and P Society £40. Despite the Rugby Union staging a counter-attraction at the Carisbrook ground, 14,000 spectators travelled by car, tram, horse, and foot to watch Jonty Parkin's team win 31-18.

In September, 1955 the first floodlit rugby league match in Dunedin was held at Tahuna Park, Celtic beating Athletic 24-20. The ground is still used for rugby league, but is only available for representative or major club fixtures on Sundays. The rugby union authorities still control the best draining surface in the city and play club games there on Saturdays.

Tahuna Park	
1924 New Zealand 18 Great Britain 31	14,000

Caledonian Ground When Jonty Parkin captained his second Lions team to New Zealand in 1928 the second test was held at Dunedin's Caledonian Ground. Unfortunately, this time the warfare was not between rival rugby codes but opposing players in a bitter encounter, won 13-5 by the British.

Affectionately known to Dunedin citizens as *"the Cale"*, the ground was New Zealand's seventh first-class cricket venue in the 1879-80 summer (only four games of that standing were played, the last in 1904-5) In 1908 the ground found a niche in rugby league history when Otago met Southland in the first match on New Zealand's South Island. About 2,000 spectators saw Otago win 11-8.

Rugby league in Otago had flourished between the 1924 and 1928 tests. The Caledonian Ground was leased and considerable money spent on improvements. A combination of the Great Depression, poor administration, rates, and other expenses forced the Otago R. L. to sell the ground in 1930. Within a few years the game was in recess. In lieu of £1,100 ($2,200) in rates the Otago R. L. gave its own ground,

The referee takes Bill Burgess by the arm before sending the British forward off the field during the 1928 test at the Caledonian Ground.

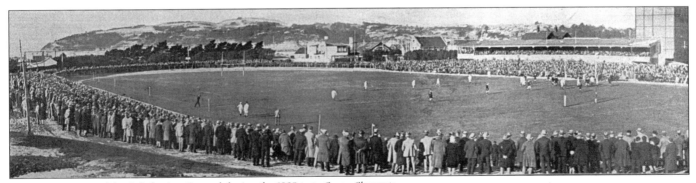

A panoramic view of the Caledonian Ground during the 1928 test - Carey Clements.

Tonga Park, to Dunedin City Council. When the code was revived in 1953 that piece of real estate was valued at about $1 million. The *"new"* Otago R. L. had to pay the council rent for one humble pitch not wanted by other sports.

The Caledonian Ground itself has in the 1990s been coveted by a supermarket chain as a suitable site for development. It has been for years the home of the Otago Football Association and the Otago Amateur Athletics Association, the soccer field also being encircled by a concrete cycling track. On 2 April, 1995 the adjacent Caledonian pub, dating from 1880, was demolished to make way for a car yard.

Caledonian Ground
1928 New Zealand 5 Great Britain 13   12,000

Wingham Park at the test in 1954 - P. E. Kerridge.

GREYMOUTH

Wingham Park More than one English writer has described Greymouth, on the South Island's West Coast, as the Workington of the south. This town (population 7,500) alongside the Grey River and its surrounding mining and milling villages of Blackball, Ngahere, Runanga, Taylorville, and Dobson has long boasted rugby league as its major sport and proudly boasts more than 50 Internationals.

In the heyday of the mines and mills, many mighty forwards came out of the Coast, among them Jim Calder and Billy Glynn in the 1930s, Chang Newton, Bill McLennan, Charlie McBride, and Frank Mulcare in the '40s and '50s, Jock Butterfield and Trevor Kilkelly through to the '60s, and Tony Coll and Ray Baxendale in the '70s. Strong three-quarters Nippy Forrest, Graham Kennedy, Reece Griffiths and Mocky Brereton complemented gifted inside backs such as George Menzies and Wigan's famed *"Blackball Bullet"* Cecil Mountford. These days West Coast has second division status, and players such as Whetu Taewa, Quentin Pongia and Brent Stuart travel east across the rugged Southern Alps to Canterbury in quest of higher honours.

Wingham Park hosted the second test against the 1954 British tourists, a tribute to the persuasiveness of West Coast administrator Tom McKenzie. The attendance of 4,240 was commendable in such a sparsely-populated district. Ron Ackland, later one of the game's finest second-rowers, made his debut in the centres, while Butterfield, who played most of his 36 tests at hooker, was a try scorer from the second-row in the Kiwis' 20-14 win.

Named in honour of J. D. Wingham, president of the West Coast Rugby League from 1919 to 1930, Wingham Park is situated on ten acres of freehold land at Coal Creek, just north of Greymouth on the road to Runanga. Late on sunnier winter afternoons the shadows of bush-covered hills creep across the field, though the districts' notorious rainfall has long been the curse of visiting teams hoping for a firm playing surface. Wingham Park is located outside the Greymouth borough because of the then town council's opposition to Sunday sport.

It was opened in 1930. The first grandstand was built a decade later, seating 450 people, and extensions in length and by adding uncovered seats boosted capacity to 1,500. Most work and maintenance was by voluntary labour. With typical initiative, the Coasters have recently constructed meeting and function rooms alongside the stand. Once encircled by a cinder speedway track, the ground has survived frequent flooding, and a high wind which deposited the grandstand roof across the road behind it. Optimism is high of an economic resurgence on the West Coast, with floodlighting installed at Wingham Park during the summer of 1994-5 to capitalise upon it.

Wingham Park	
1954 New Zealand 20 Great Britain 14	4,240

PALMERSTON NORTH

Show Grounds Oval The Palmerston North phenomenon has delighted rugby league followers in recent years. Many were surprised when its Show Grounds Oval became New Zealand's 17th and latest rugby league test venue during Great Britain's 1990 tour because the Manawatu province had traditionally been one of the sport's minnows. But Palmerston North (population 71,000) has convenient road, rail, and air links to other North island centres.

An attendance of 8,073 proved satisfactory in this rural and university city with its strong rugby union heritage as Garry Schofield masterminded an 11-10 Lions victory after the Kiwis had made a strong start. Schofield's field goal was the only score in the second half. Two years later New Zealand turned the tables in front of 11,548 spectators, winning 15-14 after trailing Britain by eight points. Replacement Daryl Halligan's 75th minute field goal completed the Kiwi come-back.

Chaotic scenes accompanied Palmerston North's first floodlit test, a Friday night encounter against Australia in 1993. The headlines next day were not so much about Australia's 16-8 victory in chilling rain but the lack of crowd control. At least 22,000 tickets were sold for a ground with an official capacity of 20,000, though some literature gives 16,000 as a comfortable maximum for the big grandstand and embankment surrounds. The overflow of spectators crossed the speedway/stock car track and encroached near the sidelines throughout the tense match. Players were left standing around in the final minutes when the last of the match balls was swallowed up by the crowd. A subsequent enquiry exonerated Show Grounds staff from any blame.

Administered by the Palmerston North Show Grounds Board of Control, the original Agricultural and Pastoral show site was gifted by the Crown in 1886 and adopted for rugby union football from the 1890s. It was used extensively by the New Zealand Army for training during the Boer War, and the First and Second World Wars. In 1974 the A and P Show Grounds were purchased by the Palmerston North City Council as a recreation and sporting complex and since then $12 million has been invested in development. The nearby indoor Manawatu Sports Stadium can cater for a multiplicity of sports and trade conventions. With the other pavilions and halls, a rugby union museum, and playing fields, the entire inner-city complex covers 42 acres.

Several grandstands had stood alongside the Show Grounds before the present 4,000-seater was built in the 1986/7 season after a major fire in the previous structure. Since 1963 a speedway and stock car track has encircled the field, which has also been the stage for a soccer test, touch football, sevens rugby union, military ceremonies, and national marching and band championships. Two adjacent fields have on occasions been used for local and regional rugby league games. Floodlighting of the oval was upgraded to television standard over the 1992-3 summer, and sand slitting of the turf completed in 1994. A new grandstand and adjoining indoor venue are planned before 1999.

Show Grounds Oval	
1990 New Zealand 10 Great Britain 11	8,073
1992 New Zealand 15 Great Britain 14	11,548
1993 New Zealand 8 Australia 16	22,000
1995 New Zealand 16 France 16	10,500

The Show Grounds Oval grandstand, 1990. Temporary seating can be added down to track level to increase its capacity - Palmerston North Showgrounds.

ROTORUA

International Stadium One of New Zealand's most renowned tourist towns, Rotorua is famed for its thermal pools which leave a distinct aroma of sulphur in the air - so much so that several British journalists on one rugby league tour sought to change their hotel rooms until they realised they had no escape.

The second test against the 1989 Australians was allocated to Rotorua's International Stadium, which had been opened 17 years earlier. There is covered seating for 1,600 spectators, and 5,000 uncovered seats, but the massive grassed embankment boosts the capacity to 54,000. That has never been achieved, the ground record standing at 38,000 for the rugby union match between the 1978 British Lions and the Bay of Plenty provincial team. A 1987 Rugby Union World Cup quarter-final, additional representative games in both rugby codes, and soccer internationals have also been held at the stadium.

Future plans include floodlighting, more seating, the establishment of a second playing field to be used in conjunction with a neighbouring seven-field complex, and the improvement of players' facilities and reception areas.

Rotorua's only rugby league test was a dour affair, won 8-0 by Australia after replacement Des Hasler scored the sole try. The Kiwis were left rueing the chances missed by goalkickers Kevin Iro, Tony Kemp and substitute Phil Bancroft. It was the first of 26 consecutive test appearances for impressive hooker Duane Mann. An estimated attendance of 26,000 was widely publicised but the correct figure was nearer 17,500.

International Stadium	
1989 New Zealand 0 Australia 8	17,500

WELLINGTON

Basin Reserve Wellington's Basin Reserve, New Zealand's second test venue and the first for a home match with arch rivals Australia in 1919, was given to sport, and especially cricket, by an act of God. Not long after the first settlers arrived in 1840 plans were drawn up for the lake at the top of Kent Terrace to become a basin, or inner port, once a stream had been widened into a canal. The proposal was delayed long enough by financial restrictions and other priorities for an earthquake in 1855 to elevate that end of the town and reduce the Basin Lake to a swamp.

Prison labour improved the area sufficiently for cricket to be played in 1868 and it gained first-class status when Wellington met Auckland in 1873-4. An original grandstand was replaced in 1923-4 but the most dramatic revamping occurred when the R. A. Vance Stand, new embankment seating, and landscaping, picket fence, semi-electronic scoreboard, and surface improvements were completed in November, 1980. It holds about 14,000 spectators at one-day internationals, and for many years had soccer as its main winter sport.

The New Zealanders lining up before their 44-21 defeat by Australia at the Basin Reserve in August, 1919.

The Basin Reserve in its modern form was used again for representative rugby league games from the 1980s, and also when the national club competition was introduced in 1994. It now bears little resemblance to the comparatively open ground, swept by a chilling southerly gale when New Zealand recovered from an 11-point deficit to beat Great Britain 13-11 on 6 August, 1924, and secured its first series success on home soil. Twenty-nine years later history was repeated when the Kiwis got home 12-11 to clinch the series against Clive Churchill's Australians in the Basin's fifth and most recent test.

Basin Reserve

1919 New Zealand 21 Australia 44	8,000
1920 New Zealand 10 Great Britain 11	4,000
1924 New Zealand 13 Great Britain 11	6,000
1949 New Zealand 26 Australia 21	7,737
1953 New Zealand 12 Australia 11	5,394

Athletic Park Back-to-back rugby union and rugby league tests against Australia were held on consecutive days at Athletic Park in 1990 to mark the 150th anniversary of New Zealand. The weather was unkind, particularly for the rugby league international on 19 August when the attendance of 25,000 was considered satisfactory in the circumstances. The visitors also spoiled their hosts' party by winning both matches.

Controlled by the Wellington Rugby Union, the ground was opened on 6 April, 1896. Its main stand was erected in 1929, and the double-decker Millard Stand in 1961. Athletic Park has been the subject of much debate in recent years because of its deteriorating condition, but of New Zealand's regular rugby union test venues it alone is not shared by cricket and thus is rectangular shaped. An attendance record of 57,000, set for a rugby union test against the British Isles in 1959, cannot be approached now that alterations have reduced the capacity to 39,425, of which 8,671 can be seated under cover. Apart from occasional soccer and hockey fixtures, and rugby league's brief appearance, Athletic Park's principal other use has been for rock concerts.

Athletic Park

1990 New Zealand 6 Australia 24	25,000

PAPUA NEW GUINEA – *Dave Hadfield*

Rugby league in the one country of the world where it can be indisputably termed the national sport began during the Second World War. Australian servicemen stationed in terrain that became one of the principal battlegrounds of the war against the Japanese brought the game with them.

After the war, many Australians went to work in a country for which Australia had been given responsibility and by 1948 they were playing competitive matches in both halves of the country. In Papua, a club competition grew up in the capital, Port Moresby. In the formerly German-run territory of New Guinea, separated from Papua by mountains which to this day have no road to cross them, the game took root in the major regional centres: Lae, Wau, Bulolo and Madang.

The main events were the annual matches between Papua and New Guinea representative sides, but for the first decade and more of the game in Papua New Guinea there were no Papuans or New Guineans in those sides. Rugby league in its formative phase was played exclusively by Australians, a restriction which was in tune with the general *"never the twain"* mentality of those times. Originally Australian expatriates who had gone to work in Papua New Guinea were the players, but as the various competitions, especially the one in Port Moresby, developed, players began to be imported specifically to strengthen teams. Many veterans from New South Wales and Queensland went to Papua New Guinea to earn a little money in the twilight of their careers. For others, Papua New Guinea could be the stepping stone, the most notable example being Mark Harris, who played for the Port Moresby club Paga until he was signed by Eastern Suburbs and went on to play for Australia.

Two factors transformed rugby league from the sport of the occupying workforce of administrators and technicians into the game of the people of Papua New Guinea. The first was the progress made in eradicating malaria which had resulted in many indigenous people suffering from swollen spleens, making it dangerous for them to play. The second was the emergence in Rabaul, on the New Guinean island of New Britain, of the first Papua New Guinea national to make his mark in the game. John Kaputin was such an obviously gifted athlete at the university in Port Moresby that he could not be kept out of the first grade league and he was soon playing for Papua as well. His success opened the door for rugby league to become an integrated sport.

Action from the test at the Danny Leahy Oval, Goroka, in 1990, when Great Britain lost 20-18 to Papua New Guinea - Dave Hadfield.

Slowly the direct influence of Australian players diminished, with Rod Pearce, who managed the 1991 Papua New Guinea tour to Britain and France, being one of the last. That process was more than counter-balanced by the way that the game spread to all corners of a country whose diversity is illustrated by its 700 different language groups. There are two things that hold the patchwork fabric of this complex nation together - the use of pidgin English and the playing of rugby league.

Apart from the early centres, the game has been particularly strong in the rugged and beautiful Highlands, where towns like Mount Hagen, Goroka, Kundiawa and Kainantu all have their thriving local competitions. Island Zone have been a major force at times, but secession in Bougaineville and the ravages of the volcanic eruption in Rabaul have inevitably disrupted the game there.

The 1990s have seen domestic competition refined into an inter city cup which supplements the club competitions in the individual centres. There is some limited professionalism for the players who are good enough to represent their cities and a handful have made a modest impression abroad. Philip Ralda played briefly at Bradford Northern and Dairi Kovae made several appearances for both North Sydney and the Newcastle Knights. Bal Numapo, however, failed to reach first grade during a season with Canterbury-Bankstown, despite being arguably the best player Papua New Guinea has produced. Aquila Emil, a mercurial stand-off, is now with the North Queensland Cowboys.

Papua New Guinean rugby league first impinged on the consciousness of the outside world through schoolboy tours to Australia, and a national squad visited New South Wales in 1971, playing sides representing the Sydney Second Division - now the Metropolitan Cup - Illawarra and the Central Coast. Papua New Guinea also took part in the first two Pacific Cups, reaching the final of the 1975 tournament in Port Moresby before losing to the New Zealand Maoris, but making less of an impact in New Zealand two years later.

The visit of the 1975 England World Cup squad gave Papua New Guinea its first full international match, losing 40-12 in Port Moresby, but the same venue two years later saw a convincing 37-6 win over France. In 1978, BARLA toured Papua New Guinea, playing in Rabaul, Lae (where rioting endangered the rest of the tour), Mount Hagen and Port Moresby, before winning the one international 28-7, also in Port Moresby.

Later that year, Papua New Guinea were admitted as the fifth full member of the game's International Board, making their international matches after November 1978 full tests. Their first were in France, following a visit to England that included no tests, in 1979.

Since then, Papua New Guinea's better moments have been confined to home tests. There was a draw with France in 1981 and victories over New Zealand in 1986 and Great Britain in 1990, all of which triggered nationwide celebrations. The most frenzied scenes, however, greeted the arrival of Australia - en route to Europe - in 1982 and again on their first and so far only tour in 1986. Australian Rugby League has a huge following in Papua New Guinea, where Winfield Cup jerseys are the height of fashion and every child throwing a ball around on a beach or in a jungle clearing imagines himself as his favourite Aussie star.

Away from Papua New Guinea, it has largely been a story of heavy defeats as the Kumuls have struggled to come to terms with unfamiliar conditions. The cold of a European winter is a torment for them when they tour Great Britain and France, but statistically the low point of their test history was a then record 70-8 defeat by Australia in Wagga Wagga in 1988.

In June, 1995, Papua New Guinea took the decision to join Great Britain, New Zealand and the Pacific Island nations under the umbrella of Rupert Murdoch's Super League, much to the chagrin of the Australian Rugby League. One reason for Papua New Guinea's disillusionment with the ARL was, ironically, their feeling that saturation coverage of the Winfield Cup was damaging the domestic game.

GOROKA

Danny Leahy Oval The very name of Goroka's ground is an introduction to the recent history of the town. The Leahy brothers were the first outsiders to penetrate the previously unknown world of the Eastern Highlands and the oval is named after the son of one of those pioneering brothers, who himself pioneered the game of rugby league in the area.

The Danny Leahy Oval is basically a cleared paddock, with a raised mound surrounding much of it and a scaffolding structure supporting seats along part of one side. It is fenced around to try to restrict the view of matches to paying customers, but little can be done about the hundreds of spectators who climb the trees surrounding the ground and thus get the best view of all. The fences have proved inadequate on more than one occasion when would-be spectators locked out of the ground have decided that they were going to get in.

In 1990, when Great Britain lost 20-18 at Goroka, rock-throwing latecomers were met with the usual police response of firing off tear gas, which in turn caused the game to be halted in the 14th minute. Because of this intimidating atmosphere in Papua New Guinea, visiting sides much prefer to drive to and from the grounds in a mini-bus from their hotel, rather than run the risk of being imprisoned in the very basic dressing rooms after a riotous match.

Scenes when police fired tear gas, which affected the players and caused the game to be halted in the 14th minute - Dave Hadfield.

Despite the cooler climate of Goroka, its altitude of nearly 5,000 feet makes it a difficult place for visiting sides, who invariably find the thin air a problem. Representatives matches used to be played at the nearby National Sports Institute, but the Danny Leahy Oval is now firmly established as the Highland's leading ground and the only feasible venue outside Port Moresby for tests.

Danny Leahy Oval		
1986 Papua New Guinea 26 New Zealand 36	10,000
1990 Papua New Guinea 20 Great Britain 18	10,500
1990 Papua New Guinea 4 New Zealand 36	12,000
1991 Papua New Guinea 18 France 20	11,485
1991 Papua New Guinea 2 Australia 58	13,000
1994 Papua New Guinea 12 New Zealand 28	13,000

MOUNT HAGEN

Rebiamul Oval Papua New Guinea have played just one test in Mount Hagen, the rugged frontier town that is the other population centre of the Highlands, although BARLA experienced the culture shock of playing there on the first full-length tour of Papua New Guinea by an overseas side in 1975. Even more so than Goroka, it was and is a regular feature of matches in Mount Hagen to see spectators arrive in full tribal dress.

Accompanied by a tribal warrior, BARLA's captain Bob Colgrave (right) and second row forward Alan Varty return the applause of the enthusiastic crowd at Mount Hagen during the tour in 1978 - BARLA.

Hagen's ground is the Rebiamul Oval, a simple cleared paddock with scaffolding-type seating on two sides. More than 7,500 packed into the picturesque arena for the match against Great Britain in 1984, when, after a hair-raising flight in bad weather from Madang, the Lions gained a consolation 38-20 win after six test defeats in Australia and New Zealand. The ground does not belong to the local league, being sited on church land, and there are plans to move to a new ground near the airport, upon which, it is hoped, it will be possible to stage bigger matches. But the construction of the new ground is beset by political problems and there is no telling when it might be ready for use.

Rebiamul Oval	
1984 Papua New Guinea 20 Great Britain 38	7,510

PORT MORESBY

Lloyd Robson Oval (formerly **Boroko Oval**) Boroko is the administrative centre of Port Moresby - indeed of the whole country - and it was here in the early 60s that the Port Moresby Rugby League laid out what was originally known as the Boroko Oval. The original clubhouse, which has now been extended to include 750 seats, dates from this time and is built in typical colonial style, with wooden panelling and very necessary ceiling fans.

In the early 80s, the name of the stadium was changed to the Lloyd Robson Oval, in honour of the president of the league and curator (groundsman in English terminology) of the ground. One of Robson's great achievements was to contrive to secure a steady supply of free water from the city council. That helped to give the oval what is by Port Moresby standards a healthy grass cover which it retains to this day.

The ground now includes scaffolding-type seating on the other three sides from the clubhouse, one of which is covered, giving it a capacity of around 14,500. Crowds larger than that have been credited in local newspapers, notably the 17,000 for the test against Australia in 1986, but these are unreliable estimates intended to include the not inconsiderable numbers who, in traditional Papuan New Guinean style, find a vantage point in the tress overlooking the ground.

The most recent addition to the oval has been a tier of private boxes atop the clubhouse. The ten boxes can hold another 150 people in air-conditioned comfort. For the rest, watching a match at a packed Lloyd Robson Oval can be a gruelling experience.

Lloyd Robson Oval

1975 Papua New Guinea 12 England 40	12,000
1977 Papua New Guinea 37 France 6	14,500
1978 Papua New Guinea 20 New Zealand 31	12,000
1981 Papua New Guinea 13 France 13	14,500
1982 Papua New Guinea 5 New Zealand 56	14,500
1982 Papua New Guinea 2 Australia 38	14,500
1986 Papua New Guinea 24 New Zealand 22	15,000
1986 Papua New Guinea 12 Australia 62	17,000
1987 Papua New Guinea 22 New Zealand 36	15,000
1988 Papua New Guinea 22 Great Britain 42	12,017
1990 Papua New Guinea 10 New Zealand 18	10,000
1990 Papua New Guinea 8 Great Britain 40	8,000
1991 Papua New Guinea 6 Australia 40	14,500
1993 Papua New Guinea 35 Fiji 24	14,500
1994 Papua New Guinea 16 New Zealand 30	15,000

Port Moresby's Lloyd Robson Oval, looking from the clubhouse, on the occasion of Great Britain's visit in 1990 - Dave Hadfield.

THE SOUTH PACIFIC ISLANDS – *Trevor Hunt*

There are no grounds in the world quite like those in the exotic locations of the South Pacific islands of Fiji, Tonga, Western Samoa and the Cook Islands. The surrounding lushness of the brilliantly coloured flora and fauna that proliferates with the humid climate, and the unique atmosphere generated by the warmth of the island hosts combine to provide an unforgettable experience, particularly for someone who has been reared on watching rugby league on cold damp British winter week-ends, for the most part in dilapidated, sparsely populated stadia. Even though all the Pacific grounds have something of a common feel about them, most being concrete and steel structures constructed to host the Pacific Games at various stages over the past twenty years, they are each unique in that they provide the focus for the islanders' culture and fervent nationalistic pride.

All of the islands are relatively new to rugby league, but since the inauguration of the Pacific Cup in 1986, and tours by BARLA teams in 1990 and 1994, plus the French visit to Fiji in 1994, each of the island grounds has seen a fair amount of international competition. The inclusion of Tonga, Fiji and Western Samoa in the forthcoming Centenary World Cup also provides a reason why their national stadiums should not be overlooked.

THE COOK ISLANDS

AVARUA Tereora Stadium Nestling in the lap of the Te Reinga O Pora mountain that towers some 438 metres above sea level and with the even higher Te Rua Manga, otherwise known as the Needle, protectively peering over its shoulder, the Tereora Stadium is provided with the most spectacular of backdrops by the luxuriantly jungle-clad Rorotongan mountains. The stadium is situated a couple of kilometres outside of The Cook Islands' capital, Avarua - every bit like the traditional image of a South Seas trading port - on an island that is only some 11 kilometres long by 6 kilometres wide and where a twenty minute car or bus ride is the furthest you ever need to travel.

The view from the main stand of the Tereora Stadium, Avarua, with Rortongan mountains in the background, as the Cook Islands (left) and BARLA line up for the national anthems in 1994 - Trevor Hunt.

WALES – *Trevor Delaney*

Following tours to Wales in the mid-1880s by Yorkshire and Lancashire's leading clubs, there were scores of Welshmen tempted to move north. Two notable examples are half-back William *"Buller"* Stadden (Cardiff to Dewsbury in 1886), who scored the only try in Wales' historic first win over England, at a snow-swept Crown Flatt, Dewsbury in 1890; and Oldham's former Swansea three-quarter, William McCutcheon, who was the first referee to dismiss a player in a rugby league international. The introduction of leagues in 1892 increased this demand for Welshmen; and, apart from the hundreds of other Welsh club players, we know, from Robert Gate's diligent research, that there have been 158 Welsh internationals who have changed codes since the formation of the Northern Union.

In the first official international, at Wigan in April, 1904, the Other Nationalities side were almost exclusively Welsh, and from 1935/6 Wales were able to win the European Championship on three successive occasions. However, despite the large exodus of talent from Wales, and the irregular staging of internationals on Welsh soil, rugby league has failed to establish a permanent base within the Principality. Apart from individual clubs at Pontypridd, in 1926, and Cardiff, in 1951 and 1981, only twice, in 1907 and 1949, has a professional league been successfully launched. And, significantly, both the latter initiatives came from within the Welsh community.

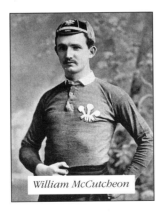
William McCutcheon

In May, 1949 the Rugby League's Welsh Commission bought Barry Town soccer club's Jenner Park, and also acquired the lease on Bridgend rugby union club's Brewery Field. An 8-club Welsh League was formed at the start of the 1949/50 season under its organiser, Harold Stacey of Neath. Although Cardiff were heavily subsidised by the Rugby League, and the Rugby League Players' Union donated a £300 trophy, there were no shortage of Welshmen and women who were prepared to back the game.

For example, Llanelli were among the league's founders, and the promoter, local bookmaker Alby Evans, had plans to develop a stadium for rugby league and speedway at the present Penygaer Fields, which he had bought for £8,000. He was prevented from doing this by the local council's compulsory purchase of the 27 acres for open space. But he was allowed to retain a portion, where games were played during the club's existence. As with the other clubs in the league, this was brie. Faced with a shortage of suitable grounds with covered accommodation, and the plundering of some of their best players by northern clubs, the Welsh League collapsed at the end of the 1954/5 season.

It was because there is no professional league in Wales at present that the Welsh side, despite impressive results against both France and Papua New Guinea in 1993/4, was originally omitted by the International Board from the Centenary World Cup. The rescinding of this decision has certainly widened the appeal of the competition, but, aware of Welsh rugby league history, it would only be a foolish man who would dare predict the date when a professional rugby league will again be functioning in Wales.

The main factor for such pessimism is to be found in the semi-professional nature of Welsh club rugby union - the very reason, ironically, why the Northern Union gained its first foothold. In January, 1907 E. M. Rees, the ex-secretary of Aberdare, who later went on to form the Northern Union club in the town, highlighted the internal problems within the supposedly-amateur game. At the subsequent Welsh Rugby Union (WRU) inquiry into the allegations of *"rampant professionalism"* it was heard that back in April, 1905 the deciding match of the Glamorgan League championship between Treorchy and Aberdare had been *"fixed"*. Unknown to the players, whom Rees alleged were paid illegal wages and exorbitant expenses, the Aberdare committee had paid £15 to Treorchy for them to play an unregistered player - the theory being that if they lost Aberdare could gain the points on appeal. The penalties, announced in September, 1907, saw the banning of the Treorchy and Aberdare committees, together with eight players. Short-term suspensions were also passed on players from Morriston, Aberdare, Swansea, Usk and Penarth, whilst a Merthyr committeeman was suspended for merely moving a resolution in favour of broken-time payments!

MERTHYR TYDFIL It was in this environment that Ebbw Vale and Merthyr Tydfil (where the first Northern Union game in Wales took place, against Oldham, on 7 September, 1907) joined the Northern Union for the 1907/8 season. They were followed by Aberdare, Barry, Mid-Rhondda (Tonypandy), and Treherbert in 1908/9. In their first two seasons, before moving to the new Athletic Ground at Rhydycar, Merthyr played at College Field, where in 1907 they lost 27-9 to New Zealand, and in 1909 beat Australia 15-13. According to the Merthyr R.U. Centenary History, College Field was on the site of the present West End Bowls Club.

Merthyr Northern Union failed to lease the nearby **Penydarren Park,** which is built on the site of a Roman fort, and was a cycling and athletics ground in the 1890s. In 1908/9 the professional soccer club, Merthyr Town, shared what is the present home of Merthyr Tydfil F.C. (formed 1945) with Merthyr R.U. (the *"Amateurs"*) before the latter went defunct.

There was clearly no love lost between the Northern Union club and its rival codes, although the Welsh League's 14-13 victory over Australia was staged on a snow-covered Penydarren Park in 1909 and watched by a crowd of 6,000. A late try by Merthyr's left-winger Cowmeadow was the decisive score of an attractive game. Looking today at the three small stands and the open terraces, it is difficult to comprehend how the ground held 21,000 for a soccer game in 1949, and that the away supporters' end was once the site of a Roman granary.

Penydarren Park, Merthyr Tydfil, 1994, looking from the end which was once the site of a Roman granary.

ABERDARE Following inspections by the tour committee, the first Northern Union international in Wales was transferred from Merthyr to Aberdare's **Athletic Ground** (earlier referred to as **Ynys Field).** This historic game took place on New Year's Day 1908, when Wales beat the New Zealand All Golds 9-8 in front of local record crowd of 15,000. This *"spectacular treat"*, gave a fillip to the game in South Wales, with at least a dozen new clubs being anticipated for the following season. The winning try was scored by Merthyr forward Dai Jones, who had played against the All Blacks in 1905. In the evening the New Zealanders watched Jim Driscoll score a second round knock-out at the Market Hall, a reminder perhaps of their afternoon's efforts when *"six of the Colonials were stretched out at different periods."*

The ground, on the Ynys Meadow to the south-east of the town, was originally owned by the Aberdare Athletic Association, who had refused its use in June, 1907 to the proposed Northern Union club. However, following the success of the above international, Aberdare were allowed to share the ground, which also incorporated a cycling track, with the Aberdare Athletic soccer club from the start of the 1908/9 season. Due to their ground being suspended, Merthyr Tydfil met Wigan, on 11 April, 1908, at the Athletic Ground immediately following the Wales-Ireland soccer international. Aberdare's first home game there was on 5 September, 1908, when they lost 56-0 to Wigan; and after finishing bottom of the league they failed to fulfil their final fixture in their only season.

Aberdare Athletic built a 1,000-seater wooden grandstand, and in 1921 plans were under way to extend this to a 4,000-seater. The ground record was set in 1921 when 20,000 watched the Wales-Scotland schoolboy international. Although the Ynys sports fields still exists, the actual stadium disappeared in the 1960s with the building of the present leisure centre, adjacent to the Aberaman RUFC ground.

Athletic Ground	
1908 Wales 9 New Zealand 8	15,000

TONYPANDY The first Anglo-Welsh international was staged by the Mid-Rhondda Social and Athletic Club, Tonypandy, at the **Athletic Ground,** Pen-y-graig, on Easter Monday, 20 April, 1908. Wales, who trailed 18-15 at half-time, and for whom Wigan's Johnny Thomas kicked a then record seven goals, beat England 35-18, in front of a crowd of 12,000.

Tonypandy, who adopted professional soccer in 1909, entertained the 1908 Australians, who won 20-6. From its opening the Athletic Ground, along Primrose Street, incorporated cycling and running tracks. It still exists today as an open rugby pitch with the bankings now overgrown.

Athletic Ground, Pen-y-graig
1908 Wales 35 England 18   12,000

EBBW VALE A company was formed to run the new Ebbw Vale club, which played its first home game against Salford on 14 September, 1907. It held a professional sports meeting, during the July Bank Holiday, 1908, to raise funds for ground-levelling, and the building of a new stand, at their former rugby union enclosure, **Bridgend Field** (later known as the **Welfare Association Sports Ground,** and now called **Eugene Cross Park**).

The first Welsh international against Australia was scheduled for Ebbw Vale in March, 1909, but was cancelled because of heavy snow. However, during their short period in the Northern Union the club hosted three internationals. On 9 April, 1910 a crowd of 4,000 saw Wales score a 39-18 victory over England, with all nine tries coming from their three-quarters. There was a similar crowd on 1 April, 1911 to see England achieve the double, having beaten Wales at Coventry. The majority of the English tries were engineered by Harold Wagstaff. In contrast to 1909, the weather was beautiful when the Australians beat Wales 28-20 on 7 October, 1911, the crowd being treated to ten tries,

Ebbw Vale circa 1908/9 season. "Chick" (T. E.) Jenkins, seated centre, was a Northern Union tourist in 1910.

including four from Will Davies, the Halifax left winger - the only player to score that number in an international whilst being on the losing side.

This first co-ordinated venture into Wales failed principally because Merthyr Tydfil, Aberdare and Barry were early strongholds of professional soccer, whilst Tonypandy, Treherbert, and Ebbw Vale were not large enough communities to support a professional rugby club. Ebbw Vale had problems in fulfilling fixtures in its rugby union days, and the expense of travelling to the north for five years finally proved too much. As the sole surviving team in Wales, Ebbw Vale resigned from the Northern Union on 3 September, 1912, their final game having been a home defeat by York on 20 April.

The Bridgend Field complex (altitude 288 metres) was renamed the Ebbw Vale Welfare Association Sports Ground in 1923, when the Association, financed by deductions from the members' wages, originally took over the 26 acres from the town's main employer, the Ebbw Vale Steel, Iron and Coal Company (Richard Thomas Ltd from 1936), before buying the freehold in 1948. Aberdare's headquarters were at the Bridge End Inn (now called the Bridgend Hotel), which is situated at the clubhouse end of the ground. All of the non-rugby facilities, which include an indoor cricket school, bowling greens, and tennis courts, are now situated adjacent to the cricket pavilion at the northern end. Until 1961 there was also an open-air swimming pool which was opened in 1931.

Following the First World War the WRU surprisingly reinstated the Ebbw Vale R.U. club, who again tenanted Bridgend Field. After the Welfare Association agreed that the Glamorgan and Monmouthshire rugby league match could be played at Bridgend Field on 2 May, 1927, the WRU, fearing that many other grounds under similar ownership were vulnerable to rugby league, made the futile gesture of threatening the rugby union club with what amounted to expulsion. The fact that Ebbw Vale RU had no control over the arrangement, and the exhibition game was in aid of the Ebbw Vale War Memorial, appeared not to matter!

On 21 September, 1974, the former Labour leader, Michael Foot, unveiled a plaque on the entrance gates to signify the renaming of Bridgend Field in honour of Sir Eugene Cross, who had been the chairman of the welfare trustees for over 50 years. In 1981 a public trust took over the management and ownership of Eugene Cross Park, which is now shared by

Ebbw Vale Welfare Ground, 1935, showing the rugby grandstand and the adjoining cricket field in the foreground

the town's rugby, soccer, and cricket clubs, as well as being one of Glamorgan's county grounds.

Before their move and change of name to Bridgend for the 1984/5 season, Cardiff Blue Dragons (see Ninian Park) transferred their fixture against Huyton to Eugene Cross Park in May, 1984. In so far as the attendance was double their meagre average at Ninian Park, this experiment proved relatively successful for the moribund club.

However, the knowledge that the woefully-weak Bridgend formed the nucleus of the resurrected Welsh side for the game against England at Ebbw Vale on Sunday, 14 October, 1984, was cause for some alarm. It was not that surprising, therefore, that with the whole game televised live throughout Wales the attendance should be a mere 2,111. However, after trailing 22-0 at half-time, the Welsh put up a spirited performance in the second half, finally losing by the respectable scoreline of 28-9. Gary Clark (Hull K. R.) scored a hat-trick of tries in this game, and Milton Huddart, the son of test legend Dick, made his full international debut.

Since that game the ground's second wooden grandstand (opened in 1959) has been replaced with a new 1,200-seater cantilever stand, and, following fire damage to the original, in 1897 a shared clubhouse, complete with electronic scoreboard, was opened.

After the demise of Ebbw Vale in 1912 there was no other rugby league played in Wales until the start of the industrial depression of the 1920s. During this period David Smith and Gareth Williams, in their superlative history *Fields of Praise*, say the South Wales coal-based economy *"fell in like a collapsed lung"*. High and long-term unemployment was the ideal climate for rugby league recruitment, and consequently, up to the start of the Second World War, literally hundreds of players were offered the ticket north, either permanently - as in the case of the great Jim Sullivan, who, as a youth, signed for Wigan from Cardiff in July, 1921 - or to play trials under assumed names.

Eugene Cross Park	
1910 Wales 39 England 18	4,000
1911 Wales 8 England 27	4,000
1911 Wales 20 Australia 28	7,000
1984 Wales 9 England 28	2,111

PONTYPRIDD The Rugby League set up a Welsh Commission in 1926, the year of the General Strike, to encourage both amateur and professional development. The Commission were more successful with the former than the latter, and it was only in Pontypridd that a professional club emerged.

Formed in 1876, Pontypridd played for a time at **Taff Vale Park** in Treforest, a ground which was bought by the Taff Vale Park Company around the turn of the century for the promotion of professional athletics and cycling. The Welsh Professional Union had been formed in Pontypridd in 1901 to foster both these sports, and in 1903 the Welsh Powderhall, a handicap event run over 130 straight yards, was inaugurated. Taking its name from the famous Edinburgh event, the Welsh Powderhall had a 26-year history at Taff Vale Park, which was also the home from 1911 of soccer club Pontypridd Dragons, who played in the Southern League until 1924.

In December, 1921 Taff Vale Park was described as *"primitive"* when Wales lost 21-16 to the Australians. Although the game was played in a continuous drizzle, it still provided top-class entertainment for both the 13,000 crowd (an excellent figure, bearing in mind the two shilling admission charge, and the high unemployment in the district) and a future cinema audience. Australia owed their victory to a superb try by winger Harold Horder, who ran clean through the Welsh defence to score near the posts shortly before half-time.

By the time that England beat Wales 30-22, on Monday, 12 April, 1926, Taff Vale Park's capacity had risen to between 30-40,000, including a new 2,850-seater stand. It also had one of the best playing surfaces in South Wales. The 22,000 who assembled for the 5 o'clock kick-off were rewarded with an exhibition-type game, Wales being handicapped by the loss of one of their centres. The Welsh crowd, showing no partisanship, were said to have been *critical rather than enthusiastic*, many of the tries being greeted with stony silence.

This game, however, really set the seal on the formation of a Pontypridd club, the new organisation being admitted to the Rugby League (along with Castleford) at the 1926 AGM. Welsh Commissioner John J. Leake, an exiled Yorkshireman from Pontefract, pointed out the fact that, with the Dragons having folded and Pontypridd RU heavily in debt, there was very little opposition in the town. Pontypridd were further helped by the Rugby League purchasing Taff Vale Park and agreeing a short-term lease with the club.

For propoganda purposes the Wales-New Zealand international on 4 December, 1926 could not have been equalled. Wales, with four Pontypridd players in the side, took full advantage of Swinton stand-off, Billo Rees' openings, to finish 34-8 winners. The crowd of 18,000 was the highest of the tour. Pontypridd also played New Zealand, on Christmas Day, 1926, losing 18-7 before a crowd of 10,000.

Unfortunately, future attendances dropped considerably, and when the ground was sold to the Greyhound Racing Association during September, 1927, arrangements had to be made with this body for its continued use for rugby league.

Action from the Wales versus England game at Taff Vale Park in 1936 - The Hulton Deutsch Collection.

As well as dogs, speedway, trotting, and boxing also flourished at the ground during the 1920s and 1930s.

Before resigning from the Rugby League Pontypridd played their last match there on 22 October, 1928 against Oldham when the receipts were a mere £24, although the scheduled Glamorgan and Monmouthshire versus Lancashire game went ahead at Taff Vale Park on 12 November, 1928. The amateur rugby league which had been established collapsed in 1929 and its players were reinstated by the Welsh R.U.

The final rugby league international to be staged at Taff Vale Park was on 7 November, 1936 when the weather was so bad that many of the other local fixtures were either postponed or abandoned after only a few minutes play. Wales created history by defeating England 3-2 in a thrilling game and clinching the championship for the second successive season. In the appalling conditions, the game was memorable for the brilliant handling of both full-backs, Jim Sullivan and Billy Belshaw (Liverpool Stanley).

At the time that an abortive attempt was made in February, 1938 to stage a Wales-Australia international there, Taff Vale Park was owned by the local authority. It is now principally used by the neighbouring school for athletics. Other than the rugby posts, as it presents today Taff Vale Park gives few indications, to the uninitiated, of its former importance as a premier sporting venue for South Wales. However, it is still possible to see the remains of the grandstand's metal stanchions, and it takes little imagination, looking at the huge playing surface, and the long steep grass banking opposite the River Taff side, to conjure up scenes of past Powderhalls and rugby league internationals on the ground.

Taff Vale Park	
1921 Wales 16 Australia 21	13,000
1926 Wales 22 England 30	23,000
1927 Wales 34 New Zealand 8	18,000
1936 Wales 3 England 2	12,000

CARDIFF The first rugby league match in the Welsh capital was the international at **Sloper Road Greyhound Stadium,** Grangetown (Welsh White City), on 14 November, 1928, when England met Wales before a crowd of 15,000. It was a proud moment for Jim Sullivan as he led out his team *"to the cheers from his own people"* but Wales had to endure a 39-15 defeat to a side containing eleven tourists. St. Helens' winger Alf Ellaby left the Welsh crowd gasping when he

sidestepped five men (including Sullivan) at the start of a 30-yard run to the line.

Covered on three sides, the stadium was situated a few hundreds yards, on the opposite side of Sloper Road, from Ninian Park (see below). The architects claimed that it had a potential capacity of 70,000, and was later named the Welsh White City. After becoming the GKN sports ground it was demolished in November, 1984 to make way for the present housing development, opposite the Ninian Park School.

Sloper Road Greyhound Stadium	
1928 England 39 Wales 15	15,000.

In 1927 the syndicate who built the Sloper Road stadium had made an unsuccessful application to join the Rugby League, and it was not until 1949, and their admittance to the Rugby League in 1951, that a Cardiff club again surfaced. They played their one and only season in the top flight at the 30,000-capacity Penarth Road Stadium, which was leased from Speedway Racing (Cardiff) Ltd. This stadium has since been built on with the appropriately named Stadium Close the only lasting reminder.

Cardiff on the attack against New Zealand in 1951 at the Penarth Road Stadium - Science & Society Picture Library.

LLANELLI Following the Cardiff international, it was 1935 before the next professional rugby league game was played in Wales. But the wait was perhaps justified with two Welsh records being set at **Stebonheath Park,** Llanelli, a former allotments site, owned by Mr W. T. Morris, the chairman of Llanelli AFC. Llanelli christened their new ground on Saturday, 2 September, 1922 with a win over Brigend, but the official opening was reserved for Monday, 16 October, 1922, when a crowd of 10,000 saw Tottenham Hotspur beaten 2-1 on Spurs' first-ever visit to Wales. At Steboneath's opening there was one grandstand (which was gutted by fire in March, 1924) opposite which was a steep grass bank, estimated to hold 25,000, with room at either end for additional Spion Kops.

During September, 1926, with the soccer club defunct, the Rugby League Commissioners tried to buy Steboneath Park. The price, however, was apparently excessive, and the Wales-New Zealand game, as we have seen, was played instead at Pontypridd. In 1927 Mr Morris transformed the soccer pitch into tennis courts and putting greens, for the benefit of the 100 female staff of his departmental store, The Realm, and

greyhound racing was introduced for a limited period from December, 1932.

On 23 November, 1935, a Welsh record crowd of 25,000 saw Wales score 11 tries in trouncing France 41-7 in the inaugural game of the European Championship. *"In some ways"*, wrote *"Nomad"* of the Llanelly Mercury, *"the display made one feel that the amateur code was an old man's game."*

Stebonheath's second international, in April, 1938, which France lost 18-2, guaranteed Wales their third successive championship and the following season, on 5 November, 1938, Wales maintained their 100% record in the tournament with an impressive win over England, despite being a man short in the second half. With the war intervening, this was to be the last game of rugby league staged at Stebonheath until 19 May, 1951 when, in front of a crowd of 6,500, an Empire XIII beat Wales 29-16 as part of the Festival of Britain.

Alby Evans, who has been referred to previously, bought Stebonheath Park from Mr Morris' family in 1950, with the

Alan Prescott (St. Helens) (left) and Tommy Harris (Wales XIII) lead out their sides for the exhibition game at Stebonheath Park, Llanelli, on 19 May, 1959 - Science & Society Picture Library.

intention of not only transferring Llanelli rugby league club there, but also reintroducing greyhound racing. However, he was thwarted on both counts due to the failure of the local council to grant him a greyhound licence, and a clause in Mr. Morris' will which protected the interests of the soccer club. Consequently, in 1958/9 Mr Evans sold Stebonheath for £9,500 to a newly-formed development committee of Llanelli A.F.C.

Although none of Llanelli rugby league club's games were ever played at Stebonheath, in 1949/50 Ystradgynlais met Cardiff in the final of the Welsh Cup and a Welsh Northern XIII played a South Wales XIII. Also, on Whit Monday, 18 May, 1959 St Helens beat a Welsh International XIII in the first of three exhibition games in Wales - the others being scheduled for Pontypool Park and Maindy Stadium, Cardiff, on the Wednesday and Saturday of that same week. Saints also played a similar Welsh combination at Llanelli in 1980 as part of Roy Mathias' benefit season.

During this year, following financial difficulties and the problem of implementing the requirements of the Taylor Report, Llanelli A.F.C. agreed that Stebonheath should be controlled by the local authority. Subsequently the council have built a 600-seater cantilevered stand, laid a tartan track, and granted the club a long term lease.

The steep grass banking, into which the present clubhouse has been built, still gives some idea of where the majority of Stebonheath's previous capacity lay. However, even allowing for the loss of the eastern side of the ground due to the inner relief road, it is difficult to imagine the crowd of 25,000 at the international in 1935.

Stebonheath Park	
1935 Wales 41 France 7	25,000
1938 Wales 18 France 2	20,000
1938 Wales 17 England 9	15,000

SWANSEA The Second World War was responsible for an important breakthrough so far as rugby league in Wales was concerned. Firstly, with the lifting of the Rugby Union's draconian rules on professionalism and the ineffectiveness of the WRU to function, the door was opened for a series of Services rugby union charity matches and internationals, organized by a group called the West Wales Rugby War Charity Effort. Such games brought together the best talent from both codes and helped raise nearly £15,000. Secondly,

the Swansea club, on whose **St. Helen's** ground several of these games were played, went out of existence during the war and surrendered their lease to the local Council. The Rugby League were therefore able to hire what was then one of the WRU's international grounds.

The first of the eleven rugby league internationals played at St. Helen's during the mid-40s and early 50s took place on 24 November, 1945 when Wales beat England 11-3. The historic occasion, and the fact that W. T. H., *"Willy"* Davies, the Bradford Northern stand-off, was returning to the ground where he first met fame as a schoolboy in the defeat of the 1935 All Blacks, ensured that new figures for rugby league in Wales were established with a crowd of 30,000 (still a record) paying £4,100.

Unfortunately, the game did not match the occasion, with such as Gus Risman and Ernest Ward, who had furthered their reputations in those war-time matches, being well below their top form. A year later, however, the same sides put on a far better performance for an appreciative crowd of 25,000, and in 1947 Wales' games against France and New Zealand impressed gatherings of 20,000 and 18,000 respectively.

Following this early post-war boom, however, support for Swansea's internationals went into decline. So much so that after the 1948 Australian tourists had taken their 65% cut, the receipts did not cover expenses; and with Swansea Council charging £250 for the hire of the ground the fixture against France in 1949 again lost in the region of £200.

Despite these financial problems, on the field of play things were definitely improving. The best game so far at Swansea was Wales' 14-10 defeat of England in February, 1949. A storming first half by the Welsh *"got the interest of the crowd so worked up"* that the Rugby League decided to stage an exhibition game at Abertillery before the end of the season. And in the final international at Swansea during this early post-war period Alfred Drewery of the *The Yorkshire Post* described the Wales versus Other Nationalities game on 31 March 1951 as, *"One of those delightful games in which every player had at least one moment of glory in this stimulating show of brilliant running and handling."* Unfortunately, the attendance was little more than 5,000, and, apart from two more internationals at Llanelli and Abertillery later that year, it was not until 1975 that representative games returned to Wales, with St. Helen's being the chosen venue.

Mel Meek (in scrum-cap) misses a tackle as the French break from their own 25 in the international at St. Helen's, Swansea, in 1947.

The home of Swansea Cricket and Rugby Club is named after the medieval Augustinian convent dedicated to St. Helen, which once stood on the site of St. Helen's Crescent. The cricket club moved there in 1873 and levelled the ground and reclaimed the sandbanks, and a year later the rugby club amalgamated with them. Today both clubs share the pavilion, which was first built in 1927, extended in 1980, and recently renovated.

Wales played their first-ever international at St. Helen's in 1882, and the ground continued to be used for such fixtures until 1954. At the game against Scotland in 1921 over 60,000 spectators passed through the turnstiles and play was interrupted by the overflow. The ground has also been the home of Glamorgan since 1888, and, in cricketing terms, is perhaps most famous for the feat of (Sir) Gary Sobers (Nottinghamshire), who hit Malcolm Nash for six sixes in a single over.

The only cover on the ground is provided by the wooden 2,000-seater stand, built in the 1920s at a cost of £12,500, which runs alongside the seaside Mumbles Road. Prior to the game against Ireland in March, 1949 the Council completed the concrete terracing of the *"Tanner Bank"* (on which loose seating is installed in summer) and later finished the sections near to the Cricketers Hotel and on the cricket banking at the Guildhall end. All this terracing is built on heaps of colliery waste taken from the Clyne Valley. Looking at photographs of this development, the original tubular crush barriers bear a striking resemblance to those in place today. By 1951 the Council had raised the capacity to 51,000, but after 1954 the WRU abandoned St. Helen's in favour of Cardiff Arms Park.

St. Helen's floodlights, which were installed in 1964, are powerful enough for night cricket, although their failure during Swansea's game against the Wallabies in 1984 resulted in the game being abandoned.

An aerial view of St. Helen's from the Mumbles end.

St. Helen's is perhaps the nearest one gets in Britain to the dual-purpose Australian ovals, although at Swansea the rugby spectator's view is hindered by the ground's horse-shoe shape, with the popular terracing running away from the touchline at an angle of something like 45 degrees. In order to achieve a more rectangular shape, and presumably to increase income, temporary seating is today installed behind the posts for major rugby union tour games. This is nothing new, however, as such structures were used on the ground in the 1940s (continued below).

The international at St. Helen's in February, 1949 was the catalyst for the second Welsh rugby league movement to take shape, with Huddersfield (the Rugby League Champions) and St. Helens being invited to play three exhibition matches prior to the formation of the Welsh League. The tour commenced on Monday evening, 16 May, at Portardulais, where a crowd of 5,000 saw the Fartowners score a 40-11 victory. 48 hours later the show moved to the Brewery Field, Bridgend, (see below) where Saints levelled matters with a 33-17 win before 10,000 spectators, the highest crowd on the rugby union ground that season.

ABERTILLERY Such was the interest generated by this attractive rugby, when the teams ran out for the final match of the series on Saturday 21 May, 1949, the organisers were staggered to find that a crowd, estimated at well over 20,000, were at Abertillery's Council-owned **The Park** to greet them - Huddersfield winning a fine game 22-16. Because of his alleged involvement in the game's promotion a town councillor was banned by the WRU, although his only motive was apparently to see that the town benefited from the £500 guarantee, based on the size of the crowd.

Unfortunately, when the Wales-Other Nationalities international was staged, on what still remains the local rugby union club's ground, on 22 October, 1949 the event lost £439. Both captains pleaded with the referee, Charlie Appleton, to abandon the match due to the heavy icy rain and lightning, but he played the full 80 minutes, Wales losing 6-5. Although this natural amphitheatre was estimated to easily hold 40,000, in 1949 there was still only cover for 650; and, perhaps understandably, the crowd, who were said to have been *"as heroic as the players"*, numbered only 2,500.

The following October Wales lost scrum-half Billy Banks after ten minutes and went down gallantly to England, 22-4, whilst on 1 December, 1951 Brian Bevan scored a first minute *"special"* from half-way for Other Nationalities in their 22-11 defeat of Wales before an official crowd of only 3,386, but estimated in press reports as 10,000.

The last professional game of rugby league at The Park was on 1 June, 1968 when Bradford Northern beat Salford 46-22 in an exhibition match watched by a crowd of 10,000. Salford had last played Cardiff there during the 1949/50 season in

The picturesque setting for the Huddersfield-St. Helens exhibition game in May, 1949 at The Park, Abertillery.

the Challenge Cup first round, first leg, and this picturesque ground was hired for several other exhibitions and Welsh League fixtures. For example, on 17 May, 1950 the Challenge Cup winners, Warrington, played Cardiff & Blaina in a game organised by the local council, but attempts to form a club in Abertillery during this period were unsuccessful.

The Park	
1949 Wales 5 Other Nats. 6	2,500
1950 Wales 4 England 22	8,000
1951 Wales 11 Other Nats. 22	3,386

BRIDGEND Following the success of the previously mentioned exhibition game at the **Brewery Field**, however, a new club was formed at Bridgend. Brewery Field, which at one time had been owned by the WRU, who had disposed of it for less than £2,000 when twice its present size. It was the traditional home of Bridgend R. U. club, who, in May, 1949, were shocked to find that their short-term lease was not renewed following the intervention of the Welsh Rugby League Commission who were prepared to pay an annual rent of over £500 to secure the ground for the next three years. With the rugby union club having to use what became known as the *Bandstand Field*" at Newbridge Fields, Bridgend rugby league club made their Welsh League home debut on 20 August 1949, losing 45-10 to Cardiff.

On 2 September, 1950 a South Wales XIII beat Italy 29-11 at Brewery Field, Castleford winger Roy Lambert and Les Lewis (Ystradgynlais) both scoring a hat-trick of tries. The relative strengths of these two sides can perhaps be measured by the fact that the previous Monday a team representing South Wales had been beaten 74-29 by Wigan at Central Park. The novice Italians had also been heavily defeated by Northern Rugby League clubs on their first tour. Watched by a crowd of only 2,500 the above *"international"* lost the Rugby League £40, which was small change compared to the thousands of pounds which they invested in both the Italian and Welsh ventures.

Following the failure of Cardiff to be re-elected to the Northern Rugby League for the 1952/3 season, the Welsh League soon lost its early momentum. Among the problems was the fact that players no longer wished to risk life bans from rugby union for playing a game with an uncertain future in Wales, and therefore recruitment was difficult. At the end of the 1954/5 campaign the league ceased to

function, with Bridgend - together with Aberavon, Cardiff, Neath and Ystradgynlais - being one of the last surviving founder members.

It was to take the Bridgend R. U. club until 1957 before they could move back to the Brewery Field, when the local council purchased the ground and granted the club a long-term lease. Since the rugby league club's occupancy the grandstand's capacity has been successively raised to 1,600 seats, and £200,000 spent on social amenities. The large popular bank has since been concrete terraced, whilst cover has been provided behind the posts at the town end.

SWANSEA (continued) From 1951 Wales' internationals were confined to grounds in the north of England until the new administration at League headquarters staged the first ever Sunday rugby league fixture in Wales on 16 February, 1975, when Wales beat France 21-8 at Swansea's **St. Helen's.** Such was the crush on the turnstiles that the gates were opened to allow in the crowd, which was originally estimated at 20,000 but later changed to 15,000.

One of the three brawls which marred the Wales-Australia game in 1975 at St. Helen's, Swansea - Andrew Cudbertson.

On 19 October, 1975 Australia virtually clinched the World Championship by winning a tense encounter during which the end-to-end excitement was marred by three brawls, principally involving props Jim Mills and Artie Beetson. After David Watkins had edged Wales ahead with his third penalty, the turning point came shortly before half-time when fullback Graham Eadie started a move from his own line, combined with 17-year old winger Ian Schubert, who scored a brilliant hat-trick of tries in the match, for the latter to put Peard under the posts at the cricket ground end.

The crowd was initially announced as being over 13,000 but this was later reduced to 11,112. There certainly seemed to be thousands more in the ground and the rugby league authorities were a little suspicious. Although no malpractice was ever proved that day, it would not have been the first time that the Rugby League had been short-changed at St. Helen's. For example, following the game against France in 1947 a temporary turnstile operator had been found guilty of embezzling money at the boys' gate where hundreds had been allowed in without being registered. Unfortunately, for the last two internationals at St. Helen's - for the World Cup game against New Zealand later in 1975, when Jim Mills' challenge on opposing prop Greengrass had international repercussions and for the disappointing test against Australia in 1978 - the crowds were so thin that there could be no disputing the final figures.

St. Helen's	
1945 Wales 11 England 3	30,000
1946 Wales 5 England 19	25,000
1947 Wales 17 France 15	20,000
1947 Wales 20 New Zealand	18,283
1947 Wales 7 England 18	10,000
1948 Wales 12 France 20	6,500
1948 Wales 9 France 12	12,032
1948 Wales 5 Australia 12	9,224
1949 Wales 14 England 10	9,553
1949 Wales 16 France 8	4,749
1951 Wales 21 Other Nats. 27	5,000
1975 Wales 21 France 8	15,000
1975 Wales 6 Australia 18	11,112
World Champ. 1975 Wales 25 New Zealand 24	2,645
1978 Wales 3 Australia 8	4,250

CARDIFF (continued) Professional club rugby league returned to Wales for the first time in thirty years with the formation in 1981 of the Cardiff City Blue Dragons in a ground-sharing move with Cardiff City at **Ninian Park**, Sloper Road. Their opening game against Salford on 30 August attracted 9,247, which is still a ground record for the code. In 1984 a consortium bought the club out of liquidation from Cardiff City's owners, but were faced with opposition from the Welsh F. A., who were then considering plans to develop Ninian Park as their permanent international headquarters. Although Cardiff Arms Park has since taken on this role, as a consequence of the Welsh F.A.'s stance, the Blue Dragons moved to Bridgend, where they were struck out of the Rugby League for failing to secure a ground for the start of the 1985/6 season.

Ninian Park staged two internationals during the Blue Dragons' existence: England's first visit to Wales since 1950, on 8 November, 1981, which resulted in a 20-15 success after a spirited late come-back by the home side who scored two tries in the last five minutes and on 24 October, 1982 when Wales lost 37-7 to the Kangaroos' second-string, for whom full-back Steve Ella scored four tries, a record for an Australian against Wales.

Following the successful re-launch of the Welsh side in 1991, the ground has hosted three further internationals, culminating in a European Championship match in 1995 as part of the build up to the Centenary World Cup. On the night of Friday, 4 March, Wales achieved a hollow 13-12 win over France thanks to an injury-time try, on his international rugby league debut, by Salford's novice forward Richard Webster and Jonathan Davies' easy conversion, which denied France their first victory on Welsh soil since their success at St. Helen's in 1948.

Unfortunately, because of a shoulder injury which he sustained at Wembley in the first test, Davies was unavailable to have a second tilt at the 1994 Australians. However, his young stand-in, Iestyn Harris, had an outstanding game but generally Wales had no answer to the Kangaroos' broken-field running and clinical finishing which gave them an easy 46-4 victory. The highly-charged game was marred by a number of brawls, Wales clearly being upset by the broken-jaw which centre John Devereux's sustained in attempting to tackle the mighty Mal Meninga. Almost all the 9,000 who braved the appalling weather were both seated and under cover - Ninian Park having undergone several changes since the days of the Blue Dragons.

Named after Lord Ninian, Ninian Park, which was formerly the site of a council rubbish tip, was opened in 1910. Its record attendance of 61,566 was set on 14 October, 1961 when Wales met England, but due to safety measures the ground's capacity was reduced to approximately 40,000 by the early 1980s. The reduction of the large standing area at the Grangetown End (which also lost its cover) was mostly responsible for the initial reduction. But since 1992 the

Ninian Park, from the Grangetown Road end, at Cardiff City Blue Dragons opening game on 30 August, 1981 against Salford - Mike Haddon.

installation of seating in both the paddock area (now covered by a £300,000 extension) of the main stand, and the covered portion of the popular Bob Bank, opposite, has brought the capacity down to its present level of 21,555. This figure includes seating for over 13,000; 5,565 in the main stand, 5,550 in the Bob Bank Stand, and 1,975 in the recently renovated Canton Stand.

Ninian Park	
1981 Wales 15 England 20	8,102
1982 Wales 7 Australia 37	5,617
1994 Wales 13 France 12 (Floodlit)	6,287
1994 Wales 4 Australia 46	8,279
1995 Wales 18 England 16 (Floodlit)	6,232

SWANSEA (continued). Ninian Park therefore appears well equipped to accommodate Wales' group matches in the Centenary World Cup, which are to be shared with Swansea City's **Vetch Field**, where the reconstituted Welsh side was given a heroes' welcome on 27 October, 1991 for their game against Papua New Guinea.

Playing under floodlights for the first time on home soil, and urged on by a partisan crowd of 11,422, Wales registered 68 points without reply, which at the time was a world record margin for a rugby league international. Jonathan Davies, with 24 points (two tries and eight goals) also set a new individual points record for Wales. The Papuans, who clearly were not only affected by the atmosphere but by the cold night air, were steam-rollered by the powerful Welsh pack. As a result, full-back Phil Ford was able to join the line with impunity to score a hat-trick of tries and take the man-of-the-match award. On the night, however, it was the game which was the real winner, with the Welsh performance - which later guaranteed games at Vetch Field against France and England during 1992 and the opening match of the New Zealand tour in 1993 - receiving rave reports in the local press.

The centrally-situated Vetch Field, which is as near to the sea as St. Helen's, only hemmed in by housing and the local prison, was opened as a sports ground in 1891. In 1913 Swansea Town (renamed City in 1970) built the present main stand on Glamorgan Street. Including the recent Jewsons family enclosure, which was previously a standing section, this quaint old stand currently seats just over 1,700. The ground's only other seats (1,647 with an unrestricted view) are to be found in the top tier of the £800,000 cantilever East Stand, which was built at the city-centre end in 1981. The monstrous floodlight pylon on its roof would not be out of place on the neighbouring docks. The wooden double-decker West Stand, which dated from 1927 and was demolished in 1990 on safety grounds, has been replaced by a £114,000 cover holding 3,500, sponsored by European Profiles. There is also cover on the North Bank for another 7,650. All told, Vetch Field's capacity for the 1994/5 season was 16,355 with saleable seating for 3,352.

From a vantage point in the East Stand it is possible not only to look out to sea but to observe the floodlight towers of St. Helen's in the distance. There is no such luxury for inmates of the adjacent prison, although, from certain cells on the gable end, it appears likely that there is a reasonable view of part of the pitch. With Vetch Field due to host one of the games in the World Cup, a competition which they will enter as European Champions thanks to their famous 18-16 victory over England at Ninian Park in February, there should plenty to cheer.

Vetch Field	
1991 Wales 68 Papua New Guinea 0	11,422
1992 Wales 35 France 6	10,133
1992 Wales 11 England 36	10,243
1993 Wales 19 New Zealand 24	6,073

This view of Vetch Field, taken at the Charity Shield game between Wigan and Widnes on 19 August, 1990, shows the East Stand and the prison behind the main stand to the right - Mike Haddon.

SUBSCRIBERS

1 Michael Jackson, Leeds
2 Niel Griffiths, Kippax
3 Don Yates, Manchester
4 David Ian Benson, Wigan
5 John H. Barker, Shipley
6 Alan James, Newton-le-Willows
7 Andrew Shepherd, Loughborough
8 Tim Jones, Pinner
9 Roger E. Davies, Morecambe
10 Tony Ackroyd, Halifax
11 K. Fillingham, Plymouth
12 John Caley, Wigan
13 D. Fletcher, Sheffield
14 Derek Smith, Bolton
15 C. Elliott, Maidstone
16 Roger Grime, St. Helens
17 George Bordessa, Liverpool
18 Don Rainger, Salford
19 M. A. Hayton, Spalding
20 Albert Phythian, St. Helens
21 C. M. J. Wilson, Wigan
22 T. J. C. Towner, Hammersmith
23 The Revd. John Wickstead, Skegness
24 E. E. Day, Warrington
25 Association of Sports Historians, Bickley
26 Karl Spracklen, Leeds
27 Graham Williams, Leeds
28 Tony Collins, Leeds
29 Barry Scarth, Bangor, Northern Ireland
30 George A. Astle
31 E. Philip Harrison, Leeds
32 G. Morris, Manchester
33 Peter Caswell (Leigh), Warrington
34 Ron Brown, Leeds
35 John Evans, Stratford
36 Richard Adams, Harlow
37 Terry Cook, Loughton
38 Orrell St. James ARLC
39 Geoff Ellis, Stockport
40 Michael McCauley, St. Helens
41 Alan Thompson, Cambridge
42 K. Stobart, Hipperholme
43 Peter A. Moir, Rickmansworth
44 Ken Harvey, Leeds
45 A. Shaw, Warrington
46 Stuart Farmer Media Services, Hinckley
47 Dave O'Connor, Widnes
48 Ian Clayton, Featherstone
49 Stephen Boothroyd, Leeds
50 Derek Hewitt, St. Helens
51 Derek Kettlewell, Bradford
52 Alan Plater, London
53 Andrew Wardrop, Wimbledon
54 David C. Makin, Leeds
55 Bill Abernathy, Brisbane
56 J. Nigel Winnard, Chorley

57 Andrew Pearson, Halifax
58 Ian David Lowe, Leeds
59 R. B. Austin, Knaresborough
60 I. A. Gray, Egremont
61 Stephen Parker, Ackworth
62 Nick Evans, Rheindahlen
63 R. A. Pepper, Pontefract
64 A. McGuire, Keighley
65 Joe Holliday, Workington
66 J. M. Sanderson, Saltaire Wines, Shipley
67 John Dotters, Manchester
68 Peter Sharples, Bolton
69 P. W. Reed, Henley-on-Thames
70 Trevor D. Standish, Leigh
71 S. J. S. Ickringill, Coleraine
72 Paul Scanlon-Wells, Carlisle
73 B. Rowlin, Hull
74 C. R. Buckton, Uxbridge
75 Barry Rennison, Pudsey
76 Lee F. Carson, Ossett
77 A. D. Hanson, Huddersfield
78 Bill Lythgoe, Wigan
79 M. J. Ferguson, Durham
80 Glen Dwyer, Alexandria, NSW
81 E. A. Patrick, Warley
82 Tim Bolton, Hull
83 M. G. Spencer, Cardiff
84 D. S. Barnes, Congleton
85 The Rev'd David Burrows, Southowram
86 D. A. Mitchell, Leeds
87 Ian Jackson, Macclesfield
88 John S. Edwards, Swinton
89 Steve Lawrence, Salford
90 Harvey Davis, Henley-on-Thames
91 Jeremy Bent, York
92 Patricia Arthur, Birkenhead
93 Geoffrey Moorhouse, Hawes
94 Kevin Hansen, Warrington
95 Mr Leslie Barron, Wigan
96 J. Rigby, Surbiton
97 Anthony Holstead, Harrogate
98 Tim Leleux, London
99 B. White, Wakefield
100 Jason Harborow, Chorley
101 A. R. Webster, Magull
102 Alastair Murray, St. Helens
103 Tony Lewis, Bridgend
104 Eric Pontefract, Huddersfield
105 Peter Brown, York
106 Mike Baxter, Hull
107 M. A. Taylor, Wakefield
108 D. Butterfield, Warrington
109 G. Jumps, Hull
110 D. E. Else, Wakefield
111 Jack Leyland, St. Helens
112 Graham Guy, Castleford

113 Alan J. Mark, Leeds
114 T. J. Hall, Hayes
115 Donald G. Lancaster, Pittsburgh
116 J. P. Simpson, Manchester
117 Harry Penna Brooks, Lincoln
118 David W. Marsh, Tyldesley
119 Stan Lewandowski, Warrington
120 David Ellicott, Salford
121 B. E. Brown, Salford
122 Alex Service, St. Helens
123 George Foster, Stanford, California
124 David J. and Marguerite Clark, Preston
125 Geoff Peters, Durham
126 Iain Peacock, Prestwich
127 P. Sunderland, Sutton Coldfield
128 Eric Anderson, Glasgow
129 Bill Nelson, Cleator Moor
130 Sam Coulter, Whitehaven
131 Edgar Clarkson, Keighley
132 C. P. Harrison, Cottingley
133 Bob Evans, Kew
134 B. Collett, Bradford
135 P. R. Catcheside, Leigh
136 Kirsty Beddard, Chester
137 R. Niall Courtney, Ulceby
138 Chris Park, Hull
139 Bryan Lamport, Sandal
140 Stephan Pieper, Herdecke, Germany
141 Bill Riley, Hohne Camp, BFPO 30
142 John Plumbley, Auckland
143 Alistair Whitehead, Huddersfield
144 D. P. Griffin and Ed. Schaurte, Sth Harrow
145 R. Ryan, Ilkley
146 Peter Lush, London
147 John Joseph Dunn, Rawtenstall
148 Phil Fletcher, Huddersfield
149 Carlos Sicilia, Guatemala
150 Gordon Broom, Hull
151 Stuart Evans, York
152 Graham Nixon, Hull
153 Henry and Andrew Skrzypecki, Halifax
154 A. G. Tucker, Carlisle
155 Canon G.C. Smith, Newmarket
156 Peter, Julie and William Howarth, Hereford
157 Jim Hope, Palmerston North, New Zealand
158 Chris, Lynne and Natalie Zarzecki, H'field
159 D. West, Harrow
160 M. Turner, Chorley
161 Michael Waring, Marsfield, Australia
162 Eric Watterson, Bradford
163 Edward M. Baker, Leeds
164 The Benatmane Family of Hunslet
165 Joe, Margaret and Christian Ratcliffe, Leeds
166 Clifford Heavisides, Salford
167 Michael Latham, Chorley
168 David Schofield, Leeds

INDEX OF GROUNDS

Australia:

ANZ Stadium, Brisbane	125
Brisbane Cricket Ground	123
Brisbane Exhibition Ground	120
Eric Weissel Oval, Wagga Wagga	129
Olympic Park, Melbourne	135
Optus Oval (Princes Park), Melbourne	137
Parramatta Stadium, Sydney	118
Pioneer Oval, Parkes	131
R.A.S. Showground, Sydney	108
Sports Reserve, Townsville	132
Suncorp Stadium (Lang Park), Brisbane	125
Sydney Cricket Ground	112
Sydney Football Stadium	117
Wentworth Park, Sydney	110

England and Scotland:

Alfred McAlpine Stadium, Huddersfield	50
Athletic Ground, Cheltenham	11
Athletic Grounds, Rochdale	78
Belle Vue, Manchester	69
Belle Vue, Wakefield	85
Boothferry Park, Hull	19
Borough Park, Workington	40
Celtic Park, Glasgow	16
Central Park, Wigan	93
Cougar Park, Keighley	53
Craven Cottage, Fulham	10
Craven Park, Hull	56
Derwent Park, Workington	41
Elland Road, Leeds	22
Fartown, Huddersfield	47
Goodison Park, Everton	17
Gateshead International Stadium	13
Headingley, Leeds	59
Herne Hill, London	18
Highbury Stadium, London	18
Hilton Park (Kirkhall Lane), Leigh	65
Knowsley Road, St. Helens	80
Lonsdale Park, Workington	39
Meadow Lane, Nottingham	16
Naughton Park, Widnes	90
Odsal Stadium, Bradford	30
Old Trafford, Manchester	20
Park Avenue, Bradford	30

England and Scotland (cont.):

Park Royal, London	12
Recreation Ground, Whitehaven	42
Redheugh Park, Gateshead	13
St. James' Park, Newcastle	12
South Devon Place, Plymouth	18
Stamford Bridge, Chelsea	10
Stanley Greyhound Stadium, Liverpool	17
Station Road, Swinton	72
The Boulevard, Hull	54
The Butts, Coventry	15
The Cliff, Broughton	68
The Willows, Salford	69
Thrum Hall, Halifax	43
Tynecastle Park, Edinburgh	16
Villa Park, Birmingham	14
Watersheddings, Oldham	75
Wembley Stadium	25
Wheater's Field, Broughton	68
Wheldon Road, Castleford	37
White City Stadium, London	19
Wilderspool Stadium, Warrington	87

France:

Le Stade de Paris, St. Ouen	143
Le Stade du Hameau, Pau	156
Le Stadium, Albi	156
Parc de Suzon, Bordeaux	144
Parc des Princes, Paris	142
Parc des Sports, Avignon	157
Parc des Sports, Roanne	152
Stade Albert Domec, Carcassonne	154
Stade Buffalo, Paris	140
Stade de Gerland, Lyons	148
Stade de l'Amitie, Narbonne	156
Stade de la Mediterranee, Beziers	158
Stade des Minimes, Toulouse	149
Stade Gilbert Brutus, Perpignan	153
Stade Jean-Laffon, Perpignan	153
Stade Malakoff, Nantes	147
Stade Municipal, Bordeaux	144
Stade Municipal, Grenoble	151
Stade Municipal, Toulouse	149
Stade Pershing, Paris	139
Stade Velodrome, Marseille	146

New Zealand:

Addington Showgrounds, Christchurch	169
Athletic Park, Wellington	177
Basin Reserve, Wellington	176
Caledonian Ground, Dunedin	172
Carlaw Park, Auckland	160
Domain Cricket Ground, Auckland	160
Eden Park, Auckland	164
English Park, Christchurch	168
Ericsson Stadium (Mt. Smart Stdm), Auckland	166
International Stadium, Rotorua	176
Lancaster Park, Christchurch	167
Monica Park (Athletic Park), Christchurch	168
Queen Elizabeth II Park, Christchurch	171
Show Grounds Oval, Palmerston North	175
Sydenham Park, Christchurch	167
Tahuna Park, Dunedin	172
Wingham Park, Greymouth	174

Papua New Guinea:

Danny Leahy Oval, Goroka	179
Lloyd Robson Oval, Port Moresby	181
Rebiamul Oval, Mount Hagen	180

The South Pacific Islands:

Apia Park, Apia	185
National Stadium, Suva	183
St. Joseph Mairist Ground, Apia	186
Tenefaira Field Stadium, Nuku'alofa	184
Tereora Stadium, Avarua	182

Wales:

Athletic Ground, Pen-y-graig	188
Athletic Ground (Ynys Field), Aberdare	188
Brewery Field, Bridgend	197
Eugene Cross Park (Bridgend F'ld), Ebbw Vale	189
Ninian Park, Cardiff	198
Penydarren Park, Merthyr Tydfil	188
St. Helen's, Swansea	194
Sloper Road Greyhound Stadium, Cardiff	192
Stebonheath Park, Llanelli	193
Taff Vale Park, Pontypridd	190
The Park, Abertillery	196
Vetch Field, Swansea	199

Robert Gate

The following books by the above author are available post free from:

Mount Pleasant Cottage, Ripponden Bank, Ripponden, Sowerby Bridge HX6 4JL

Please make cheques payable to R.E. Gate

GONE NORTH: WELSHMEN IN RUGBY LEAGUE (Volume 1)

184 pages, fully illustrated. Price £6.50 – The story of Wales' greatest Rugby League players. This volume features, amongst others, Billy Boston, Wattie Davies, Trevor Foster, Roy Francis, Jim Sullivan, Jim Mills, Tommy Harris, Emlyn Jenkins, John Mantle, Colin Dixon, Kel Coslett.

GONE NORTH: WELSHMEN IN RUGBY LEAGUE (Volume 2)

182 pages, fully illustrated. Price £9.99 – More great Welsh Rugby League players including Gus Risman, Johnny Freeman, Garfield Owen, Lewis Jones, Clive Sullivan, Johnny Ring, Ben Gronow, David Watkins, Maurice Richards, Alan Edwards, Joe Thompson, Danny Hurcombe, Johnny Rogers.

Both volumes of Gone North may be obtained for £13.50 the pair.

THE STRUGGLE FOR THE ASHES

208 pages, fully illustrated. Price £8.00 – The history of Anglo-Australian Rugby League test matches 1908-84. Match by match accounts of every Great Britain-Australia test match.

CHAMPIONS: A CELEBRATION OF THE RUGBY LEAGUE CHAMPIONSHIP 1895-1987

192 pages, fully illustrated. Price £12.00 – A pictorial and statistical record of Rugby League's most important competition featuring all Rugby League's champion teams.

THEY PLAYED FOR WIGAN – in association with Michael Latham

78 pages, fully illustrated. Price £5.99 – A complete statistical record of all the players who have appeared in the cherry and white of Wigan between 1895 and 1992.

"THERE WERE A LOT MORE THAN THAT" – ODSAL 1954

120 pages, fully illustrated. Price £11.95 – A fascinating story of the Halifax - Warrington Challenge Cup final replay and the world record crowd, including over 100 eye-witness accounts and reminiscences of the players, officials and fans.

Woods Visual Communications

500 Leeds Road, Bradford BD3 9RU

Copies of photographs used in
The International Grounds of Rugby League
**can be obtained by ringing 01274 732362 quoting the reference
number shown. Some of the older prints are black and white only.**

	8" x 6"	10" x 8"
Black and White Print	£7.95	£9.95
Colour Print	£11.75	£13.75

The above prices include V.A.T. and postage & packing in the U.K.
Prints can be supplied mounted and framed if required. Please ask for details.

Apart from the photographs used in this book, recent aerial colour photographs are also available
for the following grounds: **Headingley** Ref: AC 28724, **Wheldon Road** Ref: AC 28731,
The Alfred McAlpine Stadium Ref: AC 28563, **Cougar Park** Ref: AC 28718, **Thrum Hall** Ref: AC 28566,
Odsal Stadium Ref: AC 28714.

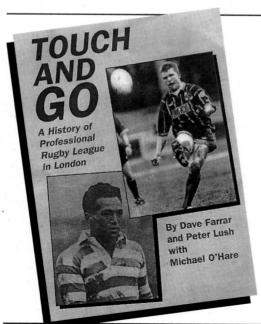

TOUCH AND GO

A History of Professional Rugby League in London

By Dave Farrar and Peter Lush with Michael O'Hare

Approximately 300 pages, softback format,
Touch and Go is published on 29 August, 1995.

Priced £9 plus £1 postage & packing,
it is available from London League Publications,
144 St. Leonards Road, London E14 0RA
Tel: 0171-515-5615 or 0171-515-2001